JUMP IN

Dow stock . . . open market stock . . . preferred stock . . . common stock . . . stock splits . . . capital appreciation . . . growth investing . . . value investing . . . fundamental analysis . . . technical analysis . . . cash flow per share . . . current ratio . . . dividend yield . . . earnings per share . . . net profit margin . . . price/book ratio . . . price/earnings ratio . . . price/sales ratio . . . quick ratio . . . return on equity . . . a sea of endless possibilities . . . thousands of stocks to invest in . . . hundreds of brokers to choose from . . . dozens of "expert" strategies to adopt . . .

AND RIDE THE WAVE TO FINANCIAL SUCCESS

With this illuminating, easy-to-use guide you can instantly turn to and follow with confidence your whole investment life.

THE NEATEST LITTLE GUIDE TO STOCK MARKET INVESTING

THE
Neatest Little
Guide to
Stock Market
Investing

JASON KELLY

A Plume Book

PLUME
Published by the Penguin Group
Penguin Putnam Inc., 375 Hudson Street, New York, New York 10014, U.S.A.
Penguin Books Ltd, 27 Wrights Lane, London W8 5TZ, England
Penguin Books Australia Ltd, Ringwood, Victoria, Australia
Penguin Books Canada Ltd, 10 Alcorn Avenue, Toronto, Ontario, Canada M4V 3B2
Penguin Books (N.Z.) Ltd, 182–190 Wairau Road, Auckland 10, New Zealand

Penguin Books Ltd, Registered Offices:
Harmondsworth, Middlesex, England

First published by Plume, an imprint of Dutton Signet,
a member of Penguin Putnam Inc.

First Printing, January, 1998
10   9   8   7   6   5   4   3   2   1

REGISTERED TRADEMARK—MARCA REGISTRADA

LIBRARY OF CONGRESS CATALOGING-IN-PUBLICATION DATA
Kelly, Jason.
    The neatest little guide to stock market investing / Jason Kelly.
        p.   cm.
    ISBN 0-452-27870-8
    1. Stocks.   2. Investment analysis.   3. Portfolio management.
    I. Title.
    HG4661.K354   1998
    332.63'22—dc21   97-34177
                                                        CIP

Printed in the United States of America
Set in Times New Roman

PUBLISHER'S NOTE
This publication is designed to provide accurate and authentic information in regard to the subject
matter covered. It is sold with the understanding that the publisher is not engaged in rendering financial, accounting, or other professional service. If financial advice or other expert assistance is required,
the service of a competent professional person should be sought.

Ten Steps to Investing in Stocks

Acknowledgments

Writing these little books has brought me in touch with some of the neatest people in business. The woman who started it all is my agent, Doris Michaels. In the days when both of us were new to the world of publishing, we gave each other a chance and haven't looked back since. She is my mentor, my friend, and a great partner.

I'm not the only one who took a liking to Doris. Charlie Michaels met her first and married her. He is the president of Sierra Global Management, LLC. Charlie's thorough understanding of the stock market kept this book from leading you down the wrong path. Helping Charlie was a team of expert reviewers including Stefan Alb, managing director, Sierra Global, and Brian Danelian, vice president, Everen Securities.

This book is packed full of content from many fine people and organizations. Thanks to Gary Pilgrim, one of the best mutual fund managers in the business, who took time on his birthday to discuss stock investing with me. Thanks to Standard & Poor's, Value Line, and Morningstar for supplying me with all the data I requested.

Finally, a toast to the dynamite crew at Plume. My editor, Jennifer Dickerson, is the only reason that "little" is still in this book's title.

Contents

1 Speak the Language of Stocks

Welcome to the world of stock investing! By picking up the phone or turning on the computer, you can own a piece of a company—and all of its fortune or folly—without ever attending a board meeting, developing a product, or devising a marketing strategy. When I was eleven years old, my grandfather explained to me in less than ten seconds why  he invested in stocks. We sat by his pool in Arcadia, California, and he read the stock tables. I asked why he looked at all that fine print on such a beautiful day. He said, "Because it takes only $10,000 and two tenbaggers to become a millionaire." That didn't mean much to me at the time, but it does now. A tenbagger is a stock that grows tenfold. Invest $10,000 in your first tenbagger and you have $100,000. Invest that $100,000 in your second tenbagger and you have $1 million. That, in less than ten seconds, is why everybody should invest in stocks.

This chapter further explains why investing in stocks is a good idea, then covers some basic information you'll use in the rest of the book when you begin investing.

Why Stocks Are Good Investments

You should know why stocks are good investments before you start investing in them. There are two reasons to own stocks.

First, because they allow you to own successful companies and, second, because they've been the best investments over time.

Stocks Allow You to Own Successful Companies

Stocks are good investments because they allow you to own successful companies. Just as you can have equity in your home, you can have equity in a company by owning its stock. That's why stocks are sometimes called *equities*.

Think of all the rich people you've read about. How did they get rich? Was it by lending money to relatives who never repay? No. Was it by winning the lottery? Not very often. Was it by inheriting money? In some cases, but it's irrelevant because nobody has control over this factor. In most cases, rich people got rich by owning something.

That something might have been real estate. You learned the first time you watched *Gone With the Wind* that land has value and that owning some is a good idea. In most cases, though, people get rich by owning a business. Schoolchildren learn about John D. Rockefeller, Andrew Carnegie, and J. P. Morgan. They all owned businesses. Henry Ford sold cars, Ray Kroc sold hamburgers from McDonald's, Thomas Watson sold business machines from IBM, and Scott Cook and Tom Proulx sold financial software from Intuit. They all owned their companies. I sold magazine subscriptions door-to-door in school to raise money for the student council. I'm not rich because I didn't own the subscription company. See the difference?

I could have taken some of that money I earned pawning off another copy of *Reader's Digest* on Mrs. Klein and bought shares of the subscription company. Suddenly, I would have been a business owner encouraging my classmates to "sell, sell, sell!" even if it meant they would win the portable radio instead of me winning it. The business they generated would have improved the subscription company's bottom line and, as a shareholder, I would have profited. If all went as planned, I could have bought a dozen portable radios.

Ah, the Beauty of Stock: You Own a Company but Never Go to the Office!

That's why owning stocks is a good idea. They make you an owner of a company. Not an employee or a lender, an owner. When a company prospers, so do its owners.

Stocks Have Been
the Best Investments over Time

That's cute, you're thinking, but does it really work that way? Let's take a look at history and a few hard numbers.

The stock market has returned about 10.5 percent a year for the past 70 years or so. Corporate bonds returned 4.5 percent, U.S. Treasuries returned 3.3 percent, and inflation grew at 3.3 percent. Notice that Treasuries and inflation ran neck and neck? That means your investment in Treasuries returned nothing to you after inflation. When you include the drain of taxes, you lost money by investing in Treasuries. You need stocks. Everybody who intends to be around longer than ten years needs to invest in stocks. That's where the money is.

Investing in stocks helps both the investor and the company. Take McDonald's, for instance. It went public in 1965 at $22.50 per share. If you bought 100 shares, the company would have had an extra $2,250 to put toward new restaurants and better hamburgers. Maybe your money would have funded the research and development of the Big Mac, one of America's great inventions. Thirty years and ten stock splits later, your 100 shares of McDonald's would have become 18,590 shares worth almost $1 million. Both you and McDonald's prospered, thanks to the stock market.

How Stocks Trade

When stocks are bought and sold, it's called *trading*. So a person might say, "IBM is trading at $140." That means if you wanted to buy IBM stock, you'd pay $140 for one share.

Every company has a *ticker symbol*, which is the unique code used to identify its stock. In magazine articles and newspaper stories, the ticker symbol is usually in parenthesis and follows the exchange on which the stock is listed. For example, IBM (NYSE: IBM), Microsoft (NASDAQ: MSFT), Oakley (NYSE: OO), and Emerson Radio (AMEX: MSN). This notation tells you that IBM and Oakley trade on the New York Stock Exchange under the symbols IBM and OO respectively. Yes, the OO is supposed to look like a pair of glasses, Oakley's product. You can see that Microsoft trades on NASDAQ under the symbol MSFT and Emerson Radio trades on the American Exchange under the symbol MSN.

A $1 move in stock price is called a *point*. If IBM went from $140 to $143, you'd say that it rose three points.

Stock prices are given in point fractions. In the real world, IBM doesn't usually trade in such clean increments as $140 and $143. Instead it would trade for 143^{3}/_{8}$, which equates to $143.38. If it rises $^{1}/_{4}$ of a point, it would trade at 143^{5}/_{8}$ or $143.63. Every $^{1}/_{16}$ point move in a stock is equal to 6.25 cents, a $^{1}/_{8}$ point move equal 12.5 cents, and so on.

With Stocks, You Don't Need to Meet the Other Buyer or Seller

Many investors purchase shares of stock in blocks of 100. A block of 100 shares is called a *round lot*. Round lots provide a convenient way to track your stock investments because for every round lot you own, a one point move up or down adds or subtracts $100 from the value of your investment. If you own 100 shares of IBM at $143, it's worth $14,300. If it rises two points to $145, your investment is worth $200 more for a total of $14,500. Simple, eh?

Preferred Stock vs. Common Stock

There are two types of stock, preferred and common. Both represent ownership in a company. Preferred stock has a set dividend that does not fluctuate based on how well the company is performing. Preferred stockholders receive their dividends before common stockholders. Finally, preferred stockholders are paid first if the company fails and is liquidated.

Common stock is what most of us own. That's what you get when you place a standard order for some number of shares. Common stock entitles you to voting rights and any dividends that the company decides to pay. The dividends will fluctuate with the company's success or failure.

How You Make Money Owning Stocks

This is really the bottom line to investors. The only reason you own a business is to profit from it. The way you profit by owning stocks is through capital appreciation and dividends.

Through Capital Appreciation

Sometimes called capital gains, *capital appreciation* is the profit you keep after you buy a stock and sell it at a higher price. Buy low, sell high is a common investment aphorism, but it is just as legitimate to buy high, sell higher.

Expressed as a percentage, the difference between your purchase price and your sell price is your return. For example, if you buy a stock at $30 and sell it later for $60, your return is 100 percent. Sell it later for $90 and your return is 200 percent. If you bought Iomega at $2^3/_4$ and sold it later for $55^1/_8$, your return was 1,905 percent.

Through Dividends

As an owner of a company, you might share in the company's profits in the form of a stock *dividend* taken from company earnings. Companies report earnings every quarter and determine whether to pay a dividend. If earnings are low or the company loses money, dividends are usually the first thing to get cut. On a *declaration date* in each quarter, the company decides what the dividend payout will be.

To receive a dividend, you must own the stock by the *ex-dividend date*, which is four business days before the company looks at the list of shareholders to see who gets the dividend. The day the company actually looks at the list of shareholders is called the *record date*.

If you own the stock by the ex-dividend date, and are therefore on the list of shareholders by the record date, you get a dividend check. The company decides how much the dividend will be per share, multiplies the number of shares you own by the dividend, and mails you a check for the total amount. If you own 100 shares and the dividend is $.35, the company will mail you a check for $35 on the *payment date*. It's that simple.

Most publications report a company's annual dividend, not the quarterly. The company that just paid you a $.35 per share quarterly dividend would be listed in most publications as having a dividend of $1.40. That's just the $.35 quarterly dividend multiplied by the four quarters in the year.

Total Return

The money you make from a stock's capital appreciation combined with the money you make from the stock's dividend is your total return. Just add the rise in the stock price to the dividends you received, then divide by the stock's purchase price.

Getting a Bit Crowded? The Right Stocks Can Buy a Bigger Home

For instance, let's say you bought 200 shares of IBM at $45 and sold them two years later at $110. IBM paid an annual dividend of $1.00 the first year and $1.40 the second year. The rise in the stock's price was $65, and the total dividend paid per share was $2.40. Add those to get $67.40. Divide that by the stock's purchase price of $45 and you get 1.5, or 150 percent total return.

All About Stock Splits

A stock split occurs when a company increases the number of its stock shares outstanding without increasing shareholders' equity. To you as an investor, that means you'll own a different number of shares, but they'll add up to the same amount. A common stock split is 2-for-1. Say you own 100 shares of a stock trading at $180. Your account is worth $18,000. If the stock splits 2-for-1, you will own 200 shares that trade at $90. Your account is still worth $18,000. What's the point? The point is that you now have something to do with your spare time: adjust your financial statements to account for the split.

Not really. Companies split their stock to make it affordable to more investors. Many people would shy away from a $180 stock, but would consider a $90 one. Perhaps that's still too expensive. The company could approve a 4-for-1 split and take the $180 stock down to $45. Your 100 shares would become 400 shares, but would still be worth $18,000. People considering the stock might be more likely to buy at $45 than at $180, even though they're getting the same amount of ownership in the company for each dollar they invest. It's a psychological thing, and who are we to question it?

Mathematically, stock splits are completely irrelevant to investors but they are often a sign of good things to come. A company usually won't split its stock unless it's optimistic about the future. Think about it. Would you cut your stock price in half or more if the market was about to do the same? Of course not. Headlines would declare the end of your fortunes and lawsuits might pile up. Stock splits tend to happen when a company has done well, driven up the price of its stock, expects to continue doing well, drops the price of its stock through a split, and expects to keep driving up the stock price after the split.

Great companies like Microsoft and Cisco have split their stocks several times in the early 1990s. A $10,000 investment in Cisco at its February 1990 initial public offering was worth more than $1,000,000 at the end of 1996. The stock didn't just run straight up 100-fold, however. It made four 2-for-1 splits along the way. It rose and split, rose and split, rose and split, rose and split until, voilà! $10 grand turned into $1 million. You can be sure that Cisco wouldn't have been splitting its stock if it wasn't excited about its future.

Not That Kind of Split!

Remember that a stock split drops the price of the stock. Lower prices tend to move quicker than higher prices. Also, the fluctuations of a lower-priced stock have a greater percentage impact on return than they do against higher-priced stocks. A $2 increase is a 4 percent gain for a $50 stock, but only a 2 percent gain for a $100 stock.

Why and How
a Company Sells Stock

Companies want you to buy their stock so they can use your money to get new equipment, develop better products, and expand their operations. Your investment money strengthens the company. But first the company needs to make its stock available. This section describes how.

Mister Magazine's Future Headquarters

The magazine subscription selling job I held in school made me think a lot about becoming a business owner. I imagined teaching all the other kids how to sell subscriptions, collecting their money at the end of the day, using some of it to buy a prize for the top seller, sending a small amount to the magazines, and depositing the rest in my bank account. Pretty simple business model, right? Pretend for a minute that I did it. I called my business Mister Magazine.

I realized early on that Mister Magazine needed office space. A treehouse would do. I needed lumber to build it, and I needed to get electricity and phones installed. That takes money that I didn't have. After all, that's why I went into business: to make money. If I already had it, I wouldn't have needed to go into business! There are two ways I could have raised money for Mister Magazine.

First, I could have drawn up a business plan and pleaded with my local bank. When I showed the officer the sketches of corporate headquarters in a tree, my guess is that our interview would have been quite short. A lot of fledgling businesses face just that problem. They aren't established enough to get a loan, or if they do get one it comes with such a high interest rate to offset the risk that it ends up strangling the business anyway. Nope, a loan wouldn't do it for Mister Magazine.

Selling Stock Is a Great Way to Raise Money

My second option was to sell shares of Mister Magazine to investors who wanted a piece of the upcoming profits. By selling shares I would raise money, I wouldn't owe anybody anything, and I would acquire a bunch of people who *really* wanted Mister Magazine to succeed. They would own part of it, after all! I chose this second option to raise money, and I decided that 10 shares made up Mister Magazine's entire operation. I could have chosen 100 shares or 100,000 shares. The amount doesn't matter. The only thing investors care about is what percentage of Mister Magazine they'll own. I decided to keep six shares for myself to retain majority ownership and sell four shares to parents in my community for $100 each. The parents were my *venture capitalists* in this case. After the sale I owned 60 percent of Mister Magazine and four parents in the community owned 40 percent. It was a private deal, though. You couldn't find Mister Magazine listed in the paper yet.

Another Subscription Sold!

The first year of operation at Mister Magazine went great. I hired twenty kids to sell magazines door-to-door, I negotiated a cheap deal with the magazines, and I found a wholesale prize distributor who sold gadgets for half their usual price. My employees were happy and Mister Magazine grew to be worth $5,000. How did my investors fare? Quite well. Those initial $100 shares became $500 shares in one year. That's a 400 percent annual return!

Clearly there was only one thing for me to do. I needed to immediately drop out of school and expand Mister Magazine to outlying communities, and then the entire United States. It was time to come down out of the treehouse and establish a ground-based headquarters, evolving as a business just as humanity evolved as a species. To fund this ambitious expansion, I decided to take Mister Magazine public.

Going Public Raises Even More Money

Instead of selling shares to just 4 parents in my community, my next step was to sell Mister Magazine to millions of investors by getting listed on a major stock exchange. There are three primary exchanges in the United States, each of which provides a place for investors to trade stock. They are the New York Stock Exchange (NYSE), the American Stock Exchange (AMEX), and the National Association of Securities Dealers Automated Quotation system (NASDAQ or OTC). Here's a description of each exchange:

New York Stock Exchange (NYSE)

This is the biggest and oldest of America's big three exchanges. Its famous floor is located along Wall Street in Manhattan. It caters to well-established companies like IBM, Ford, and McDonald's. To be listed, a company must have at least 1.1 million shares of stock outstanding, boast annual profits of $2.5 million or more, and be worth at least $18 million. As you can see, it's a big deal to be listed on the NYSE. *Outstanding*, by the way, refers to stock owned by shareholders. To make the NYSE, a company must have issued and sold at least 1.1 million shares of stock.

American Stock Exchange (AMEX or ASE)

Slightly less demanding than the NYSE, the American Stock Exchange lists smaller companies. It has five floors: Boston, Chicago, Cincinnati, Pacific, and Philadelphia. To be listed, a company must have at least 250,000 shares of stock outstanding with a total value of at least $2.5 million.

National Association of Securities Dealers Automated Quotation System (NASDAQ or OTC)

The NASDAQ gets most of the action these days and has become more prominent by trading cool high-tech companies like Microsoft, Intuit, and Gateway 2000. It's sometimes called the over the counter (OTC) market because there's no floor to see on Wall Street or any other street. Instead, the NASDAQ is comprised of brokers networked together around the country who trade stocks back and forth with computers. Some of the brokers are known as "market markers" because they supply the stock when you want to buy it. You'll never know which broker supplied the stock you're buying, and you won't care. To be listed on the NASDAQ, a company must have at least 400 shareholders, outstanding stock worth at least $1 million, assets of at least $4 million, and annual profits of $750,000 or more.

Working with an Investment Banker

As you can see, Mister Magazine didn't have a prayer of making any of the big three exchanges. But let's say a colossal exception was made and I worked with the investment-banking side of a large brokerage firm like Goldman Sachs, Merrill Lynch, or Paine Webber to make an *initial public offering*, or *IPO*. That's what a company's first offering of stock to the public is called. I told the investment banker how much money I wanted to raise, and the banker determined how many shares to sell at what price. I wanted to raise $10 million. The banker could have sold 5 million shares at $2 each, 10 million at $1 each, or 2 million at $5 each. As long as the combination produced the target amount, it didn't matter.

The investment banker committed to buy the shares if nobody else did and got to keep a small amount of profit per share for this risk. The banker initially sold shares of Mister Magazine to the *primary market*, which consists of the banker's preferred private accounts. After the primary market had dibs on the tantalizing new shares of Mister Magazine, the investment banker offered the remaining shares to the *secondary market*, which consists of everyday shmoes like you and me who read a stock's price in the paper and buy it.

Making a Secondary Offering

Once the banker made the initial public offering, I had my money and a bunch of new investors in the company. When it came time to raise more money, I sold additional shares of stock in what's called a *secondary offering*. No matter how many additional times I sell more stock, it's always called a secondary offering. I would also have the option of selling bonds to investors. When an investor buys a corporate bond, he or she is lending money to the corporation and will be paid back with interest. That means bonds have the same drawbacks that bank loans do. Mister Magazine would be forced to pay interest on the money it borrowed from investors instead of just selling them a share of stock in the company through a secondary offering.

Secondary offerings are sometimes necessary because companies don't receive a dime in profit from shares once they're being traded on the open market. After a company issues and sells a share of stock, all profits and losses generated by that stock belong to the investors trading it. Even if the price of the stock quadruples in value and it's bought and sold ten times in a day, the issuing company doesn't make any money off it. The reason is simple: the investor who buys a share of stock owns it. He or she can sell that share for whatever price the market will pay. The company isn't entitled to any of the profits from the sale because the investor is the sole owner of that share of stock until it's sold to a buyer who then becomes the new owner. Unless the company buys back its own stock, it won't own the shares again.

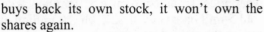

It's no different than selling your car. Do you owe Ford a share of the sale price when you finally get rid of that old Pinto in your garage? Of course not. You place an ad in the paper, deposit the buyer's check, and go on your way. It's the same situation if you own shares of Ford Motor Company. You place the sell order, take the buyer's money, pay a brokerage commission, and go on your way. Ford doesn't even know it happened.

Now, the shrewder among you might be wondering why companies care what happens to their stock price once they've got their dough. After all, they don't see any profit from you selling to me and me selling to another guy and him getting rich. That's true, but remember that companies might want to make another secondary offering later, and another, and another, and another. If a company issues 1,000,000 new shares at $40, it makes $40 million. If it issues 1,000,000 new shares at $10, it makes $10 million. Do you suppose most companies would rather make $40 million than $10 million? Of course they would, and that's why companies like to see their stock prices high. Not to mention that a falling stock price breeds ugly headlines.

What People Mean by "the Market"

You hear every day that the market is up or down. Have you ever paused to wonder what "the market" is? Usually, that phrase refers to the U.S. stock market as measured by the Dow Jones Industrial Average, often abbreviated DJIA or called simply the

Dow. The Dow is not the entire market at all, but just an average of 30 well-known companies like IBM, Merck, McDonald's, and Sears. The companies tracked by the Dow are chosen by the editors of the *Wall Street Journal*. The list changes occasionally as companies merge, lose prominence, or rise to the top of their industry.

The Dow is an *index*, which is just a way for us to judge the trend of the overall market by looking at a piece of it. The Dow is the most widely cited index, but not really the best gauge of the market. A more popular index among investors is Standard & Poor's 500, or just the S&P 500. It tracks 500 leading companies across four industries. It accounts for 80 percent of the NYSE. The Russell 2000 tracks 2,000 small companies across several industries while the Wilshire 5000 tracks—oddly enough—around 6,000 stocks of all sizes. For foreign markets there's the Morgan Stanley EAFE, which tracks stocks from overseas. EAFE stands for Europe, Australia, and Far East. Here's the average annual performance of these five indexes as of December 31, 1996:

Index	Tracks	3-Year	5-Year	10-Year
The Dow	30 Large U.S. Companies	22.85	18.42	16.66
S&P 500	500 Large U.S. Companies	19.66	15.2	15.26
Russell 2000	2,000 Small U.S. Companies	13.68	15.64	12.41
Wilshire 5000	6,000 U.S. Companies of All Sizes	15.62	12.24	11.45
Morgan Stan EAFE	1,100 Companies in 20 Countries	8.64	8.48	8.74

There are dozens of other indexes that you will encounter as you dig deeper into the world of investing. Each is an attempt to monitor the progress of a market by looking at a sliver of that market. One of my favorite indexes is the NASDAQ 100. It follows 100 top stocks from the NASDAQ such as Ascend Communications, BMC Software, Food Lion, Microsoft, and PETsMART. It's one of the hippest indexes around.

You probably already use indexes in other parts of your life, although you might not know it. We create them all the time to help ourselves compare different values. For example, let's say

One of the Hippest Indexes Around: NASDAQ 100

you are interested in buying a new Dodge Neon. If one of your main selection criteria is fuel economy, how do you know if the Neon performs well in that area? You compare its miles-per-gallon number to the average miles-per-gallon number of other midsize passenger cars, such as the Ford Escort and the Honda Accord. After several comparisons you know what is a good number, what is average, and what is below average. Notice that you don't compare the Neon's MPG to that of a Geo Metro or a Chevy Suburban. Those vehicles are in different classes and are irrelevant to your comparison. Thus, in this case, midsize passenger cars make up your index.

As you encounter different market indexes, just remember that each looks at a piece of the market to monitor how that part of the market is performing.

How to Choose a Broker to Buy Stocks

You buy stocks through a brokerage firm. A brokerage firm is a business licensed by the government to trade *securities* for investors. Brokerage firms join different stock exchanges and abide by their rules as well as the rules laid down by the *Securities and Exchange Commission*, or *SEC*.

Three Types of Brokerage Firms

There are full-service brokerage firms, discount brokerage firms, and deep-discount brokerage firms. Here's a description of each:

Full-Service Brokerage Firms

These are the largest, best-known brokerage firms in the country who spend millions of dollars a year advertising their names. You've probably heard of Bear Stearns, Goldman Sachs, Merrill Lynch, Paine Webber, Shearson Lehman Hutton, and others of their ilk. They're all the same. Regardless of their advertising slogans, the two words that should immediately come to mind when you hear the names of full-service broker-age firms are *expensive* and *misleading*. Other than that, they're great. Most full-service brokerage firms are divided into an investment-banking division, a research division, and a retail division.

The investment-banking division is what helps young companies make their initial public offering of stock and sell additional shares in secondary offerings. The brokerage firm keeps a profit on each share of stock sold. This is where the firm makes most of its money. Therefore, every one of the full-service brokerages wants to keep solid investment-banking relationships with their public companies. Never forget that full-service brokerage firms make their money by selling shares of stock for the companies they take public. They make their money whether investors purchasing those shares get a good deal or a bad deal. In other words, it doesn't make a bit of difference to the full-service broker whether investors make or lose money. The firm always makes money. To be fair, most brokers do want to find winning investments for their clients if for no other reason than future business.

"Full Service" Isn't as Good as It Sounds

The research division of a full-service brokerage firm ana-lyzes and writes evaluations, fact sheets, and periodic reports on publicly traded companies. Supposedly this information is pro-vided to you, an individual investor, to help you make educated decisions. However, remember from the previous paragraph that the brokerage firm makes its money by maintaining solid rela-tionships with companies. There are millions of investors, but only a few thousand companies. Whom do you think the broker wants to keep happy? The companies, of course. So, you'll rarely see a recommendation to "sell" a stock. Instead a broker will rec-ommend that you "hold" it. No company wants to see a firm telling investors to sell its stock. The brokerage's solution is to just never issue that ugly word. The *Wall Street Journal* revealed how blatant this directive is when it discovered a memo from Morgan Stanley's director of new stock issues stating that the company's policy was "no negative comments about our clients." The memo also instructed analysts to clear their stock ratings and opinions "which might be viewed negatively" with the company's corporate finance department.

The retail division is what you and I deal with. It's made up of brokers, who are really just sales reps, who call their clients and urge them to trade certain stocks. They charge large commissions which they split with the brokerage firm. The justification for the large commissions is that you're paying for all the research the company does on your behalf. But as you now know, that research is misleading anyway. It exists simply to urge you to trade the companies that the firm represents. So, you are paying for the way the firm makes most of its money! The only reason full-service brokerage firms have a retail division is so that they have a sales channel for the companies they represent.

Why Pay Someone to Annoy You?

When the investment-banking division takes a new company like Mister Magazine public, the research division puts the stock on a buy list and the retail-division brokers start making their phone calls. When you answer the phone and buy the stock, the broker and firm make money. It's an interesting twist on "full service," don't you think?

Discount Brokerage Firms

Discount brokerage firms do not conduct initial public offerings or secondary offerings. Most don't have in-house research divisions, either. They just handle your buy and sell orders and charge a low commission to do so. The commissions are discounted because the firms don't shoulder the expense of a full-service research department and a legion of sales reps in a retail sales department.

Compare Commissions

If you bought 500 shares of a $40 stock off the NYSE, here's the commission you should expect to pay at the different types of brokerage firms:

Full Service	$400
Discount	$100
Deep Discount	$20

Some discount brokers offer limited research assistance in the form of company reports, price quotes, news summaries, and other helpful material. But they don't have anybody call you to urge a buy or sell. The decisions are your decisions and the discount brokerage firm simply carries out your orders. Because they don't maintain investment-banking relationships with companies and because they make the same commission off any stock you trade, discount brokers don't have an interest in selling you the stock of any specific company.

To further cut costs, many discount brokers offer computer and telephone trading. That means you have the option of not talking to a representative in person. Instead you use a computer or touch-tone telephone to place your trade. Usually the discount broker will shave an additional percentage off the commission of such automated trades.

Discount brokers are gaining in popularity, and you've probably heard of a few. Charles Schwab & Company, Fidelity Brokerage Services, Olde, and Quick & Reilly are all discount brokerage firms.

Deep Discount Brokerage Firms

As their name implies, deep discount brokerage firms charge even lower commissions than those charged by discount brokers. Deep discounters exist only for the purpose of carrying out stock trades. Investors don't get much research assistance. Deep discounters are ideal for investors who conduct their own research and merely need a broker to place their trades.

As with discount brokers, deep discounters usually offer computer and telephone trading. E*Trade, Lombard, and eBroker are all deep-discount brokerage firms.

The Case for Discounters and Deep Discounters

In this book I'll show you how to rely on discounters and deep discounters to place your trades. Here's why:

Technology Has Made Full-Service Brokers Obsolete

Full-service brokerage firms are anachronisms. They're left over from the days when individual investors didn't have access to the trading mechanisms that brokers use. To place a trade on an exchange floor in the old days, investors needed brokers and runners and agents to carry out that order. Investors were accustomed to paying a commission for all that trouble.

But all that trouble doesn't exist anymore. The NASDAQ, where most of the action occurs today, doesn't even have an exchange floor! It's just a network of computers and brokers.

Even the NYSE and the AMEX don't require people to physically run around delivering orders. They got rid of the hitching posts out front too. There are still brokers on the NYSE trading floor who carry out orders, but they receive their orders via telephone or SuperDot, a computerized order-routing and reporting system that completes the trading loop in seconds.

Think about that. If you know what stock you want to buy,

The Family Stockbroker

shouldn't you just type it into a computer or punch it into a touch-tone phone yourself? Of course you should! It doesn't make any sense to call a full-service broker—or in many cases, they'll call you—and pay him a huge commission to type your stock trade into a computer. The full-service firms know this, of course, but they prefer to have you invest the way you would have in 1897 because they can get a lot of commission money out of you in the process.

You Need to Double-Check Full-Service Information

Some would argue that the extensive research and hand-holding you get from a full-service brokerage firm make it worth the extra commission money. But the only thing you'll hear from analysts in the research division of a full-service firm is what the marketing department encourages them to tell you. In other words, the stocks they want to sell in order to further their relationship with a public company will be pitched as good stocks for you to buy. Don't assume that cold call from your brother-in-law the full-service broker has your interests foremost in mind. The advice might be good, but it might not.

Don't Let a Full Service Fool Pick Your Stocks

Zacks Investment Research tracked the stocks recommended by eight full-service brokers over the three-year period begun June 30, 1993. The November 1996 issue of *Smart-Money* reported that of the eight brokers, five failed to beat the S&P 500. That's a 63 percent failure rate *before* commissions! Even if you weren't a statistics major, you know that a 63 percent chance of failure makes those high commissions hard to justify.

Because you can't just accept that a broker's advice is good, you need to conduct research for yourself. The full-service brokerage firms will usually send photocopied pages from *The Value Line Investment Survey* or *Standard & Poor's Stock Guide* for you to peruse. That's part of their full service. However, you can get the same information free from your public library or the Internet. You can get financial statements and annual reports by calling the investor-relations department at companies you're considering investing in.

You should conduct all this background research to verify the advice a full-service broker is giving you. After you conduct the research, then you could call back the broker and have her place the trade. But do you see the stupidity of this arrangement? The "full service" you got from the broker amounted to work you did on your own anyway! The better approach is to conduct the research and then place the trade with a discounter who'll simply carry out the order for a small price.

You Should Monitor Your Own Investments

Not only do you need to double-check everything full-service brokers tell you, the unsolicited phone calls you receive from them can be confusing. If you are a truly individual investor conducting your own research and placing trades with a discounter, you limit yourself to only what you need to know.

For example, say you researched a stock and decided on a suitable purchase price and a target sell price. You told your discount broker what price to buy at. Two weeks later, the stock hit that price and you automatically picked up 100 shares. Then you told your discounter the price you wanted to sell at, say 30 percent more than your purchase price. That's it. You went about your life and let the stock run its course. Six months later, it hit your sell price and you automatically sold all 100 shares and made 30 percent minus commissions.

Notice that you—and you alone—decided what happened in the course of that stock ownership. Unbeknownst to you, your stock dropped 30 percent in value before it made a roaring comeback to your sell price. If you'd gone through a full-service broker, there's a good chance he or she would have called you when it was down and provided every negative headline regarding the company's future. Maybe he would have caught

**Avoid the Heart-
Stopping Phone
Calls**

you at a vulnerable time and you would have sold at a loss, all because you couldn't choose your own information level. And, of course, the broker would make a commission on your sale at a loss and your subsequent purchase of a new stock.

When you take care of your own investments, you choose what to monitor. Maybe you want to know every uptick and downtick of your stocks and every bit of news affecting them. But it might be that you just want the big picture by checking prices once a month, perusing top stories on the Internet, and keeping an eye on a few related stocks in the same industry. The point is that it should be up to you, not up to a broker who stands to profit off your frequent buying and selling. Keep the background noise low.

How to Evaluate Stocks

Evaluating stocks is actually quite easy. Once you've done it a few times you'll develop a pattern of research that you can repeat with every new stock that interests you. But first you need to understand the difference between growth and value investing, fundamental and technical analysis, know some basic stock measurements, and understand how to read the stock pages.

Growth Investing vs. Value Investing

This is the most basic division between investors, akin to North and South. But, like North and South, there's a lot of area between each extreme that's hard to classify. Think of growth and value as being on a continuum. Most investors fall somewhere in the middle, and combining the two styles has proven to be a great investment approach.

Growth Investing

Growth investors look for companies that are sales and earnings machines. Such companies have a lot of potential, and growth investors are willing to pay handsomely for them. A growth company's potential might stem from a new product, a breakthrough patent, overseas expansion, or excellent management.

Key company measurements that growth investors examine are earnings and recent stock-price strength. A growth company without strong earnings is like an Indy 500 race car without an engine. Dividends aren't very important to growth investors because many growth companies pay small or no dividends. Instead, they reinvest profits to expand and improve their business. Hopefully, the reinvestments produce even more growth in the future. Growing companies post bigger earnings each year, and the amount of those earnings increases should be getting bigger too. Most growth investors set minimum criteria for investing in a company. Perhaps it should be growing at least 20 percent a year and pushing new highs in stock price.

Growth Investors Look for High-Flying Companies

Most new growth stocks trade on the NASDAQ. Growth companies you're probably familiar with are Microsoft, Intel, Starbucks, Home Depot, and Mailboxes Etc. Now you know what people mean when they drive past yet another Starbucks and say, "That place is growing like a weed."

Growth investors are searching for hot hands, not great bargains. They'll pay more for good companies. As a result, many growth investors don't even look at a stock's price in relation to its earnings or its book value because they know a lot of growth stocks are expensive and they don't care.

They just look at a stock's potential and go for it, hoping that current successes continue and get even better. They buy momentum, inertia, steamrolling forward movement. That's the nature of growth investing.

William O'Neil, a top growth investor whose strategy you'll learn on page 69, says in his seminar that growth investors are like baseball teams that pay huge salaries to top-ranked batters. They come at a high price, but if they keep batting .300 and winning games, then it's worth it. Likewise, you won't find many bargains among growth stocks. But if they keep growing, it's worth it.

Because a growth stock depends on its earnings and the acceleration of those earnings, the expectations of analysts and

The Panicked Earnings Fax

investors are high. That creates a risky situation. If a growth company fails to deliver the earnings that everybody expects, all hell breaks loose. Red flags fly left and right, phones start ringing off the hook, the stock price falls, reports shoot from fax machines across the world, and nobody's dinner tastes quite as good as it did the night of last quarter's earnings report.

Value Investing

Value investors look for stocks on the cheap. They compare stock prices to different measures of a company's business such as its earnings, assets, cash flow, and sales volume. The idea is that if you don't pay too much for what you get, there's less chance of losing money.

Value stocks are less expensive than growth stocks. They are companies that have been overlooked on their journey to success, have fallen on hard times after more successful years, or are in a slump for any number of reasons. Hopefully they're on a comeback and the value investor purchases shares at the bottom of an uphill climb. Here's where value and growth are tied together. In both cases, investors want to buy companies with a bright future. The difference is that growth investors usually buy those companies when they're already steamrolling ahead to that bright future, while value investors usually buy those companies when they're still getting ready to start or are recovering from a tumble.

Using O'Neil's baseball analogy, value investors comb the locker rooms for bandaged players trying to rehabilitate. They don't cost much, and you might uncover a future star. Of course, you might get exactly what you paid for: a broken player, or a broken company.

Value Investors Look for Bright Futures from Troubled Pasts

The value investor is a bargain hunter extraordinaire. From my interviews with professionals and novices alike, I gather that value investing is close to what we've been taught from the time we were kids. What did you look at when buying candy? Probably which kind you could get the most of for your pocketful of allowance money. In school, you probably bought the package of notebook paper with the most sheets for your dollar. When relatives came by for the holidays, they might have swapped stories of the great bargains or "steals" they purchased recently. We're used to examining price with an eye toward value. It's no different in the world of investing.

Value investors pay particular attention to dividends. A company that pays dividends contributes to an investor's profit even if the stock price does not rise. That's comforting. Also, among big companies the dividend yield is a great indicator of how bargain-priced a company is.

Growth investors tend to get in when things are heating up and bail out at the first sign of slowing growth. Value investors tend to be very careful about where their money goes and let it ride out fluctuations once they decide where to invest. The contrast in these two styles is why I think value investing is more suitable to the average individual investor. Most individuals do not have the time or resources to monitor split-second changes in their stocks to act accordingly. It seems that conducting thorough research periodically and letting the chosen stocks do their

**Growth and Value
Make a Good Team**

thing is the best approach for most individual investors. That being the case, why go through the hassle of all the trading that accompanies pure growth portfolios?

These are my thoughts only, and throughout this book I try to provide equal space to each style. I think most of us end up combining the styles in our personal portfolios, but with a tendency one way or the other. I've enjoyed excellent results from both growth and value investments, although I tend toward value.

Fundamental Analysis vs. Technical Analysis

There are two ways to evaluate a stock. The first way is using *fundamental analysis*, which examines information about the company's health and potential to succeed. You use fundamental information to learn about a company. The second way is using *technical analysis*, which examines the past behavior of the stock price in different market conditions and attempts to predict the stock's future price based on current and projected market conditions and trading volume. You use technical information to learn about a company's stock.

In this guide you'll learn to use fundamental analysis and technical analysis together.

Fundamental Analysis

For individual investors, fundamental analysis should form the core of their evaluations. Choosing good companies is what I consider the foundation of successful investing. Also, healthy companies make the best long-term investments, and I advocate a long-term investment strategy. By looking at a company's management, its rate of growth, how much it earns, and how much it pays to keep the lights on and the cash register ringing are easy things for you and me to understand. After all, we constantly balance the same things in our own lives. You earn a certain amount of money, budget how to spend it, and keep an eye on your habits. If you consistently run low on funds, you pull out the stack of bills and figure out how you can change that. It's very similar to running a business.

Fundamental Analysis Teaches All About a Company

Once you have a picture of a company's fundamentals, you can determine its intrinsic value. *Intrinsic value* is the price a stock should sell at under normal market conditions. The most important fundamental measure in determining a company's intrinsic value is earnings: what the company is earning now and what you expect it to earn in the future. After that, you'll want to know what the company's assets are, if it's in debt, and the history of its management. Once you have a clear picture of the company's intrinsic value, you examine its price to see if it's selling above or below its value. If it's selling below its value, it's a good buy. If it's selling above its value, it's overpriced. Of course, there's more to it than that, but for now let's leave it black and white.

Technical Analysis

Technical analysis, on the other hand, is a little harder to understand. It uses charts of price history, computer-graph patterns, and crowd psychology to evaluate a stock. The premise of technical analysis is that supply and demand drive all stock prices. Fundamental information doesn't matter until it affects demand. The main measurement technical analysts use to gauge demand is trading volume. After that, they look at trend charts, volatility, and small price movements.

Technical analysis is useful, but takes more than a nodding acquaintance to use correctly. This little guide is supposed to help you, a busy person who isn't an investment professional, learn to buy stocks. It can't teach you, nor do you care to know, the intricacies of technical analysis as a complete investment strategy.

However, there are a few simple technical measures that you'll find helpful as you embark on your stock-picking adventure. You'll use them to gauge where the overall market is at and to determine if the stocks that interest you are selling for more or less than their intrinsic value, which you'll know after conducting your fundamental research. See how the two relate? You evaluate the company behind the stock with fundamental analysis, then evaluate the price of the stock and its demand with technical analysis.

Technical Analysis Teaches All About a Stock

The bottom line is that most investors use a combination of both fundamental and technical analysis.

Some Fundamental Stock Measurements

The annoying thing about stock measurements is that even if every one of them gives a green light to a stock you're considering, it might still end up being a bad investment. It's not like measuring your inseam. Once you know that number, you know the length of pants to buy, and if they're that length, they fit. Period. It's not that simple with stocks.

Nonetheless, knowing how your stocks measure up is important. Knowing something that might make a difference is better than knowing nothing at all. In most cases the measurements do reveal valuable information. In this section I explain the most common stock measurements and also a few you won't find listed in many other places. They're my favorites.

Important Note: This section gives you an up-front, nodding acquaintance with these measurements. I just explain them here. Later in the book I show where to find them and how to use them on your stocks-to-watch worksheet. Also, you don't need to calculate most of the measurements on your own. They're already calculated for you in newspapers, reference volumes, the Internet, and other places.

Cash Flow per Share

Cash flow is the stream of cash through a business. You want it to be positive and you'd love it to be big. Sometimes even profitable businesses don't have strong cash flows because they sell their goods on credit.

You know all those ads you see to buy now with no payments until next year? Those are just the kind of business activities that boost profits without increasing cash flow. It's true that somebody buys the couch or dishwasher or weed zapper and the sale goes on the books, but the business doesn't see any money until

A Long Payment Schedule Can Kill a Company's Cash Flow

next year. That can be a problem if there isn't enough money around to keep the lights on and the water running. Bills need to be paid on time no matter what a customer's payment schedule is.

A well-managed business can do fine with buy now, pay later plans. With enough cash in the bank, the bills are covered. In the meantime, special promos do sell a lot of product that will eventually be paid for. Also, the profits that are finally realized might be higher than the advertised prices due to accrued interest and other fine print.

Cash flow per share—what we're examining—is simply a company's cash flow divided by the number of shares outstanding. That lets you see what price you're paying for a share of the company's cash flow.

Current Ratio

The *current ratio* is the most popular gauge of a company's ability to pay its short-term bills. It's measured by dividing current assets by current liabilities. The ratio reveals how easily a company can deal with unexpected expenses or opportunities. It's usually expressed in the number of times, such as "current assets are three times current liabilities." That might be a company with current assets of $300,000 and current liabilities of $100,000. Another way to state the current ratio would be 3-to-1.

A company's assets are everything it owns: cars, machines, patents, computers, and so on. Its *current* assets are things that are used up and replenished frequently such as cash, inventory, and accounts receivable. A company's liabilities are everything it owes: loans, bills, and such. Its *current* liabilities are the ones usually due within one year.

As you can see, comparing current assets with current liabilities shows you if the company is prepared for short-term obligations and able to take advantage of short-term opportunities. That's what you want. Look for companies with a current ratio of at least 2-to-1.

Dividend Yield

A stock's *dividend yield* is its annual cash dividend divided by its current price. If Mister Magazine paid a quarterly dividend of $.15, you assume that its annual dividend is $.60—15 cents per quarter times four quarters in a year give you 60 cents. Let's say its current stock price is $15. Divide .60 by 15 to get a yield of .04 or 4 percent. It's simple to figure a stock's dividend yield, but you won't need to do it. It's printed for you in the newspaper every day.

At first dividend yield probably looks pretty boring. A lot of stocks don't pay dividends anyway, and who really cares what a stock yields in dividends? If you want steady payouts, you'll go to your local bank.

But alas, amigo, the dividend yield reveals plenty about a stock's price. It tells you more about a stock's price than it does about a stock's dividend. Why? Because there are only two numbers involved in the dividend yield. If one number remains constant, then the other number drives any changes.

What's a Quarter?

A quarter is simply a three-month time period. Calendar quarters are January to March, April to June, July to September, and October to December.

Many companies define their own business year, which might not be the same as a calendar year. Company-defined years are called fiscal years. A fiscal quarter is still three months, but won't necessarily be a calendar quarter. For instance, a fiscal quarter might be August to October.

With most companies the dividend payout remains fairly constant. That leaves you with only one other number to influence dividend yield: stock price. It changes daily and its relationship to the dividend is immediately reflected in the dividend yield.

Look what happens. If Mister Magazine's price rises from $15 to $30 but it maintains a constant dividend of $.60, its dividend yield drops to 2 percent. If the price then rises to $60, the dividend yield drops to 1 percent. If the dividend remains constant and the yield changes, you know the price is moving. In this case, Mister Magazine's decreasing yield tells you that the stock price is rising and might be overvalued.

Being the astute person that you are, as evidenced by the fact that you chose this book from a crowded shelf, you might be thinking that you could find some bargain stocks by looking for high dividend yields. You are correct. Large companies that maintain steady dividends are judged all the time by their dividend yields. You'll learn in Chapter 3 that history proves that high-yielding, market-leading companies can be selected by dividend yield alone. Then, in Chapter 4 you'll learn an automated investment strategy that uses high-dividend yield to select winners from the 30 stocks in the Dow Jones Industrial Average.

Earnings per Share (EPS)

This is the king of growth measures. *Earnings per share*, sometimes called *EPS*, takes what a company earned and divides it by the number of stock shares outstanding. It's the last thing listed on a company's income statement, the famous bottom line that everybody lives and dies for. Earnings per share is usually reported for either last quarter or last year. Analysts project future earnings too.

Say Mister Magazine's earnings were $4,500 last quarter and there were 10 shares of stock outstanding. Mister Magazine's earnings per share would be $450. That's quite high. In real life, earnings per share tend to fall between $1 and $5 with occasional spikes to $10 or $20. But they can be anything, and they go negative when the company loses money.

The real problem with earnings per share is that it's subject to manipulation and market pressure. Every company knows that investors examine earnings. Every company wants to report the biggest earnings number possible. So different companies use different accounting methods and complex formulas to take into consideration their specific situation. Some companies deduct the dividends paid to preferred stockholders while other companies don't issue preferred stock; some companies need to worry about investments that can be converted to common stock while other companies don't; and every company chooses its own pace to depreciate equipment. Sometimes earnings are affected

The Endless Earnings Quest

by market conditions beyond a company's control. For instance, the cost of goods sold fluctuates as market conditions change. A computer company might sell the same computer model all year long. But if the price of memory goes up, so does the company's cost of building computers. You definitely don't want to know the details of how every company determines its earnings, but you should at least be aware that this is not a cut-and-dried number. It's subject to manipulation and market pressure.

Earnings per share remains a useful measurement. The bigger the number, the better. It doesn't take a mental giant to see why. The more a company earns, the more successful it is and the more desirable it becomes to investors. That should make the stock price rise. If the company's earnings per share increases quarter after quarter at a faster rate, that's called *earnings momentum* or *earnings acceleration* and is a popular way of identifying solid growth companies. Some of the best-performing mutual fund managers use momentum investing to choose their stocks. I've heard investors say they're searching for "the big mo," referring to a hidden company with incredible earnings momentum.

Quarterly reports from a company showing either higher or lower earnings per share than expected are called *earnings surprises*. They often cause a stock to rise or fall sharply. Analysts study surprises carefully, hoping to spot a trend early.

Net Profit Margin

A company's net profit margin is determined by dividing the earnings left over after paying all its expenses (net earnings) by the amount of revenue it had before paying expenses (total revenue). So, if a company makes $1 million and pays $900,000 in expenses, its net profit margin is 10 percent ($100,000 divided by $1,000,000). If a competing company also makes $1 million but pays only $700,000 in expenses, its net profit margin is 30 percent ($300,000 divided by $1,000,000). All other things being equal, which company's stock would you rather own? The company with a 30 percent profit margin, of course. It makes the same amount of money as its competitor but keeps more. Put differently, it spends less to earn the same income. A high profit margin tells you that the company's management is good at controlling costs. That's great news because every dollar frittered away unnecessarily is one less dollar of profit for shareholders.

Everybody Wants a High Net Profit Margin

High net profit margins are the hallmarks of companies that dominate their industries. When any industry is thriving, people notice and start new companies to compete against the existing ones. All the companies need to buy similar equipment, similar supplies, hire employees with similar skills, market to the same customers, and research similar improvements. Notice how similar the companies in an industry become? They can't all survive forever. When the shake-out comes, companies that are able to maintain a high net profit margin will make the most money and will survive. They've somehow figured a way to squeeze more profit from sales, a clear sign of superior management. Not only does the high net profit margin itself translate immediately into higher profits and a stronger bottom line, it also reveals to you a management team that is probably ahead of competitors in many areas of running a company in their industry.

Price/Book Ratio

Price/book compares a stock's price to how much the stock is worth right now if somebody liquidated the company.

In other words, if I took all of Mister Magazine's office space, magazine inventory, telephones, computers, and delivery bicycles to the local business auction, I'd get a sum of money for it. Let's say I could get $5,000. If there are currently 10 shares of Mister Magazine stock outstanding, each one would be entitled to $500 of the company's sale price. Thus, Mister Magazine stock has a *book value per share* of $500. That's the "book" part of the price/book ratio. Explained in official terms, book value per share is common stockholders' equity divided by outstanding shares. You'll find both figures on the company's balance sheet.

Next, divide the current price by the book value to get the price/book ratio. If Mister Magazine currently sells for $400 a share, its price/book is .80 ($400 divided by $500). If the ratio is less than 1, that means you're paying less for the stock than its liquidation value. That's good. If the company goes bankrupt, you should still get your money back. If the ratio is more than 1, you're paying more than the stock's liquidation value.

Of course, a lot of crucial information about a company isn't reflected in its book value. Who cares about the fax machines and desks when you've got a business that earns money and a popular brand name? The value of McDonald's goes way beyond french-fry machines and drive-through microphones. I can buy my own french-fry machines, but can I serve billions and billions of people with them? Heck no, so I'm willing to pay more than book value for McDonald's.

Price/Earnings Ratio (P/E or Multiple)

This is the king of value measures. The price of a stock divided by its earnings per share is called its *price/earnings ratio*, or *P/E*, or *multiple*. At cocktail parties, just say "P and E." Every stock has a trailing P/E and a forward P/E. The trailing P/E uses earnings from the last 12 months while the forward P/E uses next year's projected earnings from an analyst. A stock's P/E ratio fluctuates all the time from changes in its price, which happen every day, and changes in its earnings, which happen every quarter.

A stock selling for $40 a share that earned $2 last year and is projected to earn $4 next year has a trailing P/E of 20 and a forward P/E of 10.

A stock's price by itself is meaningless. If one stock sells for $100 and another for $20, which would you rather buy? You have no idea unless you can put those two prices in context with company earnings. Once you know the P/E for each stock, then you can see if the stock is selling for a good price or not. Suppose the $100 stock earned $10 last year and the $20 stock earned $1. The $100 stock has a trailing P/E of 10. The $20 stock has a P/E of 20.

**Good
Measurements
Bring Good Stocks**

The $100 stock is a better value because you're buying more earnings power with your money.

Use a stock's P/E to determine how much you're paying for a company's earning power. If the P/E is high, you should expect to get high earnings growth for the extra money you paid for the stock. It's riskier to invest in a high P/E stock than a low P/E because it's more difficult for the high P/E to meet the high earnings expectations of its shareholders and analysts. Many of today's newest technology companies trade with high P/E ratios, generally over 20. Companies with low P/E ratios usually operate in slow-growth industries. Also, mature companies with low P/E ratios often pay dividends while new companies with high P/E ratios usually do not.

Price/Sales Ratio (P/S or PSR)

This is one of my favorites. P/E compares price to earnings, price/book compares price to liquidation value, and *price/sales*, or *PSR*, compares price to sales revenue. To determine a stock's PSR, simply take the company's total market value and divide it by the most recent four quarters of sales revenue. Sometimes you'll know the price per share and the sales per share. In fact, we use both on this book's stocks-to-watch worksheet. In that case, simply divide the price per share by the sales per share to get PSR.

For instance, if there are 10 shares of Mister Magazine stock outstanding and the current price is $400, Mister Magazine has a *total market value* of $4,000. If Mister Magazine has sales of $10,000 in the past four quarters, its PSR is .40. Running the numbers per share gives us the same result. Mister Magazine's stock price is $400 and its sales are $1,000 per share. $400 divided by $1,000 is .40.

Let's look at a comparison from *SmartMoney*. In summer 1996, Microsoft had a market value of $73.5 billion and sales of $8 billion. Its PSR was around 9. IBM had a market value of $55 billion and sales of $72 billion. Its PSR was .76. These numbers revealed something very important to investors considering both stocks. People were paying $9 for each dollar of Microsoft's sales, but only 76 cents for each dollar of IBM's sales. Aha! By PSR measure, IBM was a better bargain than Microsoft.

"So what?" you might say. "It's profits I care about, not sales." That's a common objection to using PSR. But remember from the explanation of earnings on page twenty that companies can manipulate earnings all sorts of ways. They use accounting rules that are flexible to interpret how much it costs them to do business and then subtract that number from revenue to get earnings. The flexible accounting can spit out small or big numbers as needed. But with sales revenue there's not a lot to adjust. It's just what you sold—end of story.

Of course, it never hurts to see big sales *and* big earnings. The two aren't mutually exclusive.

Quick Ratio

The quick ratio is very similar to the current ratio, which is the first measurement you read in this section. The current ratio evaluates a company's short-term liquidity by dividing current assets by current liabilities. The higher the ratio, the better the company is able to deal with unseen expenses and opportunities.

The *quick ratio* provides a more accurate look at a company's ability to deal with short-term needs by dividing only the company's cash and equivalents by its current liabilities. I remember the difference between the two measures by associating "quick" with easy money, that is, cash on hand. "Current" doesn't sound nearly as speedy. The quick ratio looks at how "quickly" a company can respond to a surprise bill or sudden opportunity. If it has lots of cash, it can just write a check. But if its money is already earmarked for current liabilities, then it's not available for quick spending. The company might start using its equivalent of credit cards to pay for things—very bad.

The Quick Ratio Looks at a Company's Cash

Say a company has $50,000 cash and current liabilities of $25,000. Dividing 50 by 25 gives you a quick ratio of 2, also written 2-to-1 or 2:1. That means the company keeps cash worth twice its current liabilities. If worse came to worst, it could write a check for everything it owes in the next year and still have $25,000 in the bank. That's a comfort to any investor.

I like to see a quick ratio of at least .5. That means the company has cash worth half of its current liabilities sitting somewhere accessible. As with the current ratio, however, bigger is better.

Return on Equity (ROE)

Some people consider this the ultimate measure of a stock's success. *Return on equity* shows you the rate of return to shareholders by dividing net income by total shareholders' equity. Bigger is always better with this number because it means the company is making a lot of money off the investments that shareholders have made. A good return on equity is anything above 20 percent.

In 1995, Apple Computer reported net income of $424 million and total shareholders' equity of $2,901 million. Dividing 424 by 2,901 gives you a return on equity of 15 percent. Adding to the trouble, income dropped to a negative $816 million in 1996 with total shareholders' equity of $2,058 million. That's a return on equity of −40 percent. Generally speaking, folks, minus signs in front of investment numbers are bad.

Some Technical Stock Measurements

As I mentioned earlier, this book doesn't teach you exhaustive technical analysis. This section explains the few technical measurements you'll use to research stocks.

Also, no charts here. I rarely look at anything more than a price history with a few trend lines, something that doesn't require much explanation. If you want to learn about technical charting and terms like ascending tops, breakouts, head and shoulders, resistance levels, support levels, and dead-cat bounces, pick up a good book on technical charting.

Beta

Here's a handy measurement of risk. *Beta* shows you how volatile a stock has been compared to the market. The market, as measured by the S&P 500, has a beta of 1. That's the benchmark, our basis of comparison. A stock with a beta higher than 1 has fluctuated more than the market; one with a beta less than 1 has fluctuated less. For instance, if Mister Magazine has a beta of 1.3, you know that it has been up about 30 percent more than the market in good times and down about 30 percent more in bad times.

At the end of 1996, MCI had a beta of 2.07. Looking at that, you know that the stock has fluctuated twice as much as the market. AT&T's beta was 1.38, a bit more volatile than the market but not by nearly as much as MCI. For a more conservative stock, you could look at Wells Fargo, which had a beta of .68. You know from that number that the company keeps a pretty steady course.

Stocks Aren't the Only Things That Are Volatile

Most people's gut reaction is to lean toward stocks with low betas. But remember that fluctuation can be in the upward direction. You'd rather own a stock that beats the market by 100 percent when prices are rising than one that trails it by 40 percent. A lot of small-company investors prefer a high beta.

Although you won't use beta on this book's worksheet, you'll see it listed in a lot of places. It's good to know what it means. In place of beta, we'll use relative price strength to gauge a stock's price performance against other stocks.

Max and Min Comparison

The *max and min comparison* is a stock's projected maximum percentage gain compared to its projected minimum percentage gain. If the projected minimum is a decline from the current price, don't bother with the stock. Notice that instead of using stock prices, I use percentage gains. I find them more meaningful because everything eventually translates to a percentage gain or loss anyway. You can figure max and min for any time period for which projections exist. In this book we'll use three to five years, but I've used max and min on one-year projections.

Note that max and min is not a ratio. Some people think they can run the numbers and get a high or low result. High would mean the max is considerably higher than the min—a good sign, right? Not necessarily. What if a company has a maximum projected gain of 5 percent and a minimum of 4 percent? Dividing 5 by 4 gives you 1.25. But another stock with a maximum projected gain of 500 percent and a minimum projected gain of 400 percent also clocks in at 1.25. Each situation produces the same number, but anybody can see that a 500 percent projected gain is far preferable to a 5 percent projected gain. So, do not divide the projected max and min. Just list them side by side and look at them.

The other measurements in this section look at hard numbers from a company's financial statements. Max and min do not. The content is all theoretical, based on the opinions of analysts and not guaranteed in any way. However, analysts try their best to make accurate projections on a company's future by looking at the other fundamental measures in this section—along with tons of other material. That's why I include max and min here. Together they provide a snapshot of what professionals have concluded after studying the same company you're studying. There are no guarantees, but second opinions never hurt anybody.

Relative Price Strength

This is similar to beta. *Relative price strength* shows you how a stock's price has performed compared to the prices of all other stocks. In this book you'll learn to use relative price strength as it's presented in *Investor's Business Daily*, a national newspaper that ranks the relative price strength of all stocks from 1 to 99. Stocks that rank 90 have outperformed 90 percent of all other stocks. Stocks that rank 20 have underperformed 80 percent of all other stocks. Pretty simple system, wouldn't you say?

Volume

This is an easy one. *Volume* is simply the amount of a stock that's traded on any given day, week, or any other time period. A stock's volume is a good indicator of how much interest people have in the stock. That's important to know because the stock market is greatly affected by supply and demand. If everybody wants to buy a certain stock, its price will rise. If nobody wants it, the price will fall. Some investors like to buy stocks with low volume, hoping that major institutions will discover them and begin trading heavily. Demand soars and so do prices. Lots of investors watch stock volume in an attempt to catch trends early. As with surfing, you want to be in front of the wave.

Volume is measured in either the number of shares traded or

the dollar amount that is moved as a result of that trading. If 1,000,000 shares of Mister Magazine changed hands on Tuesday at a price of $8, the share volume was 1,000,000 and the dollar volume was $8,000,000.

Stock Orders on a Busy Day

How to Read the Stock Pages

There are dozens of places to get information about stocks, but none as readily available as the stock pages of a newspaper. Your local paper probably has a listing, and you can always access one of the national investment papers such as *Investor's Business Daily* or the *Wall Street Journal*.

The format of stock pages changes slightly from paper to paper, but if you can read one you can wing it through any other. Also, most papers include a box that explains their format. In fact, why are you reading about it here? Just turn to your paper's stock pages and read how to use them right there. On the off chance that you don't have a paper handy, I'll explain how to read the stock pages. Here's an excerpt from the March 30, 1997, *Los Angeles Times* Sunday edition that includes information for Federal Express, abbreviated FedExp:

LOS ANGELES TIMES

NYSE

Continued from D6

52-week High	52-week Low	YTD %Chg.	Stock-Div	Yld	P/E	High	Low	Last	Ch.
25¾	14⅜	+19.6	FamDir 0.48f	2.0	22	25¼	24¼	24⅜	–⅞
43¾	27½	+2.0	FanniMae 0.84f	2.2	15	40⅞	37⅜	38⅜	–1⅜
10½	5¼	+28.6	Farah		dd	10⅜	9⅞	10⅛	+⅛
26¼	24¼	+0.5	xFrmG pfA 2.11	8.3		25⅞	25⅛	25½	+⅜
7⅜	5½	–6.0	Fedders 0.08	1.4	9	5⅞	5¾	5⅞	+⅛
6½	4⅝	+7.5	FeddersA 0.08	1.5	9	5½	5¼	5⅜	...
57⅞	34⅞	+21.1	FedExp s		18	57⅞	53⅝	53⅞	–2⅜
33⅞	19⅛	+4.1	FdHmLn s 0.40f	1.4	17	31¾	28⅛	28⅝	–⅝
26⅜	25⅛	–0.5	FdHLn pf 1.98	7.9		25¼	25⅛	25⅛	...
26⅛	24⅝	+1.3	FdHL pfA 1.68	6.6		25 29/64	25⅜	25 29/64	+13/64
50⅜	49¼	–0.2	FdHL pfB 2.44	4.9		49 51/64	49 51/64	49 51/64	+19/64
26¾	16⅛	+13.1	FedMog 0.48	1.9	dd	25½	24½	24⅞	+¼
28¾	20½	–1.8	FedRlty 1.66	6.3	31	27⅜	26½	26⅝	–¼
28¼	20⅞	–0.5	FedSignl 0.67f	2.6	19	26	25¼	25¾	+⅜
38¼	29⅜	+0.7	FedrDS		27	37	34⅜	34⅜	–2¾
16¼	9⅜	+2.9	FdDS wtC			15½	13	13⅜	–2

As you can see, there are ten columns of information. The first two columns show the stock's *52-week High and Low* prices. Like the names imply, these are just the highest price and lowest price the stock traded for over the past 52 weeks excluding the previous day's trading. These figures are adjusted to reflect any stock splits. The 52-week high and low are handy because they show the range a stock has traded in. It's helpful to know if the stock is currently selling near the highest price anybody has paid for it in the past year, or if it's cheaper than anybody's seen in a year. Also, you can see if there's a huge space between the high and low or if they're close together. Sometimes the figures are within a few dollars of each other. Such a narrow trading range might appeal to you if you prefer quiet stocks that pay steady dividends. On the other hand, if you're seeking major price appreciation, you might like to see a huge differential between the stock's high and low. FedEx's 52-week high was 57 $^7/_8$, and its low was 34 $^7/_8$.

The third column shows the *year-to-date percentage change*. It's based on the price change since January 1 or the company's initial public offering if it happened after January 1. FedEx gained 21.1 percent as of March 30.

The fourth column, called *Stock-Div*, lists the name of the company, followed immediately by the dividend. The dividend shown is an annual figure determined by the last quarterly or semiannual payout. Notice that FedEx doesn't list an annual dividend. That's because the company doesn't pay one. All you see is a little "s" after the name, telling you that this stock split in the last 52 weeks. But look at the stock just below FedEx, FdHmLn or Federal Home Loan Mortgage. Its dividend is .40 followed by a little "f" which means the dividend increased at the last declaration. Divide by 4 and you know that the last quarterly dividend FdHmLn paid was .10. If you'd owned a single share, you could have purchased a gumball with your dividend check.

One Share's Dividend Would Buy You a Gumball

The fifth column provides the stock's *yield*. It's shown as an annualized percentage return provided by the dividend. You can use the figure to compare the stock's dividend performance with your savings account or CD.

More important, you can use it to find undervalued large companies, as you'll learn in Chapter 4. FedEx has no yield because it has no dividend. FdHmLn's yield was 1.4 percent.

The sixth column shows the stock's *price-earnings ratio* or *P/E*. The P/E is figured by dividing the closing price of the stock by the company's total earnings per share for the latest four quarters. It's the most common measure of whether a stock is a good deal. All else being equal, you'd prefer to buy a stock with a low P/E because it means you're paying a relatively small amount to own a share in the earnings. FedEx's P/E was 18.

The last four columns show the *high*, *low*, *last*, and *change*. The high and low show the stock's price range on the previous trading day while last shows the closing price at the end of the day. Change shows how much the closing price changed from the day before or, on Sunday, from the week before. FedEx showed a high of $57^7/_8$, a low of $53^5/_8$, a last of $53^7/_8$, and a change of $-2^3/_8$.

There are footnotes sprinkled throughout stock tables that identify things like preferred stock shares, ex-dividend dates, and new stocks. These differ from paper to paper but should be defined in your paper's explanatory notes. Nobody memorizes the letters. To tell you what the little "s" and little "f" meant in the above explanations, I read the *Times* explanatory notes.

Three Stock Classifications You Should Know

People always try to categorize objects in their lives to make them easier to deal with. If you hear the model name of a new car, your first question is probably "What type of car is it?" You know that sports cars are fast, minivans haul a lot of people, and trucks carry cargo. Stocks are categorized hundreds of different ways. In fact, from my interviews with brokers, planners, investment clubs, and people on the street, I'm convinced that there is a classification system for each investor. Our view of the world is shaped by our experiences and personalities, which is why no two people view the same stock in the same way.

Surprise! You need to know only three widely accepted classifications: the size of the company, its industry classification, and whether it's growth or value. I hate complexity as much as you do, and I think these three classifications provide all the information we need.

Perception Is Everything	I'd never survive without our products. We have the best technology and it's reliable."
I recently stopped by a local computer store to see the new IBM Aptiva. While I tested it out, two men joined me at the keyboard.	Interestingly, the first man bought IBM stock when it traded around $170 and watched it drop to $45. The second man bought it at $45 and watched it rise to $130.
One said, "I used to work for IBM and I'd never own anything from the company. It's the fattest, most bureaucratic business I've ever seen." The other said, "I still work for IBM and	Same company, different employees. Same computers, different experiences. Same stock, different prices.

Company Size

A company is either big or small. Next topic.

Although it's not that simple, company size is pretty straight-forward. To investors, company size is called *market capitalization* or just *market cap*. Market cap is determined by multiplying the number of outstanding shares of stock by the current market price per share. So if Mister Magazine has grown like Jack's beanstalk and there are 4 million shares of its stock outstanding and they trade for $10 per share, Mister Magazine's market cap is $40 million.

Is that big or small? Compared to the treehouse operation it started as, that's huge! From its $1,000 initial sale to venture cap-

italists, Mister Magazine has grown 3,999,900 percent. So from an initial investor and company founder perspective, Mister Magazine is enormous.

But compared to General Motors it's a pebble in the tire tread. GM's market cap is about $43 billion. That's 1,000 times bigger than Mister Magazine. As you can imagine, owning shares of GM and owning shares of

A Very Small Company

Mister Magazine would probably be very different investment experiences.

So let's divide all companies into the five market cap ranges used by Morningstar, the most popular mutual fund rating service, to classify the holdings of stock mutual funds:

Giant	> $25 Bil
Large	$5 Bil–$25 Bil
Medium	$1 Bil–$5 Bil
Small	$250 Mil–$1 Bil
Micro	< $250 Mil

In mid-1996, Morningstar looked at the 50 mutual funds in each category with the highest concentration in stocks of that market cap range, then measured their combined performance. Here's how they compared in average annual performance:

Market Cap	3-Year	5-Year	10-Year
Giant	14.72	12.77	10.39
Large	14.17	14.44	11.78
Medium	16.09	16.09	11.99
Small	15.19	16.83	8.7
Micro	16.45	16.56	11.45

Keep in mind that the figures are for mutual-funds investing in the different categories. I like that, though, because it examines the record of real people picking stocks instead of the performance of the stock group itself. Your record will be better or worse than the aggregate of 50 fund managers, but probably not far off. A lot of people would be happy with 5-year annual returns over 16 percent.

Industry Classification

You need to know what a company does to make money; otherwise you don't know which other companies to compare it to. Also, if you know what industry a company operates in, you can keep an eye on that industry for trends.

In many cases you'll know off the top of your head what a company does to earn a buck. You're probably aware that Boeing makes airplanes, Harley-Davidson makes motorcycles, Coke makes soft drinks, MCI provides phone service, and Dell sells computers. A lot of bigger companies make money in several ways, however, and you should know all of them. Philip Morris makes cigarettes, but it also sells food under the Kraft label.

You'll usually become aware of a company's business simply by getting interested enough to invest. If somebody mentions to you that Allamuck Corporation is going gangbusters and tripled in size over the past year, you'll probably look it up in the stock pages. Once there, you'll either rule it out based on a few key measures or get excited and want to learn more. If you call Allamuck for an annual report, search the Internet for Allamuck info, or make a trip to your local library, you're going to know what Allamuck does for a living.

You'll learn specific places to find company profiles in Chapter 6.

Growth or Value

The last label you want to place on your stocks is whether they're growth or value. You read all about growth investing versus value investing on page 20. When you're examining a potential company, know whether it's increasing sales and earnings and is expected to continue doing so. That's a growth company.

Maybe instead the company has had a rough couple of years and its stock price is at an all-time low. After reviewing everything you know about the company, you might decide that it's not as bad off as everybody thinks. That's a value company.

Growth companies and value companies behave differently. Make sure you know which type you're buying.

2 How the Masters Tell Us to Invest

Now that you speak the language of stocks and should be able to follow a discussion about them, let's talk strategy! When I decided to enter the stock market, I was nervous. Just about everybody is. At first glance it looks like there are a few people making lots of money and a lot of people making little money. Come to think of it, things look pretty much that same way at second, third, and fourth glance.

But as long as you follow an informed path and conduct your own research, you'll be fine. Buying what headlines tell you to buy doesn't work. Buying what your neighbor, friend, or relative tells you to buy doesn't work. But buying what seems best to you after thorough research can work.

This chapter and the next two contain the most important information in the book. The rest of the book deals with the mechanics of investing: learning the basics, choosing a broker, placing an order, and so on. But these three chapters help you form a strategy.

In this chapter you'll learn how the best investors make money and how you can too. Investing is full of legends. Some of their stories involve overnight profits, a lot of luck, or complex theories. Those legends don't help you and me when we're sitting at the kitchen table with a newspaper trying to figure out a good way to retire. What helped me, and will help you, is studying the masters who use an approach that has proven itself over time and is feasible for individual investors to adopt.

Sorting Through the Material Like a Proofreader

Meet the Masters

This May Be a Little Young, but a HeadStart Never Hurt Anybody

Benjamin Graham—Ben, to those who've read a lot of his stuff—is one of the most influential investment writers ever. His hallmark achievement is a book called *The Intelligent Investor*, which presents a rational value-oriented way to invest in stocks. It is to investing what *Moby-Dick* is to American literature: an absolute must-read for anybody studying the topic. Graham is the grandfather of value investing.

Philip Fisher is one of the first people to reveal growth-investing strategies. His book *Common Stocks and Uncommon Profits* discusses the characteristics of superior companies and how anybody can identify them. I suppose it is to investing what *Huckleberry Finn* is to American literature: the second must-read for serious students of the topic. Fisher is the grandfather of growth investing.

Then comes Warren Buffett, considered by many to be the world's greatest investor. Buffett is still active today, running his company from Omaha and continuing to rack up impressive performance. Through his investment skills alone Buffett amassed a fortune greater than $15 billion by achieving an average annual return of 25 percent for more than 30 years. He studied and admired both Graham and Fisher, then combined their teachings in his own style.

Next is Peter Lynch. He managed the Fidelity Magellan Fund for thirteen years and took it from assets of only $20 million to more than $14 billion. He turned a $10,000 investment into $190,000 in ten years. He is considered by many to be the best mutual fund manager in history.

William O'Neil is the founder of *Investor's Business Daily*, a newspaper that a lot of investors prefer over the *Wall Street Journal*. Before founding *IBD*, he enjoyed a successful stock-investing career that allowed him to purchase a seat on the New York Stock Exchange when he was only 30 years old. He is a committed growth investor and a great lecturer.

Gary Pilgrim is our last master and one of my personal favorites. He manages PBHG Growth, one of the best small-company mutual funds around. For the five years ended in mid-1996, PBHG Growth returned 32 percent a year!

That's our lineup. These six masters cover the spectrum of large companies to small companies, and growth style to value style. Kick back and spend a little time learning what the masters have to tell. Don't worry about knowing every piece of their advice by heart. I close out the chapter with a section pulling all their opinions together.

Benjamin Graham

Benjamin Graham wrote *The Intelligent Investor*, probably the most widely recognized investment book in the world, and *Security Analysis*, co-authored with David Dodd. Graham mentored Warren Buffett and in a preface to *The Intelligent Investor* Buffett wrote, "I read the first edition of this book early in 1950, when I was nineteen. I thought then that it was by far the best book about investing ever written. I still think it is." I didn't read it until I was twenty, which explains why Buffett is still slightly wealthier than I.

Market Fluctuation and Emotion

Graham teaches that nobody ever knows what the market will do. I want to emphasize this innocent-looking observation. *Nobody ever knows what the market will do.* That includes analysts, your wealthy aunt, every newsletter writer, and every stockbroker. Graham isn't the only successful investor to point this fact out. When J. P. Morgan was asked what the market would do, he replied, "It will fluctuate." The nice thing about nobody knowing what the market will do is that you can profit by reacting intelligently to what it does do.

We are all part of the general public, and the general public is usually wrong. To counteract our inherent emotional weakness, Graham says we should automate parts of our investment strategy. By that he means use a set formula to find good stocks. Not a formula like you used in Algebra, but a set of measurements that aren't subject to emotion. You don't want to fall victim to just "feeling good" about a company's future. Human emotions are frail beasts. Nobody's wealth should ride on them.

Party Time!

Automated, measurable criteria give us something stable to fall back on when we get confused by bold headlines and great stories. Nobody is immune to such pressures. If your whole office is talking about a new toy for the Christmas season that's already breaking retail sales records in Florida, Maine, and New Hampshire, who wants to point out that the manufacturer lost money the past two years? After your office mates buy the stock, they're going to start pinning newspaper stories about the company on their cork boards, displaying the shiny toy in their offices, and maybe hanging postcards of the exotic travel destinations they'll be visiting with their profits. It's a party! We all want to go to a party. But by developing an automatic filter that we can view such parties through, intelligent investors won't suffer lost money when the party's over.

Stock Valuations

Every stock has both a business valuation and a market valuation. The *business valuation* is simply the stock's book value and its earnings. Remember from page 30 that book value is determined by dividing all the company's assets by the number of stock shares outstanding. In other words, it's the amount you could get if you liquidated the company—sold everything the company owns like the delivery trucks, fax machines, and conference tables. However, and this is important, investors need to factor in earnings with book value to fully appreciate a company's business valuation. It's not enough for us to know what we could sell the place for; we must also know what potential profit the place holds. We get that by looking at earnings per share, which you read about on page 28.

The *market valuation* is what the stock trades for. It might be higher or lower than the stock's business valuation. You'd much rather buy stocks at prices lower than their business valuations, of course, because they're on sale.

Just as you can buy your favorite sweatshirt for $10 less during a clearance sale, you can sometimes buy stock in your favorite companies for $10 per share less than they're actually worth. In Graham's language, such a stock's market valuation would be $10 less than its business valuation.

Graham recommends that investors buy stocks at prices near their business valuations. That means you'd like price/book ratios to be around 1, and you would also like P/E ratios low, preferably below 15.

Even Stocks Go on Sale

Don't worry about the specific measures Graham uses to evaluate stocks. Instead, concentrate on the nature of those measures. He suggests measures that show a stock's value: price/book and P/E. He also suggests measures that show a stock's growth potential: financial position and earnings growth. Notice how Graham blends value and growth measures. Blending the two is going to form the foundation of this book's strategy.

When you buy stocks that are cheap compared to their worth, you can ignore market fluctuations. Sometimes the market will drop the price of a stock for no apparent reason. So our job as investors is to identify stocks with strong potential and watch the market for buying opportunities. In Graham's own words, we should "use these vagaries to play the master game of buying low and selling high."

Margin of Safety

Graham's greatest gift to investors was his concept of a *margin of safety*, which is the difference between a company's business valuation and its market valuation. That definition is sometimes too vague to be meaningful. Don't think of this as a hard number. A better way to think of it is along a spectrum so that a stock either has a big margin of safety or it has a small one. A stock with a big margin of safety can go way down in price and still be a good investment; a stock with a small margin of safety can drop only a little in price and still be considered a good investment.

Graham was deliberately vague in describing a stock's margin of safety. He said that investment analysis is not an exact science. There are hard factors like book value, financial statements, and debt, but there are subjective factors like quality of management and nature of the business. He preferred to examine measurable qualities of a business because, well, they're measurable. If you're paying less for a company than it would sell for piece by piece, there's a good margin of safety there. If you're paying a lot more for a company than it would sell for and a lot more than what it's earning just because the papers say the new team of people taking over are brilliant, there's little margin of safety. What if, just what if, those brilliant folks make a mistake? Your losses could be extreme. But if hard numbers limit those losses when the brilliant managers mess up, you're still relatively safe. There's a lot of room for management to make mistakes because there's value underlying the company they're running. That's the margin of safety. It's not reducible to a single number, but the notion makes sense.

Graham emphasized the financial health of companies when discussing margin of safety. Long-term debt is very bad because it reduces the company's business valuation. The bills need to be paid even when brilliant managers make mistakes.

The one hard figure Graham assigned to margin of safety was that investors should buy a stock for no more than two-thirds of its book value. Another way of stating that is that a stock's price/book ratio should be no more than .66. So if a company has a book value of $50 per share, you should pay no more than $33 for it. Even at that low price, Graham wanted to see a low P/E ratio, which usually accompanies a low price/book ratio.

What You Should Retain from Graham

Graham was a great investor who insisted on paying a fair price for a stock no matter how bright its prospects were. That's a value approach to investing. However, he recognized the importance of a company's ability to grow earnings. This combination of value and growth is the foundation of good investing that I recommend in this book's strategy. Other key points:

- Nobody ever knows what the market will do, but we can profit by reacting intelligently to what it does do.

- Because we are all members of the general public and the public is usually wrong, we should rely on hard measurements to counteract our emotions and give ourselves something to feel secure about.

• Stocks have business valuations and market valuations. The first is what the company would be worth if it was liquidated; the second is the price the market has placed on the stock.

• We should know a stock's margin of safety, which is a general feel for how much that stock can drop in price and still be a good investment. Central to determining a stock's margin of safety is knowing the difference between its business valuation and market valuation.

Philip Fisher

Philip Fisher wrote *Common Stocks and Uncommon Profits*. Warren Buffett was so impressed with the book that he met with Fisher personally to learn more about his strategies. In 1969, Buffett told *Forbes*, "I'm 15 percent Fisher and 85 percent Benjamin Graham."

Characteristics of Superior Companies

Fisher wrote that investors should buy businesses with the ability to grow sales and profits over the years at rates greater than their industry average. Such companies are either "fortunate and able" or "fortunate because they are able." These seem like very similar things at first blush, but Fisher distinguished them with examples. A company that is fortunate and able has a good product right from the start, solid management, and it benefits from factors beyond the company's control such as an unforeseen use of its product. A company that is fortunate because it is able might have a mediocre product to begin with, but the management team is so clever that they adapt the product to the marketplace and diversify into other areas that offer opportunity. Thus "fortunate because they are able" refers to shrewd management more than anything.

Shrewd management is hard to define. To me it's a bit like indecency: I know it when I see it but can't say in advance what it is. To Fisher, shrewd management always looks past the current set of products to new items that will grow sales in the future.

You Can Certainly Tell What's NOT Shrewd Management!

That sometimes requires trading immediate profits for long-term gains, something that's unpopular on Wall Street. Because investors scrutinize earnings regularly, it's imperative that management communicate honestly with shareholders in good times and bad. Management's integrity was vitally important to Fisher, as it is to most good investors.

Sales are the key to prosperity. A company's extensive research and development of a superior product is irrelevant if it doesn't sell! Investors should examine the capability of a company's sales organization, paying particular attention to the extent of its customer research. Microsoft is a prime example of a company that is a sales machine. Many industry experts have long claimed that Microsoft doesn't develop superior products. It copies the technology of other products—sometimes not very well—and then outsells the developer of those products with Microsoft's powerful brand name and marketing muscle. This strategy has worked wonders over the years. Microsoft's *Excel* spreadsheet outsells Lotus *1-2-3*, *Word* outsells *WordPerfect*, *Internet Explorer* is gaining on Netscape *Navigator*, and *Windows* outsells the Macintosh operating system. All of these Microsoft products were blatant rip-offs of their prime competitors, and plenty of people still feel that the Microsoft products are inferior. But they sell like life preservers on the *Titanic*.

Of course, profits must follow sales. Enormous sales growth is irrelevant if it doesn't produce corresponding profits. To make sure a company is profitable, look at its profit margins. This stuff isn't as mysterious as you thought, is it? A company's profit margins coupled with its ability to maintain and improve them will tell you everything you need to know about its earning power. You'll learn later how to check a company's profit margins.

Profits must be realized soon enough to be useful. This means keeping a positive cash flow. Bad companies sell a million widgets on credit and then resort to borrowing money or issuing more stock to keep alive while the check is in the mail. Good companies get their money soon enough to live off it. That means when it's time to expand into new markets, build new factories, hire more people, or market to a wider audience, a good company taps its bank account. IBM acquired Lotus Development in 1995 just by emptying $4 billion out of its big blue piggybank. Having cash reserves and a positive cash flow are great advantages.

The last characteristic of a superior company is its status as the lowest-cost producer of its products or services and dedication to remaining such. Companies with low break-even points and high profit margins can survive hard times. Almost any company looks

Superior Companies Know How to Stretch a Buck

good when the economy is soaring. But only the leanest operations look good when the going gets tough. This is related in spirit to Graham's margin of safety. Low-cost, high-profit operations are the safest around because they have an edge in all phases of the economy.

Characteristics of Superior Investors

To succeed at investing, Fisher thought most people should concentrate on industries they already know. He called this your circle of competence.

Within that circle of competence, investors should conduct thorough and unconventional research to understand the superiority of a company over its competitors. The best source of information is the individuals who know the company. Customers, suppliers, former and current employees, competitors, and industry associations all have tidbits of information that are useful to investors. Fisher called this information scut-

Ask Around for Good Stock Info

tlebutt, a navy term describing gossip around a ship's drinking fountain. Instead of gossiping about your mate's late-night escapades, Fisher thought you should go out and gossip about the prospects of potential investments.

Scuttlebutt and other research are time-consuming. You can thoroughly understand only so many companies. Therefore, Fisher recommended a focused portfolio. He rarely placed more than ten companies in a portfolio, and even at that most of the money was usually concentrated in three or four stocks. A few superior companies are better than a slew of mediocre ones.

What You Should Retain from Fisher

Fisher recommends investing in companies with the power to earn a profit and outpace their competition. That's a growth approach to investing. To find superior companies, he was willing to look beyond hard numbers to factors that are not measurable, such as capabilities of management and the perception of those who know the company. Other key points:

- Buy businesses with the ability to grow sales and profits over the years at rates greater than their industry average.

- Look for capable management. The best management is willing to sacrifice immediate profits for long-term gains and maintains integrity and honesty with shareholders.

- Sales are key to everything. You should examine the capabilities of a company's sales organization, paying particular attention to its customer research.

- Profits must follow sales. Sales are irrelevant if they don't produce profit. You should know a company's profit margins.

- Profits must be realized soon enough to be useful. You should look for positive cash flow and a healthy cash reserve so the company can meet obligations without borrowing.

- Lowest-cost producers have an edge in all phases of the economy. Combined with a high profit margin, low-cost production is Fisher's version of Graham's margin of safety.

- You should invest in areas you're already familiar with, your circle of competence.

- You should conduct thorough, unconventional research by interviewing people who know the company best, such as employees, competitors, and suppliers.

- Because of the extensive research needed to uncover superior companies, you should own just a handful at any given time. A few superior companies beat a slew of mediocre ones.

Warren Buffett

You wouldn't be thrown out of an investment club for saying Warren Buffett is the world's greatest investor. Some have made money faster, others have made it in flashier ways, but few can match Buffett's methodical investment methods or his long-term record.

First, some background. In 1956 Buffett began a limited investment partnership with $100,000 raised from family and friends. The partnership remained in existence for thirteen years, during which time Buffett produced an average annual return of 29 percent. As his reputation grew, Buffett accepted more investors into the fold and moved his offices from home to Kiewit Plaza in Omaha. In 1969 Buffett disbanded the partnership, sent his investors' money to safe places, and took control of a textile company called Berkshire Hathaway. Berkshire became Buffett's holding company to own businesses like See's Candy, Kirby's, Dexter Shoes, and World Book Encyclopedias.

Berkshire also bought insurance companies, which became the cornerstone of Buffett's success. Why insurance companies? Because premium-paying policyholders provide a constant stream of cash. Buffett invested this cash, called "float," until claims needed to be paid. Because Berkshire Hathaway is located in Nebraska, a state with loose insurance regulations, Buffett invested a lot of the float in stocks. Most insurance companies choose safe bonds for their investments, usually allocating no more than 20 percent to stocks. But Buffett chose stocks— sometimes allocating over 95 percent of the float to them—and both he and Berkshire grew wealthy because of his picks. Buffett amassed a personal fortune of $15 billion, give or take a few billion.

Your situation is probably not like Warren Buffett's. You probably don't enjoy a steady stream of insurance premiums to invest as you see fit. You probably can't acquire companies as permanent holdings in your spare time. If you can, you don't need this book! But if you're like the vast majority of us and are investing limited resources in the stock market, read this section for pieces of Buffett's strategy that you can apply to your own program. I'll pull them together into this book's strategy later.

The Stock Market

Warren Buffett doesn't have a quote machine in his office. The world's greatest investor doesn't check stock prices because they're unreliable indicators of a company's worth. Some days they're up, others they're down. Sometimes Wall Street thinks the market looks good, other times it thinks it looks bad. It's willy-nilly, unreasonable, and unnecessary to know. Remember that Graham felt the same way: nobody ever knows what the market will do.

You'll Kill Yourself by Watching Every Market Move

At some point every investor needs to know what the stock of a company he is interested in sells for. That part's a given. What Buffett's habits show us is the fruitlessness of knowing minute movements, hourly changes, and daily aberrations. In the 1993 Berkshire Hathaway annual report Buffett wrote, "After we buy a stock, consequently, we would not be disturbed if markets closed for a year or two. We don't need a daily quote on our 100 percent position in See's or H.H. Brown to validate our well-being. Why, then, should we need a quote on our 7 percent interest in Coke?"

Buying Quality Companies at Bargain Prices

Buffett emphasized buying quality companies rather than speculating about the direction of a stock price. Good companies are still good companies when times are bad. If you buy a good company and the price of its stock drops, that doesn't signal anything more than a chance to pick up additional shares at a discount. Buffett says you should always understand the businesses in which you invest. The simpler, the better. Once you understand a business, you can make a judgment on the company's quality. You should exercise the same scrutiny when buying shares in a company as you'd exercise when buying the company itself. In advice reminiscent of Fisher, Buffett told investors in a 1993 *Fortune* interview to "invest within your circle of competence. It's not how big the circle is that counts, it's how well you define the parameters."

Buying a quality business is vital to Buffett, far more vital even than buying at a discount. After all, what's the point of buying something on sale if you're getting junk? It won't perform well in the long term, which leaves you one option: get lucky on a price run-up and sell in the short term. Time helps wonderful businesses but destroys mediocre ones, which means you should be comfortable standing by your companies over time. Investors must evaluate companies on their individual merits before looking at stock prices.

For example, Buffett bought GEICO stock after it declined from $60 to $2. The company faced a possible bankruptcy and a growing number of class-action lawsuits from shareholders. The world thought the stock would end up worthless, but Buffett loaded up on it anyway, eventually owning half the company. Buying a stock that's declined 96.5 percent is clearly a value move because by just about any measure it's discounted. In GEICO's case, Buffett found a great company at a colossal bargain.

But then there's Coca-Cola. Buffett loved the soft drink from the time he bought and sold individual cans of it when he was five years old. He watched the company's phenomenal growth over three decades and in 1986 made Cherry Coke the official beverage of Berkshire's annual meetings. Yet he didn't invest in Coca-Cola until 1988. The stock had risen over five-hundredfold since 1928 and over fivefold since 1982. To many it looked overpriced, but Buffett invested more than $1 billion. Buying a stock that's risen fivefold in six years appears to be a growth move. In Buffett's case, however, he saw Coca-Cola selling for well under its intrinsic value, so to him it was still a great company at bargain prices.

Buffett Invested in the World's Favorite Soft Drink

In each of these two investment decisions Buffett wasn't thinking value or growth. He wasn't pondering hot tips on the street because in both situations he acted against common consensus. He bought what he perceived to be quality businesses: GEICO when everybody thought it was dead, and Coca-Cola when everybody thought the opportunity had passed. The lesson we can take from this is that it is more important to buy solid, quality companies than it is to buy stocks at certain price levels. This is Buffett's use of Graham's margin of safety. You should examine a business to determine its value, then look at the stock price to see if it makes sense to buy now. It might, in which case you should. The price might decline after you buy, but that doesn't matter. The fact remains that you bought a solid business at a fair price. After that, Buffett advises you to watch what's on the playing field, not what's on the scoreboard. A price decline is the market's frenetic, short-term interpretation of the stock's worth. Ignore it.

By now it should be clear that Buffett advocates buying quality companies at bargain prices, which is a blend of Graham and Fisher. Now let's delve deeper into Buffett's definition of a quality company and a bargain price.

Attributes of a Quality Company

First, a company's management must be honest with shareholders and always act in their interest. Integrity precedes everything in business because there's no point proceeding with a business evaluation if you don't trust the people running the place! Buffett himself is famous for his candid assessment of Berkshire in the company's annual reports. You should look for clear explanations of a company's successes and, more important, its failures in reports to shareholders. This is vital to your continued understanding of the businesses in which you invest.

Second, a company should earn more cash than is necessary to stay in business and direct that cash wisely. To Buffett this means either investing in activities that earn more than they cost, or returning the cash to shareholders in the form of increased dividends or stock buybacks. The measurement we'll use in this book's strategy to determine if management is investing excess cash wisely is return on equity. To Buffett, a company's earnings are no more important than its return on equity because they don't take into account the accumu.ation of previous earnings. In other words, I can take what I earned last year and make my company bigger and better. You would expect a bigger and better company to be able to earn more, right? Of course. And if it does, everybody's happy. Everybody but Buffett, that is. He's more concerned with whether or not that company's earnings grew enough to justify the cost of reinvesting the previous year's earnings, and the ones before that, and so on. That's why he looks at return on equity instead of plain earnings. It's just as important to know what a company does with what it earns as it is to know what it earns.

Third, a company should have a high net profit margin. Remember from page 29 that a company's net profit margin is determined by dividing the money left over after paying all its expenses by the amount of money it had before paying expenses. So, if a company makes $1 million and pays $900,000 in expenses, its net profit margin is 10 percent ($100,000 divided by $1,000,000). If a competing company also makes $1 million but pays only $700,000 in expenses, its net profit margin is 30 percent ($300,000 divided by $1,000,000). All other things being equal, which company's stock would you rather own? The company with a 30 percent profit margin, of course. It makes the same amount of money as its competitor but keeps more. Put differently, it spends less to earn the same income. A high profit margin tells you that the company's management is good at controlling costs. That's great news since every dollar frittered away unnecessarily is one less dollar of profit for shareholders.

Determining a Bargain Price

Buffett determines the value of a company by projecting its future cash flows and discounting them back to the present with the rate of long-term U.S. government bonds. I'm sure that sounds about as much fun as extracting termites from your home with chopsticks, but that's how he calculates a company's value and I felt compelled to share it with you.

After determining a company's value, Buffett then looks at its stock price. It's one of the few times he pays attention to stock price. He compares the value to the price and determines the margin of safety. In other words, if the stock is selling for just under what the company is worth, there is a small margin of safety and he doesn't buy. If it sells for well under the company's worth, there is a large margin of safety and he buys. The reasoning is simple. If he made a small error in determining the value of the company, then the true value might prove to be below the stock price. But if the stock price is well below what he estimates the company to be worth, the chances of falling below it are less. It's a straightforward use of Graham's margin of safety.

Now a few caveats and adjustments. Describing Buffett's way of determining a bargain price in two steps and characterizing it as simple is a bit misleading. It's accurate, but it's not easy to copy. I can also describe Michael Jordan's way of slam-dunking a basketball in two steps: jump toward hoop, slam ball through net. There, now do you suppose you can dunk like he does? Of course you can't, and it's no different with Buffett's determination of a bargain price. He's gifted, and if you're as gifted as he is you probably don't need this book.

Arriving at an accurate assessment using Buffett's method requires an accurate forecast of future cash flow. Buffett's good at it, most of us aren't. Even within your circle of competence, you probably don't feel comfortable culling the factors of a company's success, estimating their future success, and translating it into today's dollars.

So, in this book we're going to focus on the intent of Buffett's method instead of the technique. We want to buy quality companies at bargain stock prices.

Managing Investments

Like Fisher, Buffett believes in a focused portfolio. Because he buys businesses instead of trading stocks, Buffett insists that he understands those businesses thoroughly. That means owning just a few companies at a time. In 1985, half of Berkshire's common stock portfolio was in GEICO. In 1987, Berkshire owned just three stocks and 49 percent of its portfolio was in Capital Cities/ABC. In 1990, 40 percent of Berkshire's portfolio was in Coca-Cola. Focused investments in areas you understand are superior to blanket investments across dozens of stocks in the name of diversification. If you research thirty companies and find two that are clearly better than the rest, why place your money in the top five or ten? For diversification, you might say. But diversifying across mediocre companies is riskier than focusing on good ones.

Buffett also discourages the common practice among investors of selling their top performers. If a stock runs up 100

percent many sell it and take the profits. But
Buffett believes in managing his portfolio
the same way he manages his business. How
would you react if a division of your business consistently showed a profit? You
wouldn't sell it off. You would probably invest more in it. Buffett wrote in the 1993 Berkshire Hathaway annual report, "An investor
should ordinarily hold a small piece of an outstanding business with the same tenacity that
an owner would exhibit if he owned all of
that business."

**Own Your Stock As
If You Owned the
Whole Company**

Finally, Buffett disregards the opinions of others once he's
made up his mind. Groupthink is what kills institutional investors
because they'd rather make average, safe decisions than what
Buffett identified in Berkshire's 1984 annual report as "intelligent-
but-with-some-chance-of-looking-like-an-idiot" decisions. Do
your own research, do it well, and stand by your decisions.

What You Should Retain from Buffett

Above all else, Warren Buffett believes in examining businesses, not stock prices. Once he finds a quality business, he buys
it at a bargain price. His investment style combines the best of
Graham and Fisher because he buys thriving companies at a discount. That's a combination of value and growth investing. Other
key points:

- Ignore the stock market because it's fickle. Never speculate
  about the direction of prices. Look instead at individual companies and what makes them superb.

- Buy stock in a company with the same scrutiny you'd exercise when buying the business itself. Buy within your circle
  of competence and thoroughly understand your investments.

- After choosing your investments well, you should stand by
  them through thick and thin. Time helps wonderful businesses but destroys mediocre ones.

- Buy quality companies at bargain prices.

- Quality companies

  - *Have honest management teams that communicate with shareholders in a candid fashion and always act with the interests of shareholders in mind.*

  - *Earn more cash than is necessary to stay in business and direct that cash wisely. They either invest in activities that earn more than they cost, or return the cash to shareholders in the form of increased dividends or stock buybacks. To determine how wisely a company has directed its cash, we'll look at its return on equity.*

  - *Have high net profit margins.*

  - *Increase their market value by more than the value of earnings they retain.*

- Determine bargain prices by comparing a company's value to its stock price. Buy when the stock is considerably lower than the company's value. This is a straightforward use of Graham's margin of safety.

- Focus your portfolio on a few good companies. Concentrating on good stocks is safer than diversifying across mediocre ones.

- Just as a business puts more money into its most successful ventures, you should invest more money in your stocks that are performing well.

- Do your research, do it well, and disregard the opinions of others.

Peter Lynch

Peter Lynch managed the Fidelity Magellan Fund from 1977 to 1990. The fund held only $20 million when Lynch took over and grew to $14 billion during his tenure. In the last five years of Lynch's management, Magellan was the world's largest mutual fund and still outperformed 99 percent of all stock funds. If you had invested $10,000 in Magellan when Lynch took over, ten years later you would have had $190,000.

After retiring, Lynch wrote *Beating the Street* and *One Up on*

Wall Street. These two books explain his approach to investing. *One Up on Wall Street* targets individual investors and is the title I condense in this section. Lynch, like my grandfather, refers to winning stocks as "tenbaggers," ones that return ten times your money.

Use What You Already Know

Using what you already know is the cornerstone of Lynch's advice. This should be familiar to you by now. Fisher advised us to invest within our circle of competence, and Buffett seconded that notion, adding that we must thoroughly understand our investments. Now Lynch adds his support to the idea. I think we have enough reason to pay attention.

From your position as an employee or competitor in a field, you're conducting the best research on good investments. Professional money managers fly tens of thousands of miles to talk with people you interact with every day. Your manager, your supplier, your customers, your coworkers—and you yourself—have information that's worth a lot to other investors. Here's a shocking revelation: it's worth just as much to you!

Also, as a consumer you're conducting research all the time. You know what products you're buying and probably have a pretty good idea of what your neighbors are buying. Is there a trend afoot? Possibly, and you might see it long before Wall Street does.

It has always amazed Lynch that people who work in the aerospace industry invest in the auto industry; people who work in the auto industry invest in the computer industry; people who work in the computer industry

Being a Consumer Is Good Research

invest in the entertainment industry; people who work in the entertainment industry don't have any money to invest. Well, okay, the top .25 percent have a little. The point is that this grass-is-always-greener approach is ludicrous. Invest where you already spend most of your time.

Lynch recalls several good investments he discovered by just living his life. He found Taco Bell by eating a burrito on a trip to California. He found La Quinta by talking to people at the rival

Holiday Inn. He found Apple Computer when his children insisted on owning one and the systems manager at Fidelity bought a bunch for the office. His wife liked L'eggs panty hose from Hanes. L'eggs was convenient to purchase right at the checkout counter of most grocery stores. They resisted tearing and developing runs. They fit well. What more research was needed to conclude that this was a superior product? None, in Lynch's estimation. He bought Hanes and it grew six-fold before being bought out by Sara Lee.

Look where you work, pay attention to what you buy, and observe the buying habits of those around you.

Know Your Companies

Like Graham, Fisher, and Buffett, Lynch says to thoroughly understand the companies you're considering. He recommends looking at company size first. Big companies make small stock moves, small companies make big stock moves. It's important to know the size of companies you're considering.

Categorize Your Companies

Once you know the size of your companies, Lynch says to divide them into six categories: slow growers, stalwarts, cyclicals, fast growers, turnarounds, and asset plays. Slow growers are usually large, old companies that used to be small, young companies. Electric utilities are typical slow growers. Expect them to barely outpace inflation but to pay a good dividend. Stalwarts are large and old too, but they're still growing strong. Coca-Cola is an example of a stalwart company. Cyclicals are companies whose fortunes rise and fall along with the economy. Airlines and steel companies are cyclical. Fast growers are small, young companies that grow at 20 percent or more a year. This is the land of tenbaggers to 200-baggers. Lynch identified Taco Bell, Wal-Mart, and The Gap as fast growers. More recently we've seen Iomega and Starbucks. Turnarounds are good companies that have been beaten down. Chrysler is Lynch's example and one of the best buys he made for Magellan in the early eighties. Those who bought Chrysler at $1.50 enjoyed a 32-bagger. Asset plays are companies with something valuable that Wall Street missed. Pebble Beach in California and Alico in Florida owned amazingly valuable real estate that nobody paid attention to. The telecommunications industry was an asset play twenty years ago.

Don't be concerned with the six categories per se. Don't set out to buy a stalwart company because it's stalwart. Instead, use selection criteria to turn up attractive companies and use these categories to know what you're buying. The intent of Lynch's categories is simply to know what kind of company you're investing in. Don't expect fast growth from a slow grower. If you're buying a stock that's down in price because you think it meets all of Buffett's criteria of a quality company, know if it's down in price because it's a cyclical in a down cycle, an overlooked asset play, or a turnaround. You'll know from the extensive research you've conducted on the companies you invest in, a wise approach taught by Graham, Fisher, Buffett, and Lynch.

Components of a Perfect Company

To Lynch the perfect company is simple to understand. That should be familiar to you by now. He writes, "The simpler it is, the better I like it. When somebody says, 'Any idiot could run this joint,' that's a plus as far as I'm concerned, because sooner or later any idiot probably is going to be running it."

Any Idiot Could Run the Joint

If its name is boring or ugly and something about its business turns people off, so much the better. Lately there's been a move toward hip companies with names like TerraGyro Navigation and Internetica. Most investors steer clear of boring companies with boring names. Not Lynch. To him they're fortunes. He cites Seven Oaks International as a company that engages in a boring business. It processes grocery store coupons. Yippee! Put that Netscape manual aside and let's take 10 cents off your next purchase of Grape Nuts. That'll get your blood pumping. The stock rose from $4 to $33. That really *will* get your blood pumping. Some companies engage in business that is disgusting, such as sewage and toxic waste. Lynch remembers the executives of Waste Management, Inc., who wore polo shirts that said "Solid Waste." Disgusting, right? The company became a 100-bagger.

The business should be ignored by institutions and analysts. Not surprisingly with businesses this unattractive, a lack of institutional ownership is almost a given. Lynch loves it when a company tells him the last analyst visited three years ago. Look where others refuse to look. It's not always just boring, unattractive businesses that are overlooked, either. Remember Chrysler? Nobody wanted that stock when it fell to $1.50. They all waited until it was priced at a respectable double-digit figure again. The smart money isn't always so smart.

Fast-growing businesses are best inside a slow-growth industry or, better still, a no-growth industry. It keeps competition away. Just think how many thousands of hotheaded business students want to conquer Silicon Valley. How many do you think want to conquer the funeral business? Not many. Burials aren't a growing industry; plus they're boring and depressing.

Companies that occupy a niche have a distinct advantage. Warren Buffett bought the *Washington Post* partly because it dominated its market. Most newspaper owners think they profit because of the quality of their paper. But Buffett pointed out that even a crummy paper can prosper if it's the only one in town. Lynch writes, "Thinking along the same lines, I bought as much stock as I could in Affiliated Publications, which owns the local *Boston Globe*. Since the *Globe* gets over 90 percent of the print ad revenues in Boston, how could the *Globe* lose?" Patents, trademarks, and strong brand loyalty all constitute a type of niche. Good luck starting a soft drink company and trying to get as many people to say the name of your product before they say Coke. Even Pepsi can't do it. Owning something unique is another type of niche. Lynch sums up this advantage perfectly: "Once I was standing at the edge of the Bingham Pit copper mine in Utah, and looking down into that impressive cavern, it occurred to me that nobody in Japan or Korea can invent a Bingham pit."

Soon He'll Buy More

Get yourself a double-whammy by purchasing a company that has a niche and a product that people need to keep buying. Steady business is powerful stuff. What do you do when you percolate your last cup of coffee in the kitchen? Buy more. What do you do after smoking your last cigarette? Buy more. What do you do when your gas tank goes empty? Buy more. What do you do when you hit the plastic stopper at the bottom of your deodorant stick? Please, buy more. That phrase "buy more" drives profits to the moon. It's the wind in the sales of Coca-Cola, McDonald's, Gillette, and Starbucks. Microsoft is a company with both a niche and repeat business. It owns the Windows operating system used on most personal computers and issues periodic upgrades that everybody needs to own. Remember buyers lining up at midnight to get Windows 95? Those lines were as beautiful to Microsoft investors as snowflakes are to a ski resort. Also, guess what everybody needs after they own Windows? Applications to run. Microsoft just happens to make a lot of those too.

Protect against trouble by investing in companies with a lot of cash and little debt. This can be seen as Lynch's margin of safety. If a company has accumulated cash, you can subtract the per-share amount from the stock's selling price to see the bargain you're getting. Lynch did so with Ford in 1988. The stock sold for $38, but the company had $16.30 per share in cash. "The $16.30 bonus changed everything," Lynch remembers. "It meant I was buying the auto company not for $38 a share, the stock price at the time, but for $21.70 a share ($38 minus the $16.30 in cash)." Debt works in the opposite direction. If a company owes a ton of money, you're shouldering that burden when you buy the stock. In a crisis situation, which comes everybody's way at some point, companies with no debt can't go bankrupt. These two components together—a lot of cash and little debt—mean the same thing to a company that they mean to you. Would you rather have a big bank statement or a big credit card bill? Duh, think a second. The bank statement, of course. It's the same for companies. Those with a lot of cash and little debt are secure.

Lynch advises paying attention to the stock price relative to the company's value. You've read a lot on this already, so I won't rehash it except to point out that every one of the master investors in this section offers the same advice: don't pay too much for a stock. Check the P/E ratio and other measures of value. I think we're on to something important. Lynch's rule of thumb is that a company's P/E ratio should equal its earnings growth rate. He writes, "If the P/E of Coca-Cola is 15, you'd expect the company to be growing at about 15 percent a year. But if the P/E is less than the growth rate, you may have found yourself a bargain."

The last two components of a perfect company involve the

handling of its stock. You want two things to be going on. First, you want company insiders buying stock, and second, you want the company itself buying back shares.

Insiders Should Own Their Company's Stock

When employees and managers in a company buy the stock, they become shareholders like anybody else. If managers are shareholders, they're more likely to do good things for the stock. If they just collect a paycheck, they're more likely to use profits to increase salaries. Lynch writes, "When insiders are buying like crazy, you can be certain that, at a minimum, the company will not go bankrupt in the next six months." He's also careful to point out that while insider buying is a good thing, insider selling is not necessarily a bad thing. Remember, company insiders are people too. They need to buy new cars, send kids to college, and take vacations. Selling stock is a quick way for them to raise money. There are all kinds of reasons to sell stock that have nothing to do with the seller's outlook on the stock's future. "But," Lynch writes, "there's only one reason that insiders buy: they think the stock price is undervalued and will eventually go up."

On an even bigger scale, you want the company itself buying back shares. If a company thinks it has a bright future, it makes sense to invest in itself. After a company buys its own stock, there are fewer shares circulating among the general public. Assuming everything remains healthy at the company, those fewer shares in circulation are more valuable than before the buyback. Earnings per share go up and the stock is more enticing to investors. If you own some of the shares still in circulation, you've got a hotter hand than you had before the buyback. Lynch explains, "If a company buys back half its shares and its overall earnings stay the same, the earnings per share have just doubled. Few companies could get that kind of result by cutting costs or selling more widgets."

Know Why to Buy

Lynch uses a nifty exercise to force himself to understand why he's investing in a stock. He calls it the two-minute drill.

"Before buying a stock," he writes, "I like to be able to give a two-minute monologue that covers the reasons I'm interested in it, what has to happen for the company to succeed, and the pitfalls that stand in its path." The script should change for different types of companies because you'll want to emphasize different strengths. Lynch offers several examples. One is for Coca-Cola, a stalwart company. Keep in mind that this situation might not exist when you read this:

> Coca-Cola is selling at the low end of its P/E range. The stock hasn't gone anywhere for two years. The company has improved itself in several ways. It sold half its interest in Columbia Pictures to the public. Diet drinks have sped up the growth rate dramatically. Last year the Japanese drank 36 percent more Cokes than they did the year before, and the Spanish upped their consumption by 26 percent. That's phenomenal progress. Foreign sales are excellent in general. Through a separate stock offering, Coca-Cola Enterprises, the company has bought out many of its independent regional distributors. Now the company has better control over distribution and domestic sales. Because of these factors, Coca-Cola may do better than people think.

Isn't this a great technique? You become your own analyst when forced to provide a two-minute summary to yourself or an investment club. Of course, your knowledge runs far deeper than what's revealed in two minutes. All that knowledge is on your side when making good investment decisions.

Lynch explains that the real benefit of two-minute drills is that they make you know your companies. That's handy no matter which way the stock price moves because you can make your buy and sell decisions from information about the company instead of information from the market, the most fickle of all measurement tools. If you buy Coca-Cola because it's at the low end of its P/E range, is growing its business overseas, and has greater control over distribution, does any of that change if the stock drops 10 percent after you buy? Probably not. How about if the stock rises 20 percent after you buy?

Know Everything About Your Companies

Still, probably not. Price itself should not be the only factor you look at when buying or selling. The company behind the stock should be your focus.

What You Should Retain from Lynch

Peter Lynch believes in using what you already know to find "tenbaggers." Once you know why you're buying a company, you'll know how to behave as its stock price fluctuates. Given this approach, Lynch finds opportunities in both value and growth stocks. Other key points:

- Use what you already know to find stocks. As an employee, you know the details of your company and its industry better than most analysts. As a consumer, you're constantly researching the products and services of companies. Use that knowledge when investing.

- Categorize your companies. The exact categories you use aren't important, but know the types of companies you're investing in. Are you considering a fast grower, a stalwart, or a turnaround? Companies move from category to category over time.

- Perfect companies

  - *Are simple to understand. It's great to know that any idiot can run the place because sooner or later any idiot will run the place.*

  - *Turn people off by being unattractive in some way. Maybe they're boring, ugly, or disgusting. More people want to invest in the latest Internet company than the latest grocery-coupon company. Look where others won't.*

  - *Are fast growers in slow-growth industries or, better still, no-growth industries. This keeps competition away. Everybody thinks they can make money in Silicon Valley; few think they can make money in the funeral business.*

  - *Occupy a niche. If they own something unique or dominate a tiny market, it's hard for competition to muscle inside.*

- *Sell something that people need to keep buying. What do you do when you drink your last Coke? Buy more. Use your last disposable razor? Buy more. Steady business is powerful stuff.*

- *Have a lot of cash and little debt. Companies with no debt can't go bankrupt.*

- *Sell at a stock price that is a good value relative to the company's worth. This can be measured in several ways, including P/E ratios and price-to-book ratios.*

- *Are run by managers and employees who invest in the company's stock. When personnel own a stake in the company, they'll work harder to make it successful.*

- *Buy back shares of their own company stock. This is a show of faith in the company's future, and it also decreases the number of shares in circulation, thereby increasing their worth.*

- Know why you buy. Deliver a two-minute monologue to yourself summarizing the reasons you're buying. This forces you to understand your companies and focus on their fundamental information as the stock market bats their prices around. When in doubt, refer to the reasons you bought in the first place.

William O'Neil

William O'Neil is best known as the founder of *Investor's Business Daily*, national competitor of the *Wall Street Journal*. When he was thirty, O'Neil used profits he made trading stocks to purchase a seat on the New York Stock Exchange and to found his own investment-research organization, now based in Los Angeles.

In 1988, O'Neil wrote *How to Make Money in Stocks*, which presents everything he's learned about growth-stock investing.

Use the CAN SLIM System to Find Growth Stocks

Not another diet plan, O'Neil's strange-sounding system for finding growth stocks is actually an acronym for the attributes of great companies. O'Neil stresses that every one of the attributes must apply to a company for him to invest in it. This is not an election, where if a company boasts four of the seven attributes it wins. No, it must boast all seven attributes to be a winner. The seven attributes are:

C: Current Quarterly Earnings per Share Should Be Accelerating

O'Neil wants to see an increase in the current quarterly earnings per share when compared to the same quarter from the prior year. He writes plainly, "The percentage increase in earnings per share is the single most important element in stock selection today." Bigger increases are better than little ones, but investors should be careful not to be misled by huge increases over tiny ones from the previous year. "Ten cents per share versus one cent may be a 900 percent increase," he writes, "but it is definitely distorted and not as meaningful as $1 versus $.50. The 100 percent increase of $1 versus $.50 is not overstated by comparison to an unusually low number in the year ago quarter."

A: Annual Earnings per Share Should Be Accelerating

Similar to the quarterly earnings increases, O'Neil wants to see each year's annual earnings per share for the past five years bigger than the prior year's earnings. A company should be growing at least 25 percent per year, preferably 50 percent or 100 percent. O'Neil gives this example: "A typical successful yearly earnings per share growth progression for a company's latest five-year period might look something like $.70, $1.15, $1.85, $2.80, $4." A nice bonus is an earnings estimate for next year predicting yet another increase.

N: New Something or Other Should Be Driving the Stock to New Highs

On this attribute O'Neil is flexible, but he wants to see something new that is positively affecting the company's future. In his firm's study of the greatest stocks from 1953 to 1993, O'Neil found that 95 percent of them had either a new product or service, new conditions in the company's industry, or a new management team. Most important, O'Neil likes to buy stocks pushing new highs. Cheap stocks are usually cheap for a reason.

S: Supply of Stock Should Be Small and Demand Should Be High

Supply and demand affects the price of everything, including stocks. If two stocks are steaming upward at the same pace, the one with fewer shares outstanding will perform better. Why? Because there are fewer shares for the people who want to buy it. O'Neil provides the example of a company with 10 million shares outstanding and one with 60 million. All other factors being equal, the smaller company should be the "rip-roaring performer."

L: Leaders in an Industry Should Be Your Target

When O'Neil talks about leaders in an industry, he means the stocks with the best relative price strengths. *Investor's Business Daily* shows the relative price strengths of NYSE, AMEX, and NASDAQ stocks every day on a scale from 1 to 99 with 99 being the best. Using an interesting mnemonic device, O'Neil writes, "A potential winning stock's relative strength should be the same as a major league pitcher's fast ball. The average big league fast ball is clocked about 86 miles per hour, and the outstanding pitchers throw 'heat' in the 90s." There you have it: look for stocks with relative price strengths of 90 or better.

I: Institutional Sponsorship Should Be Moderate

Demand needs to be high to drive stock prices higher. Institutional buying is the best source of demand in the stock market. Mutual funds, pension plans, banks, government bodies, and insurance companies are all institutional investors. They buy millions of shares at once. O'Neil likes his stocks to be owned by a few institutions. Too many can mean that the stock is overowned. In that case, so many institutions own the stock that if they all react the same way to news, the stock might get dumped and its price will drop.

M: Market Direction Should Be Upward

O'Neil says that even if you get the first six factors of CAN SLIM right and choose a great portfolio of stocks but buy when the market as a whole is declining, 75 percent of your picks will sink with the market. To get a feel for the direction of the market, he suggests watching market averages every day. Keep an eye on daily price and volume charts of several different market averages such as the Dow, S&P 500, and NASDAQ composite. *Investor's Business Daily* publishes major market indicators on a single page every day.

Ignore Valuation

This is a radical departure from the previous four masters. O'Neil believes that you get what you pay for in the market. He's the quintessential growth investor, ignoring P/E ratios completely and focusing on earnings acceleration. He advises, "Don't buy a stock solely because the P/E ratio looks cheap. There usually are good reasons why it is cheap, and there is no golden rule in the marketplace that a stock which sells at eight or ten times earnings cannot eventually sell at four or five times earnings. . . . Everything sells for about what it is worth at the time."

The N in CAN SLIM specifies that a stock should be pushing new highs. That notion runs contrary to everything we've been taught as consumers. Most people don't want to buy

Higher, Higher, Higher!

a car selling for more than it ever has before, or a house, or a pair of shoes. Yet O'Neil calls it the stock market's great paradox that "what seems too high and risky to the majority usually goes higher, and what seems low and cheap usually goes lower." His firm studied stocks listed on either the new-high or new-low list in the newspaper and confirmed that stocks on the new-high list tend to go higher while stocks on the new-low list tend to go lower.

"Therefore," O'Neil summarizes, "your job is to buy when a stock looks high to the majority of conventional investors and to sell after it moves substantially higher and finally begins to look attractive to some of those same investors."

Beyond price acceleration, O'Neil looks at management stock ownership and a company's debt. He agrees with Lynch that it's a good sign for management to own a large percentage of stock and that great companies carry little debt. He writes, "A corporation that has been reducing its debt as a percent of equity over the last two or three years is well worth considering."

Managing a Portfolio

O'Neil says at his seminars to manage your portfolio like a retail business. Pretend you sell stuffed animals. As Christmas approaches, Babe the stuffed bull is outselling Smokey the stuffed bear three to one. Which animal do you stock up on for the Christmas season? Babe the bull, of course, because he's given you the most profit and will probably do so in the future. According to O'Neil, it works the same way in your portfolio of stocks. "Sell your worst-performing stocks first and keep your best-acting investments a little longer." That means you shouldn't average down, a common practice of adding more money to your stocks that have fallen in price to buy additional shares at a discount.

Automate Buying and Selling

Like Graham, O'Neil likes automation. His CAN SLIM method is one way of automating your investments. Another is to set a place to stop losses. O'Neil stops his losses at 8 percent of new money placed in a stock. He's specific on the new money requirement. If you own a stock that's risen 50 percent and it slides back 10 percent, that's not necessarily a time to stop losses because overall you're ahead 40 percent. It's only with the addition of new money, when a loss means you're actually behind, that O'Neil advocates stopping losses. Even if it's money added to a rising position, O'Neil recommends stopping losses on that money if the stock slides back while keeping your initial investment money in the stock. It's wise to limit losses because it takes a greater percent gain to overcome any given percent loss. For instance, if you lose 33 percent it takes a 50 percent gain to recover. O'Neil writes, "The whole secret to winning in the stock market is to lose the least amount possible when you're not right."

While he abhors averaging down, O'Neil advocates averaging up, also called pyramiding. This practice he learned from Jesse Livermore's *How to Trade in Stocks*. The plan is simply to move more money into your stocks that are increasing in value.

Stop Counting Turkeys

One of O'Neil's best examples shows the fallacy of hoping to recover losses from a falling stock. It's the story of an old man and his turkey trap.

There was an old man with a turkey trap that consisted of a box held up by a prop. Wild turkeys would follow a trail of corn under the box. When enough turkeys were inside, the old man would pull a string attached to the prop, thereby dropping the box over the turkeys inside. The goal was to trap as many turkeys as possible.

One day he had 12 turkeys in the box. One wandered out, leaving 11 behind. "Gosh, I wish I had pulled the string when all 12 were there," said the old man. "I'll wait a minute and maybe the other one will come back."

But while he waited for the twelfth turkey to return, two more walked out. "I should have been satisfied with 11," the old man said. "As soon as I get one more back I'll pull the string." But the turkeys kept wandering out. The old man couldn't give up the idea that some of the original number would return. With a single turkey left, the old man said "I'll wait until he walks out or another goes in, then I'll quit." The last turkey joined the others, and the old man returned empty-handed.

O'Neil writes that the analogy to the psychology of the normal investor is amazingly close.

This is the opposite of stopping losses when you're wrong. Pyramiding magnifies winnings when you're right, which is precisely what Livermore teaches. O'Neil recalls, "From his book, I learned that your objective in the market was not to be right but to make big money when you were right." I suppose you could relate pyramiding to the turkey analogy in the above textbox by suggesting that the old man place additional turkey traps in the field where he's been most successful before.

After studying his successes and failures, O'Neil devised an automated profit and loss plan for prospering in the stock market:

1. Buy exactly at the pivot point where a stock is moving to new highs after a flat area in an upward trend. O'Neil calls such flat areas consolidation periods.
2. If the stock drops 8 percent from the buy point, sell.
3. If the stock rises, pyramid more money into it up to 5 percent past the buy point. So if you bought a stock at $50 and it rose to $51, O'Neil would suggest adding more

money. However, you shouldn't add more money after the stock reaches $52.50 because at that point it's risen 5 percent.

4. Once a stock has risen 20 percent, sell.
5. If a stock rises 20 percent in less than eight weeks, commit to holding at least eight weeks. After that time period, analyze the stock to see if you think it will rise even higher.

Focus, Make Gradual Moves, and Track Your Winners

Because he's found few people who do more than a few things well, O'Neil believes that a focused portfolio is better than a diversified one. He asks if you'd be comfortable visiting a dentist who's also a part-time engineer, music writer, and auto mechanic. O'Neil sees diversification as a dilution of your strengths. He writes, "The best results are achieved through concentration: putting all your eggs in just a few baskets that you know a great deal about and continuing to watch those baskets very carefully." He emphasizes: "The winning investor's objective should be to have one or two big winners rather than dozens of very small profits."

It's best to make gradual moves into and out of a stock. O'Neil says too many people are hesitant to move their money. To overcome this hesitation, he recommends buying and selling in parcels. If you own a stock you love and it starts dropping in value, sell part of it as an insurance policy. If it rebounds, fine. You made back part of the loss with the money you kept in the stock. Like all insurance policies, you won't always need to use this one. O'Neil asks his seminar audiences, "Are you angry when you buy auto insurance and then go a year without wrecking your car? No!" He reasons that you shouldn't be angry to sell part of a losing position only to see the position fully recover. Ask yourself how much worse it would have been if you hadn't sold part of the position.

To help overcome the inherent tendency to buy more of the stocks in your portfolio that have gone down in price, O'Neil suggests keeping records in a different way. At the end of each time period, he says to rank your

Make Gradual Moves

stocks by their performance from the previous evaluation period. "Let's say your Tektronix is down 8 percent, your Exxon is unchanged, and Polaroid is up 10 percent. Your list would start with Polaroid on top, then Exxon and Tektronix." After ranking your portfolio this way for several time periods, you'll see which stocks are lagging the group. O'Neil's intent is to force you to ignore the price you paid for each stock and concentrate instead on each stock's performance. He writes, "Eliminating the price-paid bias can be profitable and rewarding. If you base your sell decisions on your cost and hold stocks that are down in price because you do not want to accept the fact you have made an imprudent selection and lost money, you are making decisions exactly the opposite of those you would make if you were running your own business."

What You Should Retain from O'Neil

William O'Neil believes earnings acceleration is more important than buying stocks cheap. He advocates buying and selling in short time periods, stopping losses while they're small, and adding more money to winning stocks. He is an unmitigated-growth investor. Other key points:

- Use the CAN SLIM system to find growth stocks. CAN SLIM is an acronym for the seven conditions that indicate an excellent investment:

  - *Current quarterly earnings per share should be accelerating*

  - *Annual earnings per share should be accelerating*

  - *New something or other should be driving the stock to new highs*

  - *Supply of stock should be small and demand should be high*

  - *Leaders in an industry should be your target*

  - *Institutional sponsorship should be moderate*

  - *Market direction should be upward*

- Ignore valuation. Low P/E ratios often indicate stocks that are cheap for a reason. They can always get cheaper too.

- Look for companies with a large percentage of management stock ownership and little debt.

- Contrary to what's taught to consumers, investors should buy stocks pushing new highs. What seems too high usually goes higher; what seems too low usually goes lower.

- Manage your portfolio like a retail business: get rid of unpopular products and acquire more of the popular ones. With stocks, sell your losers and keep your winners.

- Automate your investment strategy. Stop losses at 8 percent and add more money to winners up to 5 percent above the buy price.

- Focus on a few good stocks. Don't diversify across many mediocre ones.

- Make gradual moves into and out of stock.

- To overcome the desire to buy more of the stocks that have declined in price, rank stocks by their performance over a time period. After a few tracking periods, sell the losers and add to the winners.

Gary Pilgrim

Gary Pilgrim is the manager of PBHG Growth, a top-performing small-company mutual fund. As of mid-1996, PBHG Growth posted average annual returns of 32 percent for the past five years and 22 percent for the past ten. If you'd invested $10,000 in 1986, ten years later it would have been worth $73,000. The same amount invested in the S&P 500 would have been worth only $37,000.

Like O'Neil, Pilgrim is a dyed-in-the-wool growth investor. He uses earnings momentum to find fast-growing stocks, and his portfolio is very volatile because of it.

Automate Growth Rankings to Avoid Emotion

To help avoid emotion, Pilgrim relies on his own computer ranking system to find good growth stocks. The system examines every growth prospect on the market—those that have increased their earnings by 20 percent or more for two quarters—and then ranks them using criteria specified by Pilgrim. The two criteria he weighs most heavily are upward revisions in earnings estimates and positive earnings surprises, neither of which is open to emotional interpretation. The numbers are either there or they aren't. Period. *SmartMoney* wrote, "This dispassionate approach has insulated him from the trap of what he calls 'the good story.' 'Talk to any management, and they'll persuade you how great their company is,' Pilgrim points out."

While many fund managers fly around the country meeting company directors, tasting burritos, and walking around factories, Pilgrim watches the numbers and a news feed on his computer. He said to *Kiplinger's*, "I could spend the rest of my life trying to

Watching the Numbers, Not the Story

understand the technical side of Ascend Communications, my biggest holding, but it wouldn't help me as a portfolio manager. My objective is to know *how* these companies are doing as opposed to *what* they are doing. It's much more important to know that analysts are raising earnings estimates, that competitors aren't gaining ground, that controversies over products are being resolved. In other words, I want my knowledge to be a mile wide and an inch deep."

Elements of Good Growth Stocks

Pilgrim's momentum style of investing focuses on earnings expectations. He also looks at the rate of earnings acceleration or deceleration and company balance sheets for high profit margins and low debt. He ignores valuation, meaning he doesn't look for bargain stocks, but he takes advantage of price dips in growth stocks.

High Earnings Expectations and Positive Earnings Surprises

Pilgrim looks for upward revisions in earnings estimates and positive earnings surprises. These two elements account for 60 percent of his ranking system, a hearty testament to his belief in their importance. He wants to buy stocks that everybody thinks are going to make more than they did last quarter and that have performed even better than people expected in the past. He wrote to shareholders, "Our search for the strongest relative earnings performance will uncover companies most likely to achieve sustainable, exceptional long-term growth. And our long-term portfolio success depends on this, more than on market timing, economic forecasting, or valuation analysis."

High Earnings Acceleration Rate

While the bulk of Pilgrim's system focuses on expectations, he also looks at actual results. He wants to see a company's sales and profits getting bigger each quarter as compared to that same quarter from the previous year. Referring to his ranking system, Pilgrim told *Kiplinger's*, "It's not enough for me to know a company is growing at a 20 percent rate. If that 20 percent is down from 40 percent, I want the system to reflect that the rate of growth has been slowing. So our system figures the *rate* of acceleration or deceleration." As you can see, Pilgrim's criteria aren't easy to meet. A company needs to be growing, analysts need to anticipate that it will continue growing, then it needs to do even better than the analysts predict, and on top of it all the company needs to continue outdoing its own better-than-expected performance from the past.

Gary Pilgrim is every student's worst nightmare. Imagine bringing a report card home to a parent like him! I can just hear little Susie pleading, "But I got straight A's" and Daddy Pilgrim's stern response, "Who cares? I expected straight A's. Besides, you had straight A's last semester too. I want more classes on this report card so the number of straight A's is increasing. Sheesh! Kids these days."

Not Good Enough!

Strong Balance Sheet

Another factor Pilgrim takes into account is how the company manages its money. He considers a strong balance sheet to be a good character reference, and therefore avoids companies with low profit margins and lots of debt. This is worth noting. Every one of the investors I profile in this book, whether he uses a growth or value style, avoids companies with excessive debt. It's a killer. It kills you and me as people trying to make ends meet, and it kills companies trying to make a profit.

Ignore Valuation

Pilgrim stated bluntly to *Kiplinger's*, "Valuation has no role in a growth portfolio. It is a waste of my time to wonder if companies I like are overvalued or undervalued. . . . Everybody holds those P/E ratios out there as if they mean something by themselves. A P/E of 40 doesn't mean anything unless you look at the underlying growth characteristics of the stock. You'll find that the high-P/E stocks are all selling at numbers commensurate with their growth rates." He agrees with O'Neil that in the stock market you get what you pay for.

Pilgrim ignores valuation when making both buy and sell decisions. He focuses entirely on the growth factors discussed above. Once he makes a decision to buy, he uses the factors of the buy decision to help him decide when to sell. When the reasons he bought deteriorate—perhaps the company starts earning less than it has in the past—then he sells.

Pilgrim's insistence on the growth characteristics of a company leads him to take advantage of volatility, unlike O'Neil. Remember that O'Neil wants to stop losses at 8 percent no matter what. Not Pilgrim. He told *Kiplinger's*, "The last thing I want to do is turn loose a perfectly good company that is doing everything it is supposed to do, just because its price is falling. . . . When companies begin to deteriorate fundamentally, I sell them. But I won't sell them just because they're volatile." In fact, he'll buy more shares if one of his top-ranked stocks dips in price without losing its fundamental strengths.

Managing a Portfolio as an Individual Investor

When I spoke directly with Gary Pilgrim, I had a narrow objective in mind. I wanted to know exactly what individual investors—people like you and me working from our kitchen tables—can use from his investment style. He thought that was a swell plan.

It's Dangerous to Pursue Earnings Momentum Like PBHG

One of the first things Pilgrim told me was that it's dangerous for the average investor to pursue earnings momentum like PBHG. It takes attention to detail and the full-time commitment of an entire office staff to keep on top of small-company, high-growth stocks. Plus, remember that most of Pilgrim's stocks are attractive to him because of their high expectations. Those expectations can change in a heartbeat or the company can fail to meet them, and in such times it takes a fast trigger finger to get out of the wrong stocks and into the right ones.

"I don't see how an individual sitting there looking at his Internet or his Value Line or his whatever can do that," he said. "We sit here with hundreds of thousands of dollars worth of access to information and news of the day.... The individual investor has been coached to be a long-term holder of things. In this category of asset the temptation to hold things that are faltering, to be forgiving of unexpected negative variances, is potentially very devastating. Most individuals aren't going to own 100 stocks, they're going to own a few. It doesn't take very many problems in a few stocks to blow you up."

One Mistake Can Blow Your Whole Game

A Value Approach Might be Better for Individuals

Because most people are familiar with the concept of buying things on the cheap, Pilgrim thinks value investing might be the better approach for individuals. He reminded me, "If you're dealing with very mature, moderate-growth, high-quality companies that have very little fundamental risk, then perhaps the major attribute of whether they're attractive or not is their valuation because they never change really.... You have to learn not to buy them when they're in the top quartile of their traditional relative valuation. Buy them when they're low."

Whatever you do, though, don't mistake what he's saying to

think you can use valuation tools on the types of stocks he invests in. It doesn't work that way. You're either in the small-company-momentum camp or you're not. "These smaller and emerging and midsize companies can have their growth prospects dramatically change very quickly," he said. "Valuation tools, as I'm sure you've seen us say again and again and again, aren't very helpful. It's expectations, it's actual growth, it's whether people believe more good is going on than bad."

You'll Fail Trying to Get Information Quicker Than the Pros

We all want to think we have some sort of scoop nobody else knows about. In certain parts of investing, we might. Nobody better understands the business of flea dissection than a flea dissector. Peter Lynch feels this type of specialized knowledge that employees, managers, and owners have is an advantage. Investing in companies for their long-term prospects relies on that knowledge. But for momentum investing, based on high expectations where a company's prospects can dim in a day, you as an individual investor have little chance of knowing what the pros know. Even if you do know, you probably won't find out as quickly as they do. A quick confirmation of this lies in the fact that Pilgrim doesn't even care about most of what you can know as an employee, manager, or business owner. He said he could spend the rest of his life trying to learn the technical side of Ascend Communications, but it wouldn't help him as a portfolio manager. Instead, he watches expectations—very carefully.

"We're organized to assimilate information in the form and speed with which it is dispatched these days in the investment business," he says. When stocks report earnings, "the detailed income statement is faxed to us immediately, we're on the conference call that afternoon usually, and the next morning all the analysts write it up and give us their results."

As Pilgrim explained the factors affecting his stock prices just that day, it occurred to me that I don't want to follow my stocks on such a fine scale. It would drive me crazy, which is his point. It's the professional's job to follow the market's every move, not the individual's. I would rather do the research once, buy strong stocks, and check them now and then.

I asked if he's been aware of information long before it hits the cover of newspapers. "Oh, yeah," he answered. "There's very little that you ever learn about how companies are doing from reading the newspaper or a magazine. . . . They're largely irrelevant to people who are actively following these companies as a line of work."

Strategies to Adopt as an Individual Investor

At this point I began wondering what Pilgrim thought individuals should be looking for in their portfolios. I was convinced that trying to compete with the pros in the arena of short-term expectations is futile, but there had to be something individuals can target. I asked Pilgrim where investors should go for information if they can't call up a broker.

"They can always call the companies and have the shareholder liaison help them form expectations and give them some guidance. That's not unthinkable. I can't predict that it's going to be common because these people are used to dealing with representatives of large shareholders, like ourselves and other money managers, and whether they're going to take a call from Joe and John Doe is up to the company."

How do I take the fundamental research that I can conduct in a timely enough fashion to be useful to me, and make decisions with it? For instance, how do I know that a stock's price drop is a buying opportunity instead of a red flag signaling the time to sell? These are tough questions, truly answerable only on an individual basis after years of experience developing a "feel" for such distinctions. What was true on stock A last year might not be true on stock B this year. Pilgrim provided his thoughts.

"Let's assume that you're doing as much research as you can, you're running a portfolio of 15 or 20 stocks, and you're trying to be price opportunistic on day-to-day or week-to-week variability.

Pilgrim's Not Alone

Fidelity points to its superior resources frequently when enticing individual investors into mutual funds. The slogan for its sector funds is, "You pick the industry, we'll pick the stocks." One of Fidelity's ads read: "You can invest on a hunch. As long as it's preceded by 700,000 man hours of analysis, thousands of intense interviews with industry executives, and $55 million in technology."

You Can Always Call the Companies

You should set up some parameters and say, 'Look, no matter how much I love this stock, I'm not going to let it get to be more than 7 percent or 8 percent of my portfolio. I'll try to buy low and sell high. As long as I have a higher level of confidence in some companies than others, I'll weight my portfolio toward those. When I get concerned about how a company is doing, I may not run out and sell it, but I'll stop buying it.' I think the last thing you want to do is add to a weak position and sell strong positions."

That means that, like O'Neil, Pilgrim buys more of the stocks that are rising. "That makes sense to me," he explains, "because what's usually happening when the price is going up is expectations for earnings are going up and growth is going up. So, in a sense you're not paying any more for a dollar of earnings after the price goes up than you did when you discovered it."

A hallmark of the successful investor is consistency. It's much better to do one thing exceptionally well than a slew of things just okay. There will be times when that one thing isn't working, but successful investors stick with it through good times and bad. Changing horses in the middle of the stream can cool your returns in a hurry. Pilgrim said, "I still question the way we do things, the techniques we employ, how we can improve them. If I had to think about changing strategies, the whole thing would come unglued."

No Matter How Bad it Gets, Stay Consistent

I told him I want to convey to you, my reader, that times get tough for every investor. Too many people look at PBHG's outstanding performance and think, "Those guys never have any trouble. I'll invest the way they do." Pilgrim laughed and replied. "Oh yeah, we're just whipping along having a grand old time. Nothing to it. I guarantee you the day will come when they write, 'Have Gary Pilgrim and Pilgrim Baxter lost their touch?' We'll have two or three years of investment returns that will make people wonder how awful it can be, and it will test the patience of our shareholders. I know it as well as I'm sitting here that growth will get out of favor relative to something else, and when it gets out of favor we're going right to the bottom quartile and there's not a darn thing I can do about it." You read it here first.

The last topic of our conversation focused on developing an individual investment style. "Investment success or failure submits to your own personal conviction and work habits," Pilgrim said. He invented his computerized model of choosing high-growth stocks from his own experience, tinkered with it over the years, and knows why it works. He'd never have that kind of faith in a system developed by somebody else. "Your investment style is a reflection of what you believe the world is all about, what you believe generates value, what you believe produces great stocks. . . . What you have to do is figure out what's right and then figure out the best way to do it yourself."

I told him that I think you, my reader, should approach stock investing cautiously in the beginning. Play with 10 percent of what you've got, take a few knocks on that small amount of your money, and you'll probably be a lot wiser for it in the end. "I think so," he agreed. "Pay small amounts to learn, not large amounts. . . . Over time, if you develop confidence in your strategy, you can eventually increase the amount of money you actively manage."

What You Should Retain from Pilgrim

Gary Pilgrim is one of the best small-company, high-expectation growth-stock investors around. He recognizes that most of his success relies on resources that are not available to individual investors. Therefore, he recommends dabbling in stocks with a small portion of your money to develop a style that is uniquely yours. He even went so far as to say that a value style of investing might be better for individuals. Other key points:

- Automate growth rankings to avoid emotion. In high-expectation investing, it's hard to avoid getting caught up in "the good story." Computer rankings and an insistence on strong numbers keep emotions at bay.

- Focus only on what you need to know. In high-expectation investing, knowing *how* a company is doing is more important than knowing *what* it's doing.

- A good growth stock

  - *Has high earnings expectations and positive earnings surprises. These two factors account for 60 percent of Pilgrim's ranking criteria.*

  - *Has a high earnings-acceleration rate. A company's sales and profits should be getting bigger each quarter as compared to that same quarter from the previous year.*

  - *Has a strong balance sheet. Consider this a character reference. Avoid companies with low profit margins and lots of debt.*

  - *Should* not *be judged by valuation measures. A high P/E ratio usually accompanies high growth rates. You get what you pay for.*

- Manage a portfolio as an individual investor with the following in mind:

  - *It's dangerous to pursue earnings momentum like PBHG. You don't have access to resources worth hundreds of thousands of dollars. Most individuals have been taught to buy and hold for the long term. That doesn't work in momentum investing.*

  - *A value approach might be better for individuals. It's safer to watch mature companies that don't change much and buy them low than it is to try to catch high-fliers the way PBHG Growth does. However, don't use measures of value on high-fliers—they don't work.*

  - *You'll fail trying to get information quicker than the pros. You can't possibly compete with a full-time staff of professionals who have direct lines of communications with the companies they own. By the time you read it in the paper, it's old news to the pros.*

- Strategies to adopt as an individual investor:

  - *Read quarterly earnings reports, look at earnings growth from quarter to quarter to determine acceleration or deceleration, and get hold of analysts' estimates. Most information is available from the investor relations department of companies themselves.*

- *Set up parameters to limit the percentage of your portfolio available to any given stock. For example, don't let anything take up more than 8 percent.*

- *Buy more of what's rising; stop buying what's falling and reevaluate.*

- *Don't necessarily sell when a stock is down in price. Look at the fundamentals. Is it really a bad stock, or is it a good stock with a great buying opportunity?*

- *Stay true to your strategy. Every investor experiences good and bad times. Don't change everything when times are bad.*

- Only experience and your own unique view of the world can create a truly successful investment system for you. Get that experience with a small portion of your portfolio at first, then gradually manage bigger amounts.

Where the Masters Agree

Now that you've read a lot of advice from six great investors, let's take a moment to boil it down. You still have further reading ahead before I present this book's strategy, but pausing here to review what you should have picked up so far is time well spent.

Automate Your Strategy with Proven Criteria

No matter what investment strategy you create over the years, it should be clearly defined and measurable. This helps you instantly separate a company from its story, the latest buzz, and your inherent human frailty. None of us are immune to emotion, but we can use superior reasoning to counteract our emotions and make good decisions. Every great investor, from the most insistent value types to the most aggressive growth types, relies on a set of specific criteria to find superior companies. You should too.

Look for Strong Income Statements and Balance Sheets

Every company is helped by high profit margins, lots of cash, and little or no debt. Each investor in this book wants to see these factors. They assure value investors that a beaten-down company has the wherewithal to recover, and they assure growth investors that a rising star will keep rising.

A high profit margin means the company keeps more of what it earns, plain and simple. If two companies each sell $10 million worth of products and one company spends $8 million to do it while the other spends only $4 million, you'd rather own the second company.

You would rather own a company that has a lot of cash on hand than a company that has a little. A big bank account means the company can expand easily, buy better equipment, pay off unexpected expenses, and buy back shares of its own stock.

Avoid debt. This applies to nearly every walk of life. Don't invest in companies with a lot of debt, don't go into debt yourself. Debt is a monster. It eats companies trying to prosper, and it eats the futures of people like you and me.

Avoid the Sea of Debt in Your Life and Your Investments

A company can go bankrupt only if it's in debt. Debt and death sound a lot alike, and that's no coincidence. You don't even need a finance book to arrive at this conclusion. All you need is a good literature class. Emerson wrote in *May-Day and Other Pieces*, "Wilt thou seal up the avenues of ill? Pay every debt, as if God wrote the bill." As an investor, you want those avenues of ill sealed up before you buy the stock.

Look for Insider Stock Ownership and Company Buybacks

Not everybody places a high value on this, but enough mention it to make it important. It makes sense that managers and employees will work harder to make their company successful if they own stock in it. Plus, nobody knows the fortunes and follies of a company better than the people who run it and work there. If a hot product is going to trounce every competitor, company insiders will know about it first. If a new service has produced the highest focus group scores in history, company insiders will know about it first.

Philip Fisher liked management teams that were honest with shareholders and were willing to sacrifice immediate profits for long-term gains. Like Fisher, Warren Buffett looks for a management team that communicates honestly and makes all decisions in the best interests of shareholders. There's a compelling reason to do so when managers themselves *are* shareholders. Peter Lynch writes, "There's only one reason that insiders buy: they think the stock price is undervalued and will eventually go up."

In addition to insider ownership, you want the company buying back shares of its own stock. Investing in itself indicates that the company believes in its future. The action also decreases the number of shares in circulation, which increases the earnings per share—as long as the company's earnings remain constant or grow. All in all, investors are left with more potent stocks after the buyback than they had before the buyback: Peter Lynch explains, "If a company buys back half its shares and its overall earnings stay the same, the earnings per share have just doubled. Few companies could get that kind of result by cutting costs or selling more widgets."

Compare Stocks to a Proven Profile

In addition to the factors above, you should compare stocks you're considering to a profile of key measures that have uncovered winners in the past. Some investors emphasize value measures such as P/E and price-to-book while others focus on earnings acceleration and analyst expectations. We'll develop a set of specific criteria later in this book that you'll fill in after you . . .

Conduct Thorough Research

Every great investor believes in thorough research. Warren Buffett says to exercise the same scrutiny when buying shares in a company as you'd exercise when buying the company itself. When conducting research, don't forget your own circle of competence. You work in an industry, you consume products, and you talk to other consumers. Your life experience counts as research—use it! Your base knowledge is a great way to find leads. Follow those leads to more thorough research conducted through your library, the Internet, company investor-relations departments, magazines, newspapers, and other investors.

Your style of research will vary based upon your personality and what you're looking for. Philip Fisher interviewed a company's customers, suppliers, former and current employees, and competitors to learn vital information. Peter Lynch likes to eat burritos, kick tires, watch consumers in stores, and feel hotel linen to confirm his interest in companies. Gary Pilgrim watches numbers and a news feed on his computer screen.

Develop Your Own Research Style

Whatever your research approach becomes, make sure that you conduct thorough research to find the information you need. Once you've assembled the information, you can determine whether to invest. Then you'll be prepared for the next section . . .

Know Why to Buy

It's important to know the reasons that led you to buy a stock so you know the right time to sell. If you have no idea why you bought, the only information you can rely on to decide when to sell is the current price, which is subject to a million mysterious factors, and the current word on the street, which is about as reliable as kindergarten romance. Think of Warren Buffett, Peter Lynch, William O'Neil, and Gary Pilgrim. If I asked any one of them why they held stock X, they would be able to answer me in a second.

If you own a stock because of the company's excellent earnings acceleration and high expectations for the future, know so. If it's because the company has been unfairly punished by the market and is selling for a ridiculously low P/E ratio, know so. Then you can watch those earnings and watch that P/E for a change. As they change, you can reevaluate your decision to own the stock. If you're like Buffett, the factors may not involve price at all. If that's the case, know so and watch the company's management team, return on equity, and other non-price factors to make sure they don't erode.

Investing Is No Time to Play Dumb

I think the best way of forcing yourself to know why you buy is to recite a two-minute stock script, as Peter Lynch suggests on page 66. In two minutes you should be able to run down the factors that made the stock attractive to you. That way you'll always know why you own your stocks, and you'll avoid making rash decisions to either sell out or buy more.

Once you know the reasons to invest in a company, try to . . .

Buy at a Price Below the Company's Potential

At first this looks like advice for value investors only, but it's not. Every investor, whether value or growth, must buy stocks at a price lower than they sell them. Value investors try to buy low, sell high. Growth investors try to buy high, sell higher. Both look at a stock's current price and compare it to what they see as the company's potential to drive that price higher. The difference between the two types of investors lies in the information they use to determine a company's potential.

A value investor looks at a company's assets, how much it's sold, its profit margins, and other factors before determining whether the price is more or less than the company is worth. A growth investor looks at earnings per share, the acceleration or deceleration of those earnings, analyst expectations, and positive surprises.

William O'Neil relies on the components of his CAN SLIM system to select winning stocks. One of those components—the N—wants the stock to be pushing new price highs. However, he buys only if the other factors of CAN SLIM apply too. The company must have accelerating earnings, a small supply of stock and high demand, a leading industry position, and moderate institutional sponsorship. What do these other factors show O'Neil? The company's growth potential. He doesn't simply flip through the paper looking for stocks that are expensive. He looks for stocks that are expensive for a reason, and that reason is that they have the potential to grow and produce even more expensive prices.

Gary Pilgrim insists on very strong potential in his companies as well. He wants to see high expectations, positive earnings surprises, and earnings acceleration. He assembles these numbers on every company of interest to him and buys the ones with the most potential. He doesn't care if the company passes traditional measures of value such as a low P/E ratio or low price-to-book, but he buys the high-growth companies with the most potential. Put another way, he buys the stocks that are selling today for the biggest amount below what he thinks they'll be worth in the future. If he thinks two stocks are headed for $100 per share and one sells for $20 while the other sells for $60, which do you think he'll buy? Both, probably, but if he had to choose one it would be the $20 stock. The decision didn't require him to compare P/E ratios; it simply required him to compare each stock's current selling price with what he projects to be its future potential. Most of the time he doesn't have an actual price in mind, but he certainly has an upward direction and a range in mind.

Warren Buffett, the investor who blends growth and value better than anybody, bought GEICO after it declined from $60 to $2. He saw it being worth a lot more than $2 because of the company's unrewarded potential. He bought Coca-Cola in 1988 after it rose fivefold over the previous six years. Many thought it was overpriced, but he bought more than $1 billion worth because he saw that it held plenty of unrealized growth potential. He was right in both of these purchases, which appear to employ juxtaposed investment strategies. Dig a little deeper, though, and you see that they don't. Buffett is actually quite consistent. In both decisions he projected the company's performance into the future, determined the company's potential, and bought at a price well below that potential. It's incidental that GEICO was on a path to recovery and Coca-cola was on a roll. Both had potential beyond their current price.

Whether you tend toward value investing or growth investing, you must be able to estimate the potential of your investments. Of course, you'll never be able to do it perfectly, but by conducting thorough research and understanding a company's strengths, you should be able to form a decent forecast. Once you've assembled a portfolio of companies that you own . . .

Buy More of What's Working

Business owners constantly evaluate the different parts of their operation to see what's working and what's not. They put more money into the successful parts and slowly phase out the unsuccessful parts. Eventually, the business becomes a stream-lined collection of winning pieces. Successful investors manage their portfolio in this same fashion. However—and this is key—different investors define "working" in different ways.

For Warren Buffett, a company is doing everything right if its fundamental strengths remain healthy. He watches things like the company's profit margins, its return on equity, and honest communication with shareholders. Buffett does not look at daily or weekly stock price fluctuations because they're too fickle. If he bought a quality company and it still boasts all of its quality attributes, Buffett considers it a success and keeps it in his portfolio. He doesn't think of himself as an investor in his companies; he thinks of himself as an owner. He wrote, "An investor should ordinarily hold a small piece of an outstanding business with the same tenacity that an owner would exhibit if he owned all of that business."

For William O'Neil, the only measure of a successful stock is its performance. He watches the prices of his holdings, pyramids more money into the winners, and dumps the losers. O'Neil says the objective in the market is not to be right all the time but to make big money when you are right.

For Gary Pilgrim, a stock is a combination of its fundamental story and its price. "When I get concerned about how a company is doing," he says, "I may not run out and sell it, but I'll stop buying it. I think the last thing you want to do is add to a weak position and sell strong positions. . . . I would much rather chase strength than chase weakness in the area of growth-stock investing."

While you hope the stock of every strong company you own rises in price, it ain't always the case, not even for the pros. Every investor can recall a list of failures that taught them a lesson. I learned growing up in Colorado, "There are those who *have fallen* from a horse, those who *will fall* from a horse, and those who *don't ride* horses." The only people who never fall off a horse are those who don't ride. The only people who never own a falling stock are those who don't invest. The good news is that if you've chosen quality companies you can . . .

Take Advantage of Price Dips

Well now, doesn't this seem like an odd bit of advice following the previous section? I just finished showing that the experts buy more of their winners. Now it looks like I'm telling you to buy more of the losers too. Bear with me a second and you'll see that these two pieces of seemingly incompatible wisdom can actually coexist, like darkness and light, or Democrats and Republicans.

Everything depends on your buying quality companies in the first place and knowing why you bought, as you read in "Know Why to Buy." If you bought a company because of its outstanding new products, high profit margins, and accelerating growth rate and the company still boasts those attributes, there's no reason to sell. In fact, there's every reason to buy more—regardless of price. If the stock is marching steadily upward and the company is still a great company, the previous section advises you to take advantage of that by investing more money. What this section points out is that if the company is still great but its stock is dropping, that can be just as good a reason to buy more. You're getting a discount on additional shares of a great company. Remember, though, that the reasons you bought must still apply. Don't put more money into a falling stock that also has falling profit margins, falling sales, employees on strike, and a management team that sold all of its stock and quit the company for an extended vacation in Negril. Invest only in quality companies whether buying your first shares in them or adding more shares to existing positions.

Benjamin Graham was a stickler on this point. He emphasized that nobody ever knows what the market will do but that you can profit by reacting intelligently to what it does do. Good companies drop in price every day, often for no apparent reason. A lawsuit perhaps, maybe a manufacturing glitch, or maybe just because the market's a weird place where you'd never want to hang out if there weren't so darned many ways to make money there.

Warren Buffett points out that time helps wonderful businesses but destroys mediocre ones. Even if the stock price is a bit down today—or this week, or this month, or this year—if the company is still the great company you bought, then this momentary price dip is an opportunity to invest more money at a bargain price. Robert Hagstrom, Jr., wrote in *The Warren Buffett Way* that you've approached Buffett's level of investing if you look at the market and wonder only if something foolish happened to allow you to buy a good business at a great price. That could easily be additional shares of a good business you already own.

Time Helps Wonderful Businesses

Gary Pilgrim takes advantage of the volatility of his growth stocks to buy more. He told *Kiplinger's*, "The last thing I want to do is turn loose a perfectly good company that is doing everything it is supposed to do, just because its price is falling. . . . When companies begin to deteriorate fundamentally, I sell them. But I won't sell them just because they're volatile." In fact, he'll buy more shares if one of his top-ranked stocks dips in price without losing its fundamental strengths.

This section and the one before it underscore what should be clear by now: you must understand the strengths of your companies and the reasons you bought shares in the first place. Only then can you decide if rising prices mean you've got a winner and should invest more on the way up, or falling prices mean you've still got a winner and should invest more at a discount.

I know it's a fine line. Nobody said this was easy.

What You Should Retain from This Section

When excellent investors with different styles of investing agree on a few basic truths, it's worth paying attention. This section outlined powerful advice taken from the six master investors profiled. Specifically:

• Automate your strategy with proven criteria. Don't select

stocks with your emotions, current hype, or stories from your friends. Use measurable information to compare stocks to a profile of key measures that have uncovered winners in the past.

- *Look for strong income statements and balance sheets.*

- *Look for insider stock ownership and company buybacks.*

- *Compare stocks to a proven profile.*

- Conduct thorough research. Warren Buffett sums it up best when he says to exercise the same scrutiny when buying shares in a company as you'd exercise when buying the company itself.

- Know why to buy. After conducting your thorough research on a company, outline exactly why you want to invest in it. Later you'll monitor the company to see if the factors that led you to buy deteriorate.

- Buy at a price below the company's potential. This applies to both value and growth investors because both look at a stock's current price and compare it to what they see as the company's potential to drive that price higher. The difference between the two types of investors lies in the information they use to determine a company's potential. Using your own thorough research, you should estimate a company's potential and buy at a price below it.

- Buy more of what's working. Like a business owner looking at the different parts of your business, you should constantly evaluate the different stocks in your investment portfolio to see what's working and what's not. Put more money into the successful stocks and phase out the unsuccessful stocks.

- Take advantage of price dips. If all the reasons you bought a stock are still present but the price is dropping, that can be a good time to buy more. You're getting a discount on additional shares of a great company. Make absolutely sure, however, that it is still a great company. Don't buy more shares of a stock that's falling due to company failings.

3 How History Tells Us to Invest

In 1946, Benjamin Graham observed, "It is amazing to reflect how little systematic knowledge Wall Street has to draw upon as regards the historical behavior of securities with defined characteristics....Where is the continuous, ever growing body of knowledge and technique handed down by the analysts of the past to those of the present and future?" More than a half century later, you can finally benefit from that perspective Graham desired.

Among the countless studies of stock market data completed since Graham's observation, one effort stands alone and is documented between the covers of a single book: *What Works on Wall Street* by James O'Shaughnessy. His study explored 43 years of results from 1952 to 1995 contained in Standard & Poor's Compustat database. In the preface to his book, O'Shaughnessy writes that Compustat is "the largest, most comprehensive database of United States stock market information available. This is the *first* time the historical S&P Compustat data have been released in their entirety to an outside researcher."

O'Shaughnessy gathered popular stock measures like the P/E ratio, price-to-book ratio, and relative price strength to see how they fared over the years when used to find both large and small companies. Then he combined the successful measures in ways that aren't often used. What he found—and what I'm delighted to share—is going to give you an advantage that has been available only since 1996. You, as a newcomer forming your own stock strategy, have 43 years of research to help you develop the correct habits.

Let's have a look inside *What Works on Wall Street*.

Testing Popular Measurements

Rather than take you laboriously through each measurement that O'Shaughnessy tested, I'm going to cut straight to the conclusions. Before I get started, though, you need to understand the ground rules of these studies. Bear with me if this gets complicated. The attention to detail should make you a believer in the results.

O'Shaughnessy separated the universe of stocks into two groups by company size. The first group he called "All Stocks." It consisted of all companies with an inflation-adjusted market capitalization of at least $150 million. Inflation-adjusted means that for any given year the companies were worth $150 million of today's dollars. After all, a $150 million company in 1955 was colossal. But by today's standards it is small. So the All Stocks group contained just that: all stocks of interest to this study.

The Two Stock Groups

The All Stocks group consisted of every company worth at least $150 million in today's dollars.

The Large Stocks group consisted of companies bigger than the average company size. This was usually the largest 16 percent of all companies. The Large Stocks group was a subset of the All Stocks group. In other words, every company in the Large Stocks group was also in the All Stocks group. But only the biggest companies from the All Stocks group made it into the Large Stocks.

He defined a second group of larger, better-known companies with market caps greater than the Compustat average. This second group usually consisted of the top 16 percent of the database by market cap in any given year. These companies went into the "Large Stocks" group as well as the All Stocks group.

As you can see, the All Stocks group included both smaller companies and those companies found in the Large Stocks group. The Large Stocks group contained only the large stocks.

In each of his tests, O'Shaughnessy began with $10,000 hypothetically invested in 50 stocks from the All Stocks group and 50 stocks from the Large Stocks group. He chose the 50 by applying the measurement being tested and then rebalanced every year in the study to capture the current 50 best meeting the measurement.

For instance, when testing P/E ratios O'Shaughnessy selected the 50 stocks with the lowest P/E ratios from each group. He then rebalanced the hypothetical portfolios each year to invest in the new 50 stocks with the lowest P/E ratios. He used this same method to test each measure.

O'Shaughnessy's study covered December 31, 1951, to December 31, 1994. During that time period the All Stocks group averaged 12.81 percent per year and the Large Stocks group averaged 11.41 percent. O'Shaughnessy used these group returns as benchmarks to test each measure.

The Best Value Measures

First, O'Shaughnessy examined measures of value to see how they fared in the market. The most reliable measure turned out to be price-to-sales for companies of all sizes and dividend yield for large companies.

Price/Sales

The 50 lowest P/S stocks from the All Stocks group returned 16.01 percent a year, better than the group's return of 12.81 percent. The 50 lowest P/S stocks from the Large Stocks group returned 13.75 percent, better than the group's return of 11.41 percent.

The 50 highest P/S stocks from the All Stocks group returned 4.72 percent a year, worse than the group's return of 12.81 percent. The 50 highest P/S stocks from the Large Stocks group returned 9.06 percent a year, worse than the group's return of 11.41 percent.

P/S works better with small companies but still works with large companies. In both the All Stocks group and the Large Stocks group, the 50 lowest P/S stocks beat their group in more than 90 percent of all rolling ten-year periods. The highest P/S stocks from the All Stocks group underperformed Treasury bills. Now, that's lousy!

It's interesting to note that O'Shaughnessy found P/S more reliable than P/E, the most popular stock measurement around.

Conclusion: Look for stocks with low P/S ratios.

Dividend Yield

The 50 highest dividend-yielding stocks from the All Stocks group returned 11.58 percent a year, worse than the group's return of 12.81 percent. The 50 highest dividend-yielding stocks from the Large Stocks group returned 13.13 percent, better than the group's return of 11.41 percent.

O'Shaughnessy writes, "The effectiveness of high dividend yields depends almost entirely on the size of the companies you buy."

Dividend Yield Is Great for Large Companies

Dividend yield is such an easy way to screen large companies that on page 113 you'll learn an automatic way to harness its predictive power.

The reason dividend yield works for large companies and not for small ones is that small companies rarely pay a dividend. Obviously not every small company with a yield of zero is a bad buy.

Conclusion: Don't use dividend yields with small stocks. Look for high dividend yields among large stocks.

The Best Growth Measure— Relative Price Strength

Next, O'Shaughnessy examined measures of growth. "Generally, growth investors like *high* while value investors like *low*," he notes. "Growth investors want high earnings and sales growth with prospects for more of the same. . . . Growth investors often award high prices to stocks with rapidly increasing earnings." O'Shaughnessy's characterization of value and growth investors is consistent with the styles of our six master investors profiled in the last chapter.

I could run you through the studies O'Shaughnessy conducted on a variety of growth measures, including earnings-per-share change, profit margin, and return on equity. But guess what? Only relative price strength proved to be a useful measure, so let's focus on just that one.

Remember from page 36 that relative price strength looks at a stock's price history. Did it rise or fall last year? Momentum-growth investors think you should buy stocks that have risen; many value investors think you should buy stocks that have fallen.

The 50 stocks with the best one-year price appreciation from the All Stocks group returned 14.45 percent a year, better than the group's return of 12.81 percent. The 50 stocks with the best one-year price appreciation from the Large Stocks group returned 14.17 percent, better than the group's return of 11.41 percent.

The 50 stocks with the worst one-year price appreciation from the All Stocks group returned 2.54 percent a year, much worse than the group's return of 12.81 percent. The 50 stocks with the worst one-year price appreciation from the Large Stocks group returned 9.45 percent a year, worse than the group's return of 11.41 percent.

How about that? Newton's first law of motion seems to apply to stocks as well as physical objects: prices in motion tend to stay in motion. The winners keep winning and the losers keep losing.

Things in Motion Tend to Stay in Motion—Even Stock Prices

Conclusion: Look for stocks with high relative price strengths. Avoid at all costs last year's biggest losers.

Combining the Measurements

People rarely make decisions with a single factor. A woman in search of an evening gown probably has a certain color in mind. Perhaps all black dresses are prettier to her than all red dresses, but within the black dress universe there are still plenty of choices. She narrows down the field by specifying a certain cut, a certain fabric, a certain overall panache. Soon she's presented with a handful of choices from which to make her final selection.

So it is with stocks. Single measurements are a start, but that's all. Combining measurements yields far better results by either reducing risk, increasing performance, or both. O'Shaughnessy experimented with several different combinations to come up with what he identified as a cornerstone value strategy and a cornerstone growth strategy. I'm going to skip the research process and jump to the final winning combinations.

Cornerstone Value Strategy

O'Shaughnessy found that value measures, particularly dividend yield, work best against market-leading large stocks.

Remember that a high-dividend yield does not find good small-company stocks but does find good large-company stocks. By limiting his target group to the leading large companies, O'Shaughnessy obtained even better results with the high-dividend-yield screen.

For O'Shaughnessy's purposes, market-leading large stocks came from the Large Stocks group, had more common shares outstanding than the average stock in the Compustat database, had cash flows per share greater than the Compustat mean, and had sales that were at least 1.5 times the Compustat mean. In 1993, that was only 328 of the 7,919 stocks in Compustat—a mere 4 percent of the database. These are your household names like GE, IBM, McDonald's, and Chrysler.

The 50 stocks with the highest dividend yield from the market leaders group returned 15.04 percent a year, much better than the Large Stocks return of 11.41 percent. $10,000 invested in the 50 highest yielding stocks grew to $4,141,129 compared to only $1,042,859 in the Large Stocks group. In overview of the powerful high-yield results, O'Shaughnessy wrote:

> The most extraordinary thing about this high-yield strategy is that the *worst* it ever did was a loss of 15 percent. That's nearly half Large Stocks' largest annual loss of 26.7 percent. This strategy outperformed Large Stocks in 8 of the 11 bear market years, and *never* had a negative 5-year return. It had only one 10-year period in which it failed to beat Large Stocks, then losing to the group only by a minuscule 0.78 percent. With such excellent downside protection, you would expect the strategy to perform more modestly in bull markets than Large Stocks did. But this strategy *beat* Large Stocks in 9 of the 13 years in which market gains exceeded 25 percent! Indeed, in the super bull years of 1954, 1958, and 1975—when large stocks gained 40 percent or more—the strategy *always* did better.

It's interesting that the only additional criteria added to the dividend-yield measure was in the size and success of the companies screened. O'Shaughnessy didn't combine high dividend yields with low P/E ratios, price-to-book, or any other measure. He simply looked for high dividend yields from the biggest, best companies on the market.

You may be wondering how to locate the biggest, best companies on the market yourself. After all, you don't have access to the Compustat database from your living room. You'll be thrilled to know that a tiny group of 30 successful large companies is listed everywhere you look. The returns of this group are averaged every day and posted for the world to see. Can you guess what I'm referring to? The stocks of the Dow Jones Industrial

Dow Stocks Are Listed in the Paper Every Day

Average. Starting on page 108 you're going to learn how to use the Dow with a high-yield strategy.

O'Shaughnessy concludes his cornerstone value finding by recommending it as a replacement for investors who currently index their portfolio to the S&P 500 or other Large Stocks style indexes. Indeed, with very little work you can outpace market index funds with this simple two-step process: locate the biggest, best companies and invest in the ones with the highest dividend yield. Keep reading for more information.

Cornerstone Growth Strategy

While value measures work best against the Large Stocks group, growth measures work best against the All Stocks group. After experimenting with several different combinations of growth factors, a few value factors, and different company characteristics, O'Shaughnessy developed a growth model that outperforms the market.

To focus on five-year variables, O'Shaughnessy began the tests on December 31, 1954, instead of his usual start date of December 31, 1951. He still ended the tests on December 31, 1994, to complete a tidy 40-year period. His winning combination selected 50 stocks from the All Stocks group that boasted earnings gains for five consecutive years, had price-to-sales ratios below 1.5, and displayed the best one-year price performance in the All Stocks group.

The 50 stocks returned 18.22 percent a year, much better than the All Stocks return of 12.45 percent. $10,000 invested in the 50 winning growth stocks grew to $8,074,504 compared to only $1,091,933 in the All Stocks group. This strategy returned more than other growth strategies and did so with less risk. It outpaced the All Stocks group in 73 percent of single years, 89 percent of rolling 5-year periods, and 100 percent of rolling 10-year periods.

Reflecting on the reasons that the three factors work together, O'Shaughnessy wrote:

Not Only Can Growth and Value Coexist...

It's worth noting that our best growth strategy includes a low price-to-sales requirement, traditionally a value factor. The best time to buy growth stocks is when they are cheap, not when the investment herd is clamoring to buy. This strategy will never buy a Netscape or Genetech or Polaroid at 165 times earnings. That's why it works so well. It forces you to buy stocks just when the market realizes the companies have been overlooked. That's the beauty of using relative strength as your final factor. It gets you to buy just as the market is embracing the stocks, while the price-to-sales constraint ensures that they are still reasonably priced. Indeed, the evidence in this book shows that *all* the most successful strategies include at least one value factor, keeping investors from paying too much for a stock.

O'Shaughnessy's growth finding confirms an important conclusion we arrived at by studying the six master investors: always buy at a price below the company's potential. At first this sounds silly. It doesn't take much thought to decide that buying stocks whose prices will rise is a good idea. But forcing yourself to evaluate why you think a stock's price will rise is another story altogether. O'Shaughnessy's three factors are a good way to take the emotion out of the decision. If a stock's earnings gains are increasing, its price is still cheap compared to its sales, and if its price is rising, history suggests that you have good reason to believe you're buying below the company's potential.

Combining the Strategies

O'Shaughnessy's cornerstone value and growth strategies are great complements to each other. The first provides good returns with little risk while the second provides outstanding returns with more risk. Combining the two in a 50-50 mix provides excellent returns with moderate risk. O'Shaughnessy recommends a greater allocation to the growth strategy in your younger years and more toward the value strategy as you near retirement. But for testing, he settled on an even 50-50 mix.

Over the 1954 to 1994 time frame, O'Shaughnessy split a portfolio of $10,000 evenly between his value and growth strategies and rebalanced the mixture every year to maintain the even split. The combined portfolio returned 16.74 percent a year, much better than the All Stocks return of 12.45 percent. $10,000 invested in the combined portfolio grew to $4,887,389 compared to only $1,091,933 in the All Stocks group. The combined portfolio provided the best risk-adjusted return, meaning that it returned the highest amount for the risks it took. It outpaced the All Stocks group in 83 percent of single years, 89 percent of rolling 5-year periods, and 100 percent of rolling 10-year periods.

Of this potent combination, O'Shaughnessy wrote:

The united strategies do so well in any given year because if one is coasting, the other is often soaring. Consider 1967, a frothy, speculative year. Had you invested only in the market-leading stocks from the cornerstone value strategy, you'd have gained 23.7 percent. That beat Large Stocks' return of 21.30 percent, but did only half as well as the All Stocks gain of 41.1 percent. By adding the cornerstone growth stocks, which soared 83.3 percent, you increase your overall return to 53.5 percent, beating

... Growth and Value Actually Work Best Together

both the All Stocks and Large Stocks groups. That's with *half* your portfolio safely invested in large, conservative market-leading companies paying high dividends.

Conversely, when growth stocks are getting clobbered, the conservative, high-yielding stocks from cornerstone value buffer the portfolio's performance. Cornerstone growth really suffered during the bear market of 1973–1975, but the market leaders from cornerstone value fared much better. Splitting your money between the two strategies allowed you to do better than both the Large and All Stocks universes during the two-year debacle.

Here's a breakdown of the strategies against the All Stocks group over the 40 years from December 31, 1954, to December 31, 1994:

Strategy	Compound Annual Return	$10,000 Became	Standard Deviation
All Stocks	12.45%	$1,091,933	19.83%
Value	14.62%	$2,347,560	16.76%
Growth	18.22%	$8,074,504	25.99%
Combined Value and Growth	16.74%	$4,887,389	19.94%

Standard deviation measures the amount an investment has deviated from its normal, or standard, return. A low number indicates steady returns while a high number indicates widely varying returns. Thus, a high standard deviation means high risk. Looking at the table above, notice that the value strategy returned twice as much as the All Stocks group with less risk. The growth strategy returned over 7 times as much as the All Stocks group by taking more risk. The combined strategy returned 4.5 times as much as the All Stocks group with just slightly more risk. O'Shaughnessy's work paid off.

To somebody looking for a way to win in the stock market, this table should have brought the crescendo from Beethoven's Ode to Joy flooding to your ears. If you need to pause your reading to dab the corners of your eyes, I understand. These moments in life are rare.

What You Should Retain from History's Lessons

Benjamin Graham wished for a historical perspective on the stock market. Now we've got it, thanks to the work of James O'Shaughnessy and the meticulous data maintained by Standard & Poor's. Near the end of *What Works on Wall Street*, O'Shaughnessy wrote, "Forty years of data prove that the market follows a purposeful stride, not a random walk." Here are the prevailing lessons of that stride:

- The best all-purpose value measure is price-to-sales.

- Dividend yield is a great value measure against large, market-leading companies.

- The best growth measure is relative strength. Specifically:

  - *Buying stocks that did well last year is a component of every winning strategy.*

  - *Last year's biggest losers are the worst stocks you can buy.*

- Avoid paying too much for any company. Even growth strategies need to include some measure of value. Price-to-sales is the best all-purpose value measure.

- The simplest and one of the best value strategies is to buy large, market-leading companies with high dividend yields. You'll learn a way to automate this strategy starting on page 108.

- The simplest and one of the best growth strategies is to buy small, young companies that

  - *Have posted earnings gains for the past five consecutive years.*

  - *Have price-to-sales ratios below 1.5.*

  - *Display the best one-year price performance.*

- Combining a value and a growth strategy is an excellent way to boost your returns while keeping risk tolerable.

4 Dow Dividend Strategies

Now that you've read advice from six master investors and studied the lessons from Wall Street history, let's take a look at market-beating strategies that work on autopilot. Actually, they work on cruise control because you need to be present to keep an eye on things, but you don't have to do much. They're called the Dow Dividend Strategies, and they make it easy for you to choose the most attractive stocks from the Dow Jones Industrial Average. I say the strategies are automated because you follow a simple set of steps to determine which stocks to purchase. The steps are easy and profitable.

Gary Pilgrim, one of America's premier small-company growth investors, said in my interview with him that individual investors might be better off buying established companies at bargain prices. You'll be pleased to know that all the Dow strategies lead you to invest in established companies at bargain prices.

James O'Shaughnessy's study of 43 years on Wall Street confirmed Pilgrim's comment. O'Shaughnessy found that one of the simplest and most effective strategies was to buy large, well-established companies with high dividend yields. A high dividend yield means a bargain price on stocks of large companies that provide steady dividends.

In O'Shaughnessy's study, large companies constituted roughly 16 percent of his database. If we apply that same measure to the number of stocks listed in the paper, we're left with too large a group to monitor. The NYSE lists 2,809 companies, the ASE lists 794, and the NASDAQ lists 5,430. Add them up and you get 9,033 listings, 16 percent of which leaves you with 1,445 stocks to screen for a high dividend yield. Life is way too short to

grind pencil leads writing 1,445 dividend
yields on a sheet of paper. Wouldn't it be nice
if there was a smaller group of large, well-
established companies that paid constant dividends? You bet it would, and there is: the
Dow Jones Industrial Average, consisting of
only 30 companies. That's right, just 30 stocks
to watch instead of 1,445. This chapter shows
how buying the Dow stocks with the highest
dividend yield and lowest price leads to
market-beating results.

**Life's Too Short to
Grind Pencil Leads**

Although the Dow Dividend strategies have been around for
decades, the basic strategy is best presented and validated in the
1991 book *Beating the Dow*, by Michael O'Higgins. Here we go
with another O'lesson from one of those guys. First O'Neil, then
O'Shaughnessy, and now O'Higgins. That's O'kay, though. They
all know how to make money.

O'Higgins's work has been admired and improved upon at
The Motley Fool online site. You'll read about The Motley Fool
on page 171. For now, just know that it's an Internet site with
a ton of investment information and excellent discussion forums.
I factored information from The Motley Fool's Dow enhance-
ments into this chapter and combined them with O'Higgins's
work into seamless strategies for you to follow. I do not always
identify the source of each component of the plan. If you want
details, read *Beating the Dow* and visit The Motley Fool.

A Short, Sweet Look at the Dow

The Dow Jones Industrial Average, or DJIA, was created by
Charles H. Dow in 1884. He chose 11 very active stocks, nine of
which were railroads. At the end of each trading day, he simply
added up their closing prices and divided by 11 to get that day's
measure of the market. In 1896, the *Wall Street Journal* published the first real industrial average, which measured a whop-
ping 12 companies. One of them, General Electric, remains on
the Dow today. In 1916 the Dow increased to 20 stocks, and on
October 1, 1928, it grew to 30 stocks.

The Dow is a benchmark for the entire stock market. It's an
imperfect one, but popular because of its simplicity. Other

Everybody Watches the Dow

indexes like the S&P 500, NASDAQ Composite, and Wilshire 5000 capture larger cross sections of the market and provide better benchmarks for comparing the performance of mutual funds, hedge funds, and other stock pools. But the Dow persists. It's listed in every paper, reported by talking heads on the news every evening, and whizzes past light screens in brokerage offices every few minutes. When the Dow broke 3,000 for the first time, then 4, then 5, then 6, the whole world knew about it. Few could tell you where the S&P 500 stood on those days.

And, impressively, the Dow keeps pace with the S&P 500. They've both returned an average annual 10.5 percent over the past fifty years. More recently the Dow has performed better than other indexes. Over the 10 years ended December 31, 1996, the average annual return of the S&P 500 was only 15 percent and the NASDAQ Composite's was only 14 percent. But the Dow posted 16.7 percent! That's a rousing testimony to the dominance of the 30 Dow companies. Each is powerful enough in its industry to stand for its competitors not listed on the Dow. Think of the Dow as a mini senate representing the various parts of our economy. The senators vote daily on how the market is doing. There's a senator from the computer industry (IBM), the food industry (McDonald's), the drug industry (Merck), the entertainment industry (Disney), the auto industry (GM), the aerospace industry (Boeing), the banking industry (J.P. Morgan), and so on.

Here are the 30 current Dow companies and their ticker symbols:

Alcoa AA	Eastman Kodak EK	McDonald's MCD
Allied Signal ALD	Exxon XON	Merck MRK
American Express AXP	General Electric GE	3M MMM
AT&T T	General Motors GM	Philip Morris MO
Boeing BA	Goodyear GT	Procter & Gamble PG
Caterpillar CAT	Hewlett-Packard HWP	Sears S
Chevron CHV	IBM IBM	Traveler's Group TRV
Coca-Cola KO	International Paper IP	Union Carbide UK
Disney DIS	Johnson & Johnson JNJ	United Technologies UTX
Du Pont DD	J.P. Morgan JPM	Wal-Mart Stores WMT

Heard of any of them? If not, put down this book, pick up your wooden staff, and head back to the mountaintop. You've risen to a plane of existence beyond the needs of commerce and profit.

Dow Companies Will Endure

The defining characteristic of all 30 Dow companies is their gargantuan size. Each does billions of dollars in annual sales, most are diversified into a bunch of different businesses, and they're international contenders. Even though the list reads like a who's who in American business, you probably spend even more money with these companies than you think.

Dow Companies Could Throw the Whole Party

Let's say you created invitations to your daughter's birthday party using Lotus Word-pro on your IBM computer. Lotus is owned by IBM, so money for both the software and the hardware goes to IBM. After one little boy spilled his glass of Minute Maid and a little girl spilled her glass of Hi-C, you got a headache and popped a Bayer aspirin. Minute Maid and Hi-C are owned by Coca-Cola, and Bayer is owned by Eastman Kodak, the same company whose film you were using to take pictures of those little headache producers. You quickly served up bowls of Kraft macaroni and cheese and then ducked behind the house to smoke a Marlboro. Philip Morris owns Kraft and Marlboro. Once the kids finished their macaroni, you gave them each a slice of Duncan Hines cake. They all finished their cake and went outside to play while you spruced up the kitchen with Mr. Clean. At halftime of the backyard football game, you passed around a few cans of Pringles chips. After the kids went home, your daughter washed her face with a bar of Ivory soap, brushed her teeth with Crest, and went to bed. You laundered her grass-stained jeans with Tide and finally relaxed with a cup of Folgers coffee. Procter & Gamble owns Duncan Hines, Mr. Clean, Pringles, Ivory, Crest, Tide, and Folgers.

I'd bet my bottom dollar that your grandchildren will do business with Dow companies. In fact, I'm sure of it because editors of the *Wall Street Journal* quietly update the Dow by eliminating laggards and welcoming current market leaders. At any point in history, the Dow represents the best of the big guns.

There you have it. Dow companies are enormous, pervade all parts of our lives, tread internationally, and they don't easily disappear. If you're looking for battleships in a market full of kayaks, look no further than the Dow.

High-Yield Dow Companies Make Great Investments

Dow companies are a huge part of your life; they might as well be a huge part of your portfolio. Then, at next year's birthday party, all that money you spend will help your bottom line by boosting the profits of companies you own. Remember, Wall Street loves earnings. Your dollars are as green as anybody's.

Dow companies are here to stay. They also pay a steady dividend, which makes the dividend yield a reliable indicator of how good a bargain their stock prices are at any given time. Remember from page 27 that you determine a stock's dividend yield by dividing its annual dividend by its price. So a $100 stock paying $5 a year in dividends has a yield of 5 percent (5 divided by 100 gives you .05, or 5 percent). Even though it's a piece of cake to calculate dividend yield, you'll be pleased to know that you won't need to do it. It's printed for you in the paper each day. But it's good to know how they come up with the number.

Because there are only two numbers involved in the dividend yield, if one number remains constant, then the other number drives any changes. With Dow companies, the dividend payout remains fairly constant. These big companies don't like to shock people by reducing the dividend, and they don't like to throw their books out of whack by giving too much money away. So they sit comfortably within a narrow range. That leaves us with only one other number to influence dividend yield: stock price. It changes daily, and its relationship to the dividend is immediately reflected in the dividend yield.

Now, watch the magic as our 30 Dow darlings fluctuate in price. Say IBM is trading at $86 a share and is paying a dividend of $.35 per quarter, or $1.40 per year. You could look up its dividend yield in the paper or calculate it yourself: $1.40 divided by $86 equals .016, or 1.6 percent. In the next few months, IBM declines to $42 a share but maintains the same $1.40 dividend: $1.40 divided by $42 equals 3.3 percent. Aha, it's a higher dividend yield because the stock price dropped. A lower stock price for the same company is a bargain and could indicate that a turnaround is on the way. Do you think IBM is going out of business because its stock dropped over 50 percent? Nope. Dow companies don't stay down and out forever. IBM is going to find a way to climb back up to its former glory prices, and you might as well accompany it on the journey by purchasing a few shares. When it reaches high prices again and its dividend yield goes down to reflect that, you know it's time to move your money to one of IBM's 30 Dow brethren with a low price and a high yield to accompany it on the path to recovery.

How to Invest in High-Yield Dow Stocks

Now you're thoroughly convinced of the reliability of Dow companies, and you understand why high dividend yields are a good indicator of bargain stock prices. It's time to look at ways to harness that information for profit.

The plan is to spend fifteen minutes once a year finding the 10 highest-yield Dow stocks, then invest in each of the 10 or a select number of the 10. Every year thereafter, you repeat the process and adjust your portfolio by selling the stocks that no longer make the select group and buying the ones that replaced them. Your eyes haven't failed you—this is, indeed, an investment strategy requiring fifteen minutes of research *once per year*. O'Higgins wrote that each Dow strategy "involves reviewing and updating your portfolio once a year and fastidiously and deliberately ignoring it in between." For convenience, historic returns tracking the Dow dividend strategy begin on January 1, but you can begin your plan on any day of the year.

First, I'll show how to list the 10 highest-yield Dow stocks. Then I'll review five strategies for you to choose from: the Dow 10, the Dow 5 Plain, the Dow 5 Focus, the Dow 2, and the Dow 1.

Listing the Ten Highest-Yield Dow Stocks

On the day you begin your Dow investment program, pull out the *Wall Street Journal*. If you're not sure which companies make up the 30 current Dow stocks, check page C3 of the *Journal*. There it charts the performance of the Dow Jones Industrial Average and shows each stock on the chart. In the stock tables, highlight the listing for each of the 30 Dow stocks. One of the columns in the stock tables is titled *Yld%*. That's the dividend yield. Using your keen faculties of observation and a process of elimination, circle the ten highest-yield Dow stocks. If there's a tie among the dividend yields, choose the stock with the lower price. Rank the ten circled stocks 1 to 10 from lowest to highest stock price and write the rank beside each stock's listing in the paper. The cheapest stock will have a 1 beside it, the second cheapest a 2, and so on.

List on a sheet of paper the company names, symbols, dividend yields, and prices of all 10 stocks in the order you just ranked them. If the #1 stock—the one with the lowest price—also has the highest dividend yield, cross it out. If the #1 stock does not have the highest dividend yield, leave it there. I promise there's money on the other side of this silliness. On February 11, 1997, my sheet looked like this:

	Company Name	Symbol	Dividend Yield	Price
1	AT&T	T	3.4	39
2	International Paper	IP	2.4	42
3	Goodyear	GT	2.1	53 $1/4$
4	General Motors	GM	3.5	56 $3/8$
5	Chevron	CHV	3.3	65 $1/8$
6	3M	MMM	2.3	83 $1/2$
7	Exxon	XON	3.2	100 $1/8$
8	Texaco	TX	3.3	102 $1/2$
9	JP Morgan	JPM	3.4	104 $3/8$
10	Philip Morris	MO	4	120 $1/4$

Let's discuss the #1 and #2 stocks for a second because they're the biggest source of confusion and also constitute the best profit zone. Michael O'Higgins calls the second-lowest-priced stock the *Penultimate Profit Prospect,* or *PPP.* In case your SAT study sessions have worn off, penultimate means next to last. It's the stock that has historically returned more than all the other Dow stocks. The lowest-priced stock is often facing genuine trouble, which is the reason for its low price. The second-lowest-priced stock, on the other hand, is not usually in trouble. It's simply the most bargain-priced of the high-yielders that are faring well, and therefore has the best prospects for stock performance.

The loony bunch of investors at The Motley Fool online site decided to experiment with the Dow strategy and the Penultimate Profit Prospect explained by O'Higgins. They wanted even more profitable formulas.

In their book *The Motley Fool Investment Guide,* David and Tom Gardner detail how all the Dow 10 stocks performed over 20 years ending in the fall of 1994. Here are their findings, listed from the lowest to highest price position, adjusted every year on January 1 to reflect the new stocks in each position:

Dow 10 by Price Position	Performance
1 Dow (lowest-priced stock)	8.38%
2 Dow (second-lowest-priced, or PPP)	29.82
3 Dow	17.93
4 Dow	17.54
5 Dow	19.60
6 Dow	12.25
7 Dow	11.80
8 Dow	13.01
9 Dow	11.48
10 Dow	10.82

As you can see, the Gardners' research bears out the advice of O'Higgins. The lowest-priced stock is a dog, and the second-lowest-priced, what O'Higgins calls the PPP, is a shooting star. A 29.82 percent return over a twenty-year period turns $10,000 into $1.85 million before taxes and commissions! That's acceptable to me, and probably to you too.

However, those Motley Fools weren't finished yet. Lead fearlessly by a Fool named Robert Sheard, the Fools conducted further research and discovered something very important about the lowest-price stock. It's not always a dog. In fact, sometimes it performs quite well. In the years it was a dog, it usually sported both the lowest price and the highest dividend yield of all the Dow stocks. Aha! Now you know why to cross it off your list when those conditions apply and leave it there when they don't.

The Lowest-Price Stock Isn't Always a Dog

The strategies in the rest of this section are identified with a number: Dow 10, Dow 5 Plain, Dow 5 Focus, Dow 2, and Dow 1. The name of each strategy describes the number of stocks it invests in from your initial list of 10 *assuming you did not cross off the #1 stock*. That means in a year you do cross off the #1 stock, each strategy will use one less stock than shown in its name, with the exception of Dow 1.

Ta-da! You have now completed all the research needed for the first year of your Dow investment program, and you understand why the weirdness works. From here, simply decide on one of the five strategies.

The Dow 10

In this strategy you divide your money equally among all ten stocks. It's the safest way to capture the market-beating performance of Dow Dividend investing because it's the most diversified. However, it doesn't return as much as the other strategies. You know the drill: less risk, less reward.

Let's say you have $10,000 to invest. Here's how your portfolio would look in the Dow 10:

	Company Name	Amount	Shares
1	AT&T	$1,000	25.6
2	International Paper	$1,000	23.8
3	Goodyear	$1,000	18.8
4	General Motors	$1,000	17.7
5	Chevron	$1,000	15.4
6	3M	$1,000	12
7	Exxon	$1,000	10
8	Texaco	$1,000	9.8
9	JP Morgan	$1,000	9.6
10	Philip Morris	$1,000	8.3

Over the 20 years ended December 31, 1996, the Dow 10 strategy achieved an average annual return of 18.43 percent. Your $10,000 would have turned into $294,601 before taxes and commissions, just by spending 15 minutes annually to find the 10 current highest-yield Dow stocks. The cost is low too. At E*Trade, a discount broker I recommend on page 127, NYSE trades cost $15. If the entire list of 10 highest-yielders changed in a year, you'd need to sell the 10 old stocks and buy the 10 new ones, which is a total of 20 trades. 20 trades times $15 equals $300 per year in trading commission *at most*. So your maximum trading costs would start at just 3 percent of your portfolio and decline each year as your portfolio grows. In a lot of years the list of 10 highest-yielders wouldn't change completely, and you would spend even less on commissions.

The Dow 5 Plain

In this strategy you divide your money equally among the five lowest-priced stocks from your list of the ten highest-yielders. They're simply the first five on your list, four in years that you cross out the #1 stock. This strategy returns more than the Dow 10, but is less diversified and therefore slightly riskier. With only five stocks, you can get started with less money, and you'll trade fewer times per year.

The reason that further narrowing the Dow 10 into the Dow 5 produces superior returns is that lower-priced stocks tend to be more volatile. Because they're priced lower than their siblings, the same dollar amount up or down results in a greater percentage change. For instance, a $200 stock that gains $5 is up 2.5 percent. A $20 stock that gains $5 is up 25 percent. Over the years, a portfolio of the 5 lowest-priced of the Dow 10 stocks has been more volatile and more profitable than the Dow 10 itself.

Here's how your $10,000 portfolio would look in the Dow 5 Plain:

	Company Name	Amount	Shares
1	AT&T	$2,000	51.3
2	International Paper	$2,000	47.6
3	Goodyear	$2,000	37.6
4	General Motors	$2,000	35.5
5	Chevron	$2,000	30.7

Over the 20 years ended December 31, 1996, the Dow 5 Plain strategy achieved an average annual return of 20.47 percent. Your $10,000 would have turned into $414,551 before taxes and commissions. Because you're managing only 5 stocks instead of 10, your maximum trading costs would be half that of the Dow 10. Thus, the most you would spend per year is $150. That's a mere 1.5 percent of your portfolio in the first year and even less in subsequent years when your money has grown.

The Dow 5 Focus

This strategy is exactly like the Dow 5 Plain except that you double up—or focus—on the #1 and #2 stocks on your list. You take the extra money needed to double up on those two stocks from what you would invest evenly across all five stocks in the Plain strategy. Thus in the Focus strategy you'll invest less in stocks #3, #4, and #5. All these # signs are making me look like a cartoon character swearing. Hopefully you'll make a #$!?*@! lot of money after reading them. The Dow 5 Focus evolved from a similar strategy on The Motley Fool site called "The Foolish 4," which always drops the #1 stock and doubles up on the #2. The Dow 5 Focus drops the #1 stock only when it is crossed off your initial list of 10 for having both the lowest price and the highest yield.

In years that the #1 stock is crossed off your list, simply use the money you would have invested in the #1 stock and add it to your investment in the #2 stock.

Here's how it all pans out. With a $10,000 portfolio during a year when stock #1 is crossed out, you would invest $8,000 in stock #2 and $666 in each of stocks #3, #4, and #5. In a year when stock #1 is kept, you would invest $4,000 in stock #1, $4,000 in stock #2, and $666 in each of stocks #3, #4, and #5. It might seem pointless to bother investing the little amounts of money in stocks #3, #4, and #5, but remember that you will have more than $10,000 to invest someday. The numbers get bigger in a hurry. However, if you're currently investing smaller amounts of money and don't see the point of allocating the "leftover" amount to stocks #3, #4, and #5, take a look at the Dow 2 strategy. It invests only in stocks #1 and #2.

Here's how your $10,000 portfolio would look in the Dow 5 Focus:

	Company Name	Amount	Shares
1	AT&T	$4,000	102.6
2	International Paper	$4,000	95.2
3	Goodyear	$666	12.5
4	General Motors	$666	11.8
5	Chevron	$666	10.2

If AT&T had the highest yield, it would be crossed off your list and you would have invested $8,000 in International Paper.

Over the 20 years ended December 31, 1996, the Dow 5 Focus strategy achieved an average annual return of 24.53 percent. Your $10,000 would have turned into $804,414 before taxes and commissions. Because you're managing only 5 stocks, your maximum trading costs would be half that of the Dow 10. Thus, the most you would spend per year is $150—only 1.2 percent of your portfolio the first year, less as you get richer.

The Dow 2

This strategy is exactly like the Dow 5 Focus except that you invest only in stocks #1 and #2. In years that stock #1 is crossed out, you invest everything in stock #2 and this strategy mirrors the Dow 1, which always invests everything in stock #2.

Of course, the Dow 2 strategy does not lead to a diversified portfolio. The most you'll ever hold in it is two stocks, and in many years you'll hold only one stock. However, in my opinion this is the king of all Dow strategies because it has returned more than any other and has been less volatile than the Dow 5 Plain, the Dow 5 Focus, and the Dow 1—but not the Dow 10. I'm not overly concerned with diversifying across a lot of Dow stocks. The companies themselves are so big and sprawling that any one of them is diversification enough for me. Remember Procter & Gamble's product line? I can't walk through my house without bumping into something they make. If one product does poorly, they have dozens more to boost profits.

Here's how your $10,000 portfolio would look in the Dow 2:

Company Name	Amount	Shares
1 AT&T	$5,000	128.2
2 International Paper	$5,000	119

Over the 20 years ended December 31, 1996, the Dow 2 strategy achieved an average annual return of 27.33 percent. Your $10,000 would have turned into $1,254,916 before taxes and commissions. Because you're managing only 2 stocks instead of 10, your maximum trading costs would be just 20 percent that of the Dow 10. The most you would spend per year is $60—only .6 percent of your portfolio the first year, decreasing as your money grows.

The Dow 1

In this strategy you put all your money in stock #2, what O'Higgins calls the Penultimate Profit Prospect or PPP.

This is clearly the simplest of all the Dow strategies since it invests in only one stock. Not only does the Dow 1 require little money to get started, it requires a mere 2 trades per year at most.

Here's how your $10,000 portfolio would look in the Dow 1:

Company Name	Amount	Shares
1 AT&T	$10,000	256.4

Over the 20 years ended December 31, 1996, the Dow 1 strategy achieved an average annual return of 26.25 percent. Your $10,000 would have turned into $1,058,346 before taxes and commissions. Because you're managing only 1 stock instead of 10, your maximum trading costs would be one-tenth that of the Dow 10. The most you would spend per year is $30. That's a minuscule .3 percent of your portfolio the first year, becoming more minuscule over time.

Choosing a Dow Strategy

It's up to you to choose a Dow strategy. I recommend choosing between the Dow 5 Focus, the Dow 2, and the Dow 1 because they provide the best returns and lowest transaction costs. To choose between the three of them, decide if the volatility of owning one or two stocks in Dow 2 or Dow 1 is worth the higher returns. In 1974 the Dow 1 stock was Chrysler and it lost 41.70 percent. If you can stomach years like that, consider using the Dow 2 or Dow 1 strategies. If not, take the Dow 5 Focus.

On the other hand, more diversification might be your style. The biggest loss for the Dow 10 is -7.58 percent in 1990, and for the Dow 5 it's -15.22 percent that same year. Even if you won't gain as much in the end, smoother sailing might make the journey more enjoyable. It's your call.

Let's lift a mug to Michael O'Higgins and the Motley Fools

for their hard work. With little risk, these simple Dow strategies outperform most mutual funds and the broader market averages. They require fifteen minutes of research annually, cost little, and are simple to understand. With a Dow dividend strategy, your money is betting on some of the world's most powerful corporations—a bet that will pay off in the end. Michael and all you Fools, here's to some of the neatest little investment strategies I've ever seen.

5 Get Ready to Invest

This chapter contains the planning you need to do before investing. I discuss your investment goals, then go into stock-investment necessities: opening a brokerage account, putting money into it, and placing trades.

Know Why You're Investing

You must know why you're putting money in the stock market. What could have gone toward a beautiful two-week vacation in Beaverton, Oregon, is instead going toward 100 shares of Nike, which is headquartered there. Why is that? "To make money, you moron." Fine, but let's get a bit more specific.

Precisely Define Your Goals

You need to invest differently for your retirement than for your next doctor's appointment. These days they seem to cost about the same. Your retirement is a long ways off; the doctor's appointment is right around the corner. Therein lies most of the information you need to know, namely, how much time you have to invest.

The more time you have, the more risk you can withstand. The stock market fluctuates. It always has, always will. If you have twenty years, your money can recover from short-term losses. Moreover, if you invest regularly during that time period you can take advantage of price dips along the way. When money you don't need for twenty years takes a 20 percent nosedive, there's no need to sell. It has time to climb back up to its former

Make Sure You Can Recover from Losses Before Time's Up

glory and it will do so. Instead, you can move more money into that investment at the 20 percent discount. When the price recovers, you will make money on the rebound rather than just recouping the paper loss.

That's a good term to know, by the way. A *paper loss* occurs when your investment declines in value but you don't sell. The loss is apparent only on a paper statement showing the investment's current value. Only when you actually sell the investment does the loss become real. If you don't sell, hopefully the investment will recover and the only loss you'll ever see is the one that showed up temporarily on your statement.

Make Them Specific and Exhilarating

In *The Neatest Little Guide to Mutual Fund Investing*, I wrote about my desire to buy a Lexus Sport Coupe. That's something I can picture in my mind and think about when I see the numbers starting to add up. Numbers by themselves are pretty dull. Fast cars, nice vacations, new suits, surprise gifts, and a dinner that doesn't involve an order number are real-life reasons to invest. They're why you're trying to get more money.

The most common investment goal is retirement, then college funding. Those are exhilarating too, particularly when you consider the alternative to not investing for them. That'll get you moving in the right direction.

Write Them Down

Put your financial goals on paper. Doing so clarifies the big picture so that when the paperwork starts to mount and the markets are every which way, you know why you're in the middle of it all. I won't digress into a treatise on life planning and reaching your ultimate state of consciousness, but writing your financial goals on paper is a worthy exercise.

Assign Time Frames to Those Goals

Once you know your goals, decide how long you intend to wait for them. If it's retirement, probably a long time. If it's a new car, perhaps several years. If it's a plane ticket to see your brother graduate from the Urban Hang-gliding Academy this spring, you have only a few months.

The most important distinction between those goals is the amount of time available to reach them. Money invested for retirement has a lot of years to rise and fall, rise and fall, withstanding fluctuations and recovering from them. Money for this spring's graduation has almost no time to recover from losses.

It's good to group goals by their time frames. Long-term goals are more than ten years away, medium-term goals are five to ten years away, and short-term goals are less than five years away. Looking over those time periods, here's how our three earlier goals stack up:

Goal Time Frames	
Retirement	Long-term
New car	Medium-term
Spring graduation	Short-term

Draw up a similar table for your goals. Once you know your time frames, you'll be ready to choose an acceptable level of risk. That's our next topic.

Choose Acceptable Risk Levels for Your Goals

Now you know how far away your goals are. From there you can quickly determine the amount of risk you're willing to accept for each of them. The more time involved, the more risk your investments can withstand.

The stock market involves a great deal of risk. Nobody knows where the economy is going, how the market will react to where the economy is going, or how your individual stocks will behave when the market reacts to where the economy is going. In short, you're screwed! Not really, but you don't want to subject short-term goals to the vagaries of the stock market. There isn't enough time for them to recover from losses.

Medium- and long-term goals, on the other hand, do have

time to recover. They are good candidates for the stock market. The long-term goals can withstand even more risk than the medium-term because they have even more time. That means you can feel comfortable investing in small companies, which tend to be more volatile than large companies.

This is a book on stock investing. That means you should use it to invest money intended for medium- and long-term goals. Your short-term money should be invested somewhere safe like a bank account or a money-market mutual fund.

Choose a Discount Broker

As you read on page 17, I like discount brokers a lot. After reading this book and conducting your own research on companies, you don't need the expensive opinion of a full-service broker. Save some money, consolidate your investments, and continue forming your own opinions.

This section presents six solid discounters to choose from. Look over the list, select a few that interest you, call their toll-free numbers or visit their Web sites for more information and an account application, then choose a broker to handle your stock trades. Fill out the application and send it in. If you choose a broker that has an office nearby your home, such as Schwab or Fidelity, you can always walk in and talk to a live human being. Some people actually prefer that. Go figure.

Ceres

Ceres is a one-fee online brokerage firm. Any number of shares of any stock costs you $18. Here's an excerpt from the Web site: "We make our money by providing our clients with excellent order execution at a low price. We act only as your execution firm. We offer no advice and maintain no research staff, analysts, commissioned sales force, or branch offices. In other words, we've streamlined our operation to offer only the services you need to manage your own account, allowing us to offer an $18 flat rate for equity transactions—one of the lowest in the industry. . . . It's as simple as that."

You can place trades over the phone or through the Web site for the same $18. The only added value at Ceres is a daily online column by Andrew Tobias. You won't find research like the kind provided by E*Trade. So, if you're thinking of going with Ceres, be sure to compare them with E*Trade first. The costs are about the same, but E*Trade provides free research.

Contact Information: 800-669-3900, www.ceres.com

E*Trade

E*Trade is the pioneer that kicked off the entire online-investment revolution. The company trades only stocks. You won't find a mutual fund network here, which means you can't consolidate your investments at E*Trade. Its stock trades are pretty darned cheap, though: $14.95 for listed orders, $19.95 for over-the-counter orders. That's the entire price menu. Whether you call over the phone to trade through a person, type your order on the telephone keypad, or click your order over the Web site, the cost is always the same. That's a nice convenience.

The company also offers some great free research on its Web site. Customers can get account balances, historic price charts, current quotes, and view fundamental research data from BASE-LINE Financial Services that includes earnings estimates from First Call. All this is free to customers. When viewing company information, customers simply click on a button to place an order. I've traded several times through E*Trade and am quite happy with its service. In one instance the company improved my buy price by $1. That is, I said to buy 100 shares at $25, and it bought them at $24. A nice bonus, wouldn't you say? You can see the E*Trade stock order screen on page 139.

Contact Information: 800-786-2573, www.etrade.com.

eBroker

This is the ultimate bargain-basement broker. The entire operation revolves around one simple number: $12. That's what it costs to buy or sell any number of shares of any stock. There's not a whole lot more to explain. There are no phone numbers, no people to talk to, nothing whatsoever available to you except a place to stash your cash and push buttons on a Web site to trade stocks for $12. Have fun.

Contact Information: info@ebroker.com, www.ebroker.com.

Fidelity

Fidelity Investments is worth considering if you want to consolidate your investments in one place. It offers discounted stock trading—although not very discounted—hundreds of mutual funds through its FundsNetwork program, and lots of good research via its On-Demand Research system. You can get company reports from Argus, learn about earnings surprises from First Call, and read a few Renaissance IPO reports. Fidelity maintains branch offices around the country. This may seem a small benefit, but one of my favorite parts about doing business with Fidelity is its outstanding TouchTone Xpress telephone-transaction system. It's the fastest quote system around, offering customized watch lists, abbreviated and full quote options, and speedy keys for skipping forward and back.

If you're leaning toward Fidelity, give a good hard look at Schwab first. Schwab offers many of the same benefits as Fidelity and lower stock trading prices. Conduct your own competitive analysis by getting more information from each company.

Contact Information: 800-544-8666, www.fidelity.com.

Jack White & Company

Highly rated in every broker survey, Jack White & Company is one of the most comprehensive brokerage firms around. It's the ultimate one-stop shopping for investors, offering stocks, mutual funds, bonds, commodities, futures, variable annuities, and more. The company has a program called CONNECT that allows you to buy front-end load funds without paying a load. White simply matches buyers and sellers. You do pay a $200 fee for the service, however. Thus, you need to be investing at least $3,500 in a fund with a 5.75 percent load to break even. At the end of 1996 White was preparing to implement a similar program for stocks. Instead of paying a spread—the difference between the bid and ask price of a stock—you would simply pay a flat fee to White. The program could save a lot of money on large trades.

Through its Web site or custom software, White charges $25

per trade. If you call and trade through one of White's brokers, the charge is $33 plus 3 cents per share.

Contact Information: 800-753-1700, http://pawws.secapl.com/jwc.

Schwab

Charles Schwab & Company is the biggest discounter in the nation, handling more than 3.6 million accounts. The firm offers $29 stock trades through its Web site, access to more than 500 mutual funds through its OneSource program—many of which can be traded with no sales load or transaction fee, and a slew of research tools through its Research on Request system. Such tools include First Call earnings estimates, Vickers insider-trading reports, and Standard & Poor's stock sheets. One of Schwab's biggest selling points is the number of physical locations it boasts. I seem to bump into a Schwab office everywhere I go.

Schwab is one of the best bets for consolidating your entire portfolio in one place. There are cheaper places to trade stocks, and there are other brokers with mutual fund networks, but few blend the two as well as Schwab. If you're leaning toward Schwab, take a peek at Fidelity. It runs neck and neck with Schwab on features, although its stock trades are more expensive. Conduct your own competitive analysis by getting more information from each company.

Contact Information: 800-435-4000, www.schwab.com

Others

There are hundreds of discount brokers. Others worthy of a look include AccuTrade (800-882-4887), Datek (www.datek.com), Lombard (800-566-2273), Muriel Siebert (800-872-0711), Pacific (800-421-8395), and Scottsdale (800-619-7283). For a directory listing, point your Web browser to www.yahoo.com and search on "discount brokers." It'll list a few specific ones, but what you really want is the category listing. Click on that (probably at the top of the list) and you'll find pages of discount brokers to peruse.

Get Money to the Broker

Now you've chosen a discount broker. You need to have money in your account, or you won't be able to invest in anything. You'll have a core account which receives your deposits and the proceeds from your stock sales. You'll start out with an asset transfer to get your initial money to the core account. After that you can take advantage of direct deposit and electronic bank transfers to keep it full and ready to buy investments. This section explains your core account and the three ways to put money into it.

Your Core Account

Your core account is where everything begins and ends. Money you send to your broker lands in your core account. When you buy a stock or invest in a mutual fund, the money comes from your core account. When you sell a stock or withdraw from a mutual fund, the proceeds go into your core account. You can call your broker at any time to have a check mailed to you with money from your core account. In some cases you can even set up your core account to work just like your checking account. You can write checks against it and even use an ATM card to access your money there.

In fact, many people use their discount broker as a bank. Their paycheck is deposited directly into their brokerage core account. From there money is automatically disbursed among different investments. The rest sits in the account to pay bills and everything else we do with our money. A brokerage core account is just like a regular checking account, except that it pays more interest and the funds are immediately available for investing.

Core Accounts Are a Great Place for Cash

Most core accounts are money-market accounts. They don't fluctuate, which means you can feel safe leaving money there. When you hear gurus and other unsavory types warn of an impending market crash, they usually recommend putting everything in "cash." That means the money market. So if the gurus succeed in scaring you out of stocks, you'll sell all your shares and move everything into your core account. Beware the gurus, by the way. As you'll read on page 242, they're best used for entertainment—not money management.

Putting Money into Your Core Account

There are three ways to get new money into your core account for investing: asset transfer, direct deposit, and electronic bank transfers. This section covers all three.

Asset Transfer

Asset transfer is a fancy term for sending money to your broker. You can either send it "in-kind," which means you don't actually send money but send investments instead, or by just mailing a check. In-kind transfers are most common when you're switching from one broker to another. Instead of selling all your investments at the old broker and then rebuying them at the new, you simply fill out a transfer form at your new broker that authorizes them to get all your goodies from your old broker. Hopefully, the old broker will be a full-service house and the new broker will be a discounter.

When you've chosen a discounter from the previous section, they'll tell you how much money is needed to open an account. They'll also see to it that you've got all the forms you need and will talk you through them over the phone, if necessary. If you chose a broker with a nearby office, walk in with all your paperwork and your checkbook and say, "Can anybody here help me invest my millions?" I guarantee that somebody will help you.

Make Your First Deposit

After you've made your initial deposits, you can make subsequent ones by writing additional checks or through one of the two automated programs I'll discuss next: direct deposit and electronic bank transfers.

Direct Deposit

Once you're set up with your new broker, you can automate deposits into your core account. Direct deposit establishes an automatic deduction from your paycheck just as your employer does for your taxes and possibly for your retirement program. In addition to taking money out for Uncle Sam, you can take money out for your core brokerage account. Like magic, you'll have money there when you want to invest.

To take advantage of this program, simply request a direct-deposit authorization form from your broker.

Electronic Bank Transfers

Another option for keeping your core account brimming with funds is to establish an automatic transfer from your bank account to your core brokerage account. This is the only choice for people who are self-employed and don't receive paychecks. You specify what time period you'd like the transfers to take place—such as weekly, monthly, or quarterly—and the amount of money you'd like to transfer each time. If you ever need to skip an automatic transfer, simply call your broker and tell them to do so.

To take advantage of this program, request an electronic bank-transfer authorization form from your broker.

Place Orders

Once you've chosen a discount broker and you've got money in your account, you're ready to invest. This section explains the bid, ask, and spread; discusses different types of orders available to you; and shows how to place orders by phone, by computer, or in person.

Bid, Ask, and Spread

The *bid* is the highest quoted price that buyers are willing to pay for a security at any specific moment. In that same specific moment, the *ask* is the lowest quoted price that sellers are willing to accept for the security. The bid is the price you get when you sell the stock; the ask is the price you pay to buy the stock. The *spread* is the difference between the two numbers and is kept by a dealer who's called a "market maker" on the OTC and a "specialist" on one of the exchanges. The dealer maintains fair and orderly trading by keeping an inventory of stock to satisfy demand when buyers and sellers can't be matched up. He's a middleman just like the owner of the bookstore where you bought this fine title. All middlemen purchase inventory at a price lower than they sell it. The spread is biggest for stocks that are thinly traded because it takes fewer dealers to satisfy demand. Fewer dealers means less competition and thus bigger spreads. Now you have career advice for your children: become dealers in thinly traded stocks.

Let's take a closer look at these three numbers. If Mister Magazine bids $15^1/_2$ and asks $15, the spread is $^1/_2$. Placing a market order buys your shares at $15^1/_2$. The instant after you buy your shares, they're worth only $15 because that's the price other sellers are asking. In my seminar called Stocks 101, a gentleman once questioned whether he could ask for the extra $^1/_2$ to recoup his purchase price. Ahem, well, no. First of all, nobody's actually asking anybody for anything. It's a figure of speech. The market knows the bid and ask prices based only on supply and demand. Second, even if you could ask for a higher price, nobody would pay it. If everybody but you is selling at $15, why would I pay $15^1/_2$ to buy from you? Don't

The Bid vs. the Ask

try telling me it's because you're a nice person. Lemonade stands might work on that premise, but the stock market doesn't. Besides, it's not so nice trying to fleece me for the extra fifty cents a share, pal.

As you see, the spread can translate into a serious investment cost if you sell right away. In our Mister Magazine example, fifty cents represents a full 3.2 percent of the $15^1/_2$ bid price. A flat brokerage commission of $18 on a 100-share trade is only a 1.2 percent cost. The spread is more than $2^1/_2$ times the expense of the commission! Before you get too riled up and embark on a dealer hunt, remember that you don't actually suffer the burden of the spread unless you sell right away. Hopefully, your stock will appreciate far beyond the spread and it will become irrelevant. Always be aware of the spreads, though, because your stock must move beyond the combined spread and commission costs just to break even. If you consistently trade unpopular stocks that have huge spreads, consider opening a brokerage account at Jack

White & Company. White matches buyers and sellers itself and takes a commission that's smaller than the market spread.

Orders

Giving an order to your broker is a thrilling moment. It means you've done your research, thought about your situation, and are ready to take action. There are two types of orders: market and limit.

Market

A *market order* is very easy to understand. It instructs your broker to buy a security at the current ask price. That's it. Your buy price is whatever the thing is trading for when the order reaches the floor. With today's fast communications, that price is going to be fairly close to where it was when you placed the order, if not the exact same price. For instance, say Mister Magazine is trading at 15\frac{1}{2}$ per share and you place a market order for 100 shares. If you don't buy your shares for precisely 15\frac{1}{2}$, you'll probably pick them up somewhere between 15\frac{1}{4}$ and 15\frac{3}{4}$.

Limit

A *limit order* instructs your broker to buy or sell a security at a price you specify or better. That means if you say to sell a stock at $10, your broker will sell either at $10 or at a higher price. If you say to buy a stock at $20, your broker will buy either at $20 or at a lower price.

Limit orders and stop orders (next section) have a time period associated with them. When you place a limit order, it is either a *day order* or a *good-till-cancelled* (*GTC*) order. A day order expires at the end of the current trading day regardless of whether or not its conditions were met. A GTC order remains open until its conditions are met, which might never happen.

I love limit orders and use them almost exclusively. There's no better way to remain calm about the markets than to evaluate a company, decide on a fair price to pay for its stock, specify that price to your broker in a GTC limit order, and forget about it. If the stock hits your buy price, the broker buys and mails you a confirmation statement. If not, you never hear about it. It works the same on the sell. If a stock you own is bouncing around what you consider to be a good sell price, just call your broker and specify your sell price and number of shares to sell. Then forget about it. A few days later, perhaps, the stock will spike up for a brief moment, hit your sell price, and go on its way up or down. You'll get a statement in the mail confirming your sale.

You shouldn't really forget about your limit orders, of course. The last thing you want is for a stock to hit its buy limit when you don't have any money sitting in your core account. You'll get to know your broker real well if that happens. When I say to forget about your limit orders, I mean to relax and let the market do its silly thing. Nine times out of ten, my limit orders come through and I never sweat a drop waiting for the precise right time to buy and sell. I specify it in the limit order. If it happens, great. If not, I let it go.

Don't Forget About Your Limit Orders

Of course, this is pure hooey to some people. They would say it's lunacy to place limit orders and forget about them. They are assuming that they can watch a stock and pick the right time to buy and sell. If you bought Mister Magazine at $15\frac{1}{2}$ and it rose to $30, would you sell? You could reevaluate and, if you thought it might go higher, place a limit order to sell half your shares at $31. Some would say that's foolish because the stock might rise to $35. Might, could, would have, almost did, it happened once to a friend of mine, nearly came through—anybody can surmise this way forever. I would be happy to have tacked on an extra $1 to my sell price and to have kept half my shares. Then you could place another limit order for the remainder at $36. Ah, the critics say, but what if it rises to $40? Then you made a mistake.

In truth, you shouldn't be playing the markets like that. You should always examine the worth of the companies you own and determine whether they're still worth owning. Who cares what the market says they're worth? Think like Warren Buffett and treat your stocks like your own companies. They *are* your own companies, a certain percentage of them, at least. When you do decide to buy and sell, consider using limit orders. They take away some of the pressure and usually allow you to save a few bucks on the buy and make a few extra on the sell.

Stop

A stop order becomes a market order when a price you specify is reached. Like limit orders, stop orders are either good for the day or good-till-cancelled. If you own a stock and instruct your broker to sell it at a price lower than it currently trades for, that's called a *stop loss* because you're stopping your potential loss and protecting the profit you've already gained. You can use a stop order in the other direction too. Technically it would be called a stop gain, but nobody calls it that because it sounds silly. What you're really doing is ratcheting up the point that you want to sell.

When the price you specify in a stop order is reached, the stop order becomes a market order. That means your broker will then trade the stock at its current price. If the price is moving quickly, that might be higher or lower than your stop. This is an important distinction between limit orders and stop orders. A limit order trades the stock at the price you specify or better; a stop order trades the stock at its current price after it touches the price you specify. Thus, with a stop order your trade might occur at a price better or worse than the stop price.

To get around this inherent problem with stop orders, you can use a *stop limit order*. As its name implies, it combines the features of a stop order and a limit order. First, you specify the price at which you want the stop order to kick in. Then you specify the price at which you want the limit order to trade. If the price you specify in the limit order isn't reached, your order never executes. That guarantees that you won't trade at a price worse than you specify in the limit order.

No Matter How Fast Your Order Moves, the Market Can Move Faster

Let's run through an example. Say, you're eyeing Mister Magazine at $15½ per share. You want to buy 100 shares if it starts moving upward considerably. You could place a stop order at $17. That means that if Mister Magazine suddenly spikes up to $19, your stop order will become a market order to buy 100 shares. If the price is moving quickly, the order might not go through until Mister Magazine asks $18. Perhaps that's fine with you because you just want to pick up your shares when the stock breaks out. It's more important that you actually buy the 100 shares than it is to buy them at a specific price.

On the other hand, it might annoy you to pay more for Mister Magazine than you think it's worth. You still want to buy 100 shares if it starts moving up. You could place a stop limit order with the stop at $17 and the limit at 17^{1}/_{2}$. If the stock hits $17, your stop order becomes a limit order to buy 100 shares at 17^{1}/_{2}$ or better. If your broker can get only $18, the order won't execute.

Once you buy your 100 shares, let's think positive and say they rise to $30. You don't want to lose the profits you've already gained, so you place a stop loss at $28. If Mister Magazine hits the skids and plummets to $18, your order will kick in at $28 and sell at the next opportunity, which might be lower than $28. That really bugs you, so on further consideration you decide to cancel the stop order and replace it with a stop limit order with a stop at $28 and a limit at $28 as well. Now if Mister Magazine plummets to $18, you might go with it. Why? Because your limit order to sell at $28 or better won't kick in if the price hits $28 and immediately falls lower without ever coming back up. Know what you want to do and place the right kind of order.

Ways to Place Orders

You can place your order by phone, by computer, or in person. This section explains all three.

By Phone

Investing is one of the few areas where touching keys on your phone can be rewarding. Instead of navigating a 17-level phone directory at the IRS or your favorite insurance company, you can dial up your broker and punch your way to wealth. At any time of day or night, you can call to get account balances, quotes, or to place orders.

When you open an account with one of the discount brokers, your welcome kit will include directions for using a touch-tone trading system. Though each is slightly different, the process is always roughly the same. You identify stocks by their symbols.

Each letter of a symbol is identified by pressing two keys on the pad. First, press the key displaying the letter, then press 1, 2, or 3 to identify the letter by its position as the first, second, or third letter on the key. For instance, Harley-Davidson's stock symbol is HDI. To identify Harley on your keypad, you would type 42-31-43 and then usually hit # to indicate that you've finished typing in the symbol. The letters "Q" and "Z" don't appear on phone keypads. Q is entered as 77 and Z is entered as 99. Refer to your brokerage firm's phone-trading documentation for more detail.

You need to enter trading symbols to get quotes and place orders. Most phone-trading systems include clear menus that point you in the right direction and also offer help if you sit idle long enough or ask for it by pushing *H or something similar.

By Computer

This is all the rage these days, and will probably continue to be. There's eSchwab, E*Trade, eBroker, and plenty of other e's on the way. If you've got a computer and a modem and access to the Internet, you should try computer trading. It's convenient, plus it's easy to specify exactly what you want to do by checking boxes and clicking buttons.

Zap the Orders in Yourself

It's also a way to save money. Many brokers give an additional discount on orders placed over the computer because they're cheap to fulfill. Nobody needs to answer the phone, fill anything out, or otherwise deal with you. You just go to the Web site or fire up the custom software and do it all yourself.

I have an account at E*Trade. I like the E*Trade Web site because it allows me to enter all the stock symbols from my stocks-to-watch worksheet in a list and check every price with a single mouse click. Then, if I want to enter an order, I simply click on a button next to the stock symbol and an order page appears onscreen. If you can read and fill out a door-prize drawing form, you can fill out an onscreen stock order. The top of the next page shows what E*Trade's looks like.

E✲TRADE   **stock** order   [new messages]

Account: EP2784-0001 4687-8751 Switch Accounts   For help, click on any ▼

▼ **Transaction:**   ▼ **Number**   ▼ **Stock**   ▼ **Price:**
  ⦿ Buy   of shares: symbol: ⦿Market
  ○ Sell   ○Limit:
  ○ Sell Short   Find Symbol   ○Stop:
  ○ Buy to Cover   ○Stop Limit:

▼ **Term:** | Good For Day | ▼ | *Optional:* ▼ All or none ☐ (300 shares and over)

Trading password: [   ]   Review the order carefully.   [**Preview Order**]
[Cancel]

| what's new | message center | switch accounts | e+watch | help | **main** |

the markets   **trading**   **your account**
Investor Resources   Enter Stock Order   Account Balances
Markets at a Glance   Open Stock Orders   Account Records
Quotes/News/Charts   Options Trading   Portfolio Manager NEW!
Stock Watch   Transaction History   Portfolio Summary

E*Trade Online Stock Order

See how simple it is? Just click on the type of transaction, fill in the number of shares and the stock symbol, click on the type of order and enter a price, specify whether it's good for the day or good until canceled, then preview your order. You can print the preview screen for your records and then send it on its way. If you need help on any step, just click the little arrow next to it, and a complete explanation appears onscreen.

Can you believe that people are still paying full-service brokers to do this for them? It's insulting! If you want to start investing over the computer, contact your discount broker and ask for information on doing so. If you opened an account at one of the brokers listed in "Choose a Discount Broker" on page 126, you're all set to begin computer trading.

In Person—How Quaint!

If your broker has an office nearby, you can walk in and place an order in person. I'm serious—I saw it happen once. A lady walked into a Schwab office, sat down with a representative, and simply spoke to him. He understood her spoken words, filled out a form with her, and then typed commands into a computer on her behalf. It was better than an exhibit at the Smithsonian.

They're Waiting for You

These days it seems that everything is done over a phone or computer. Even that in-person order I witnessed at Schwab involved a computer. But there are times when it's nice to hold real pieces of paper in your hand and sit in a real office chair and talk to a real person.

I've felt it myself. Sometimes investing over the phone and computer feels like Never Never Land. You never see the stock certificates, you never see money change hands, you never get assurance from somebody that all is well. You simply receive confirmations in the mail with numbers printed on them.

So, if you want a dose of the real world, stop by one of your broker's nearby offices. If being able to do so is an important option for you, consider opening an account at Schwab or Fidelity. Both companies have branches across the country.

6 Research to Riches

It's time for you to learn how and where to conduct research, the most critical part of investing. Every master investor swears by it. Your returns will be directly proportional to the quality of the companies you buy. That quality depends on your research.

Have no fear! There is more information available to you than you can use. Peter Lynch wrote in *One Up on Wall Street*, "I can't imagine anything that's useful to know that the amateur investor can't find out. All the pertinent facts are just waiting to be picked up." After reading this chapter, you'll laugh at people who say they can't invest because they don't know where to get information. I submit that it is now more difficult to avoid investment information than to get what you need. It's everywhere: from your Christmas list to your library to the magazine rack at your local grocery store, investment research is there for you to snatch it up, file it away, and turn it into profit.

This chapter shows where to get the information. The next chapter shows what to do with it.

Publications

Even though it's an electronic world these days, printed publications form the backbone of most individual investment research. It's nice to curl up with your favorite investment magazine, peruse the paper over a cup of coffee, or receive a newsletter targeted to your situation. This section covers all forms of printed publications.

Magazines

The first money you spend on investment research should go toward a magazine subscription. They're cheap and they're packed with helpful how-to articles and some pretty darned good investment advice. Nobody considers it cool to get a good stock lead from a $3 magazine purchased along with a carton of yogurt, but I've found some good investments that way. One of my favorite techniques is to monitor the model portfolios shown for different money managers or a list of stocks chosen by the magazine editors for one reason or another. The magazines monitor the performance of their picks, making it easy to wait for some of them to decline in price.

Finance Magazines Turn Up Some Great Ideas

These are my three favorite investment magazines:

SmartMoney

This is the "Wall Street Journal Magazine of Personal Business," and it's excellent. Flipping through the magazine gives you an impression of quality. There's no tabloid feel to it like you'll find in many of the investment magazines. *SmartMoney* runs articles on every aspect of investing, but does a particularly good job with mutual funds and stocks. The editors hold themselves accountable for their stock picks and are always striving to improve their methods. By following their progress, your own skills will improve along with theirs.

Contact Information: 800-444-4204. Annual subscriptions cost $24.

Worth

I love *Worth*. Its columnists are second to none—Peter Lynch is one of them—and its regular features are dynamite. For instance, it runs a global-investing section that highlights returns of every major country in the world and comments on a few specific regions. It also shows stocks that successful mutual fund managers are buying and their reasons for doing so. Another section picks the brains of newsletter editors for hot tips. The magazine reveals stock measurements that aren't widely used, such as price-to-sales and quality of earnings ratio. Finally, its periodic mutual fund surveys are among the best available.

Contact Information: 800-777-1851. Annual subscriptions cost $24.

Kiplinger's

This magazine has a broader scope than either *SmartMoney* or *Worth*. Instead of talking just about investing, *Kiplinger's* moves into other issues of personal business such as credit card spending, loans, college tuition, and vacation planning. The other magazines touch on these subjects too, but not as often as *Kiplinger's*. The magazine's real claim to fame, however, is its mutual fund surveys. With clear graphics and easily digested tables, they lead the industry year after year. Its columns are nothing to sneeze at, either.

Contact Information: 800-544-0155. Annual subscriptions cost $20.

Newspapers

Just about every newspaper includes stock tables. You probably receive a newspaper every day that has the latest numbers right there for you. But there are times when you need more than a quote or volume information. During those times it's a good idea to check out one of the three papers in this section.

The Wall Street Journal

This is certainly the Big Kahuna among investment newspapers, although its authority isn't as unquestioned as it used to be. Everybody who's anybody glances at the *WSJ* from time to time. It's a good idea for you to do the same.

The front page contains top news summaries in a section called "What's News." A quick skim of the summaries will alert you to items of interest. You can follow a page number to read the complete article.

The heart of the paper is section C, "Money & Investing." That's where you can see how the Dow is performing, what interest rates are doing, whether the dollar is falling or rising against foreign currencies, where commodities are headed, and a

The Daily Dow Dosage

slew of other information. Read the top investment stories, get quotes on every stock you own, and track the performance of your mutual funds.

Don't expect much in the way of innovation from the *WSJ*. Fifty years ago it might have been the only game in town, but it's not anymore. Its quotes contain little more than a stock's price and a mutual fund's NAV.

Contact Information: 800-778-0840, http://wsj.com. Annual subscriptions cost $175. You can also buy individual issues of the *WSJ* off the newsstand for $1.

Investor's Business Daily

Investor's Business Daily is the result of William O'Neil's frustrations in finding what he considered the most important information about stocks. Because he couldn't find it anywhere, he decided to publish it himself and thus was born *Investor's Business Daily*. You can read all about O'Neil's investment approach on page 69.

IBD covers news in an executive news summary on the left side of the front page. It contains key national and international news in single paragraphs. The right side of the front page covers important news stories in depth. Inside the front page is a feature called "To Make a Long Story Short," and it does exactly that. You'll find around 150 news items that you can cover in a glance. The streamlined front page combined with the long stories made short gives you "twice as many news items in a page and a half as you'll find in 60 pages of other publications," in *IBD*'s own words. The paper prints a ton of features too numerous to outline here. I have never purchased an issue of *IBD* that was worthless. There's always something good.

IBD's stock tables are O'Neil's main reason for starting a new paper. They contain four measurements you won't find anywhere else: earnings per share rank for the past five years, relative price-strength rank for the past 12 months, accumulation/distribution for the past three months, and a daily percentage change in volume. Here's a snapshot of the four measurements from *IBD*'s NASDAQ table for Microsoft on October 25, 1996:

E P S	Rel Str	Acc. Dis.	Stock & Symbol	Vol.% Chg.
93	83	B	Microsoft MSFT	+42

Let's have a closer look at the four unique measures from *IBD*.

Earnings per Share Rank

This measurement compares the earnings growth of all companies and then ranks them from 1 to 99, with 99 being the highest. Thus, by looking at this one simple number, you know how IBM's earnings growth stacks up against Microsoft's, Hewlett Packard's, Hamburger Hamlet's, and Gillette's.

The paper takes each company's earnings per share for the two most recent quarters and computes their percentage change from the same two quarters a year ago. That result is combined and averaged with each company's five-year earnings growth record. The final figures for every company are compared with each other, giving each company a rank from 1 to 99, with 99 being the best. Thus, a company with an EPS rank of 95 has earnings figures in the top 5 percent of all companies in the tables.

Microsoft had a 93, placing its earnings growth in the top 7 percent.

Relative Price Strength Rank

This measurement looks at a stock's price performance in the latest 12 months. That's it. It doesn't look at stories, earnings, or price ratios. It simply reports the hard numbers and answers the question, how did this stock perform compared to all others?

IBD updates the numbers daily, compares all stocks to each other, and ranks them from 1 to 99, with 99 being the best. That means a company with a relative price strength of 90 outperformed 90 percent of all other stocks in the past year.

Microsoft had an 83. It outperformed 83 percent of all stocks.

Accumulation/Distribution Rank

This measurement looks at whether a stock is being heavily bought or sold by comparing its daily price and volume. Each stock receives a letter grade A through E, with A being the best. An A grade means the stock is under heavy accumulation, or being bought frequently. An E grade means the stock is under heavy distribution, or being sold frequently.

IBD is trying to convey the direction that the price is likely to head as a result of trading trends. In other words, is the trend one of accumulation, where the price should rise as a result of high demand, or is the trend one of distribution, where the price should fall as a result of low demand?

Microsoft was graded B. That's above average accumulation.

Volume Percent Change

IBD calculates the average daily trading volume of each company's stock during the last 50 trading days. Then it compares each day's trading volume to the 50-day average and prints the difference as a percentage.

Microsoft's daily volume was 42 percent higher than usual.

Contact Information: 800-831-2525, www.investors.com. Annual subscriptions cost $189. You can also buy individual issues of *IBD* off the newsstand for $1.

Barron's

If the *Wall Street Journal* lost your business, *Barron's* might catch your fancy. Either way you're dealing with Dow Jones & Company. It owns both papers.

I like *Barron's* a lot. It's published once a week instead of every morning. Weekly information is plenty for me. Also, *Barron's* is published in a convenient magazine style that's easier to read on restaurant tables and

Barron's Arrives airplanes. I hate bending and folding the pages
Just Once a Week of standard-size papers to keep reading the

current story. With *Barron's*, you just turn the pages like a magazine. So, on the publishing side of customer satisfaction this paper wins two thumbs up. Its frequency is just right, and it's easy to use.

The center of each paper contains "Market Week," the meat-and-potatoes data. It shows vital signs of the economy, the week's biggest winners and losers from each exchange, and superbly designed stock and fund tables. Unlike the typical paper's crunched, overlapping columns, *Barron's* prints tables that have white space between different pieces of information. Though the tables don't contain data as valuable as that in *IBD*, they do display the most recent earnings and compare them to earnings from a year ago. The mutual fund tables show performance for the last week, year-to-date, and three years. Finally, "Market Laboratory" will give you plenty to think about for the next week as you ponder how every relevant index performed, how much volume the markets moved, every economic indicator, and so on.

Contact Information: 800-277-4136, www.barrons.com. Annual subscriptions cost $145. You can also buy individual issues of *Barron's* off the newsstand for $3.

Newsletters

A good newsletter is a trusty friend that accompanies you through good times and bad. Investment newsletters make or break their relationship with you based on one simple measurement: how they perform. Never subscribe to a newsletter without seeing a sample copy first.

There are good places to find newsletter information. One is *The Oxbridge Directory of Newsletters* at your library. It lists thousands of newsletters by category. A quicker alternative is the World Wide Web. Point your browser to www.yahoo.com and search on "newsletters." Call any newsletters that interest you and request a sample copy.

This section shows eight good stock newsletters.

Dick Davis Digest

The strangest thing about the *Dick Davis Digest* is that

there's no Dick Davis listed in the masthead. Beyond that interesting aside, the publication is chock full of information. Companies covered in each issue are listed alphabetically on the first page, making it easy for you to monitor the latest on stocks you own or are watching. The stories assemble expert information from other newsletters into this one convenient source. For casting a wide net, it's hard to beat the *Dick Davis Digest*. Too bad Dick's not around to enjoy it. Actually, he's the publisher, but it's so much fun to joke about his absence.

Contact Information: 800-654-1514. 24 issues per year, 12 pages, $165.

John Dessauer's Investor's World

This is a good general-purpose publication. John Dessauer is a former Citicorp investment officer based in Zurich. His rambling letters discuss global investment issues and contain stock recommendations within the narrative. Much of his writing teaches investment lessons through stories of his childhood, family vacations, and discussions with friends. You won't find detailed charts or model portfolios here.

Contact Information: 301-424-3700. 12 issues per year, 8 pages, $100.

Louis Navellier's MPT Review

Even the title makes this one look serious, and it is. In place of Dessauer's chatty advice, *MPT Review* prints mostly numbers—ones that add up to a lot of profit. It is one of the top-performing newsletters around, listing hundreds of volatile growth stocks from which to choose. It groups them into several different model portfolios that you choose based on how much money you have to invest and how aggressive you want to be.

Contact Information: 800-454-1395. 12 issues per year, 16 pages, $275.

The NeatSheet

This is my stock newsletter. It's written in the same informal style used in this book. It lists stocks to watch and tracks my own portfolio. *The NeatSheet* is published for people who do not have a lot of time to research and monitor stocks. It fits on the front and back of one sheet of paper and reports just the facts on my favorite companies. Subscribers also receive a straight-shooting annual report.

Contact Information: 800-339-5671, www.neatmoney.com. 12 issues per year plus annual report, 2 pages, $75.

Louis Rukeyser's Wall Street

Certainly one of the most attractive investment newsletters around, *Louis Rukeyser's Wall Street* is a good balance between Dessauer's conversational letters and the hard data contained in many other newsletters. It's conversational enough to keep your attention and gives you some meat to chew on. The publication hosts guest experts each month, prints interviews, profiles companies, and answers subscribers' questions. It doesn't provide enough content for serious researchers, but is a great rag for beginners.

Contact Information: 800-892-9702. 12 issues per year, 12 pages, $99.

The Outlook

Published weekly by Standard & Poor's, *The Outlook* is one of the most widely read investment newsletters. S&P analysts provide clear market commentary, stock updates, stock screens based on S&P's STARS rankings and Fair Value rankings, and investment recommendations. You can find *The Outlook* in a three-ring binder at most public libraries. Just ask for it at the reference desk. To read more about STARS and Fair Value, see "S&P STARS/Fair Value" on page 219.

Contact Information: 800-852-1641, www.stockinfo.standard-poor.com. 48 issues per year, 8 pages, $298.

Outstanding Investor Digest

Of *Outstanding Investor Digest*, Warren Buffett wrote, "I'd advise you to subscribe. I read each issue religiously. Anyone interested in investing who doesn't subscribe is making a big mistake." That's about as much endorsement as any publication should ever need. *Outstanding Investor Digest* is a collection of the best ideas from the brightest investment minds around. It prints exclusive interviews, excerpts from letters to shareholders, conference-call transcripts, and other "inside" scoops. The front table of contents shows the names of investors featured in that issue and an alphabetized list of companies covered inside. Next to the table of contents are the beginning paragraphs from several key articles. *Outstanding Investor Digest* is an eclectic publication that varies in length and is delivered on a sporadic schedule. It's expensive, but an investment gold mine.

Contact Information: 212-777-3330. 10 issues, 32 pages or so, $495.

The Red Chip Review

Here's a comprehensive small-cap investment publication. *The Red Chip Review* covers around 300 stocks with market caps under $750 million. Each gets a two-page summary of information that includes almost everything you'd want to know, including the investor-relations phone number in case there ever is more you need to know. To be considered by *Red Chips*'s analysts, a company must pass the "20/20" screen:

- 20 percent compound annual growth

- 20 percent return on investment

- Less than 20 percent institutional ownership

- At least 20 percent insider ownership

The Red Chip Review rates companies and gives them a letter grade. That quick screen and many others will help guide you to good stocks. You can subscribe to the full publication which covers 45 stocks in each biweekly issue, or you can subscribe to *The Red Chip Highlights*, which is a monthly collection of the best *Red Chip* ideas. This is the *Value Line* for small-company investors.

Contact Information: 800-733-2447, www.redchip.com. *The Red Chip Review*—24 issues per year, 100 pages, $349. *The Red Chip Highlights*—12 issues per year, 8 pages, $99.

Value Line

Value Line publishes the premier stock-research tool, *The Value Line Investment Survey*. It covers around 1,700 companies. Almost everything you could want to know about each company is condensed to a single page. When you get to this book's strategy and begin filling out the stocks to watch worksheet in the back, you'll use *Value Line* exhaustively.

Begun by Arnold Bernhard during the Great Depression, Value Line boasts more than 100,000 subscribers today. If you count the number of people who look at reports from libraries or photocopies from brokers, Value Line's users number in the millions. The company's analysts have learned a thing or two about stock research over the past seven decades. Let's take a closer look at *The Value Line Investment Survey*.

The Parts of a *Value Line* Page

Let's say you got a hot tip from your neighbor that IBM has fully recovered from its dark days in 1993 and is poised for great things. You decide to check it out by looking up IBM in *Value Line*. Look at the next two pages to see what you'd find.

Doesn't that look like light reading? Actually, it is once you familiarize yourself with the most important parts—which I've conveniently numbered and highlighted for you. Now I'll take you on a tour of IBM's Value Line page.

1. The Rankings   Value Line ranks every stock from 1 to 5 for timeliness and safety, with 1 being the best. Timeliness is a gauge of the stock's projected performance over the next 12 months as compared to all other stocks followed by Value Line. The measure examines a company's earnings momentum and the stock's relative strength. The rankings are distributed along a bell curve. Stocks ranked 1 or 5 each account for about 5 percent of all stocks, those ranked 2 or 4 each account for about 17 percent of all stocks, and the remainder get the average 3 rank.

The safety measure looks at a stock's volatility and financial stability, then assigns a rank of 1 to 5 just like the timeliness rank. Stocks ranked 1 for safety are the least volatile and most stable, those ranked 5 are the most volatile and least stable.

Are the rankings foolproof? No. If they were, stock research would consist of simply choosing stocks from those ranked 1. *Worth* ran a story on Value Line's ranking system in February 1997. Value Line's research chairman, Samuel Eisenstadt, remarked on the usefulness of the ranks: "Just get rid of the fours and fives from your portfolio and you'll do well. The system

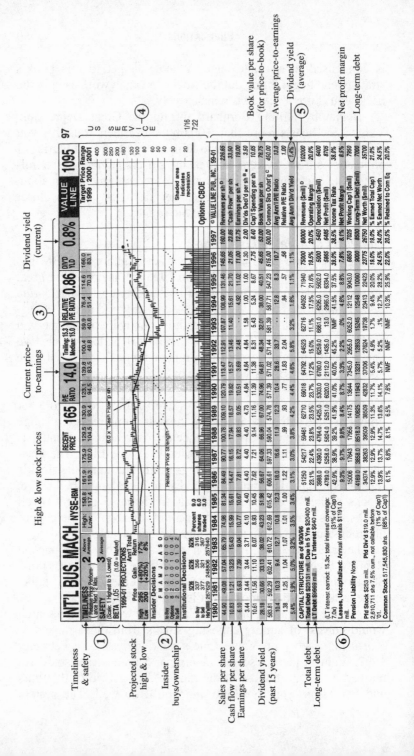

Timeliness & safety — ①

Projected stock high & low — ②

Insider buys/ownership

Sales per share

Cash flow per share

Earnings per share

Dividend yield (past 15 years)

Total debt

Long-term debt

⑥

Current price-to-earnings ③

Dividend yield (current)

High & low stock prices

Book value per share (for price-to-book)

Average price-to-earnings

Dividend yield (average) ⑤

Net profit margin

Long-term debt

④

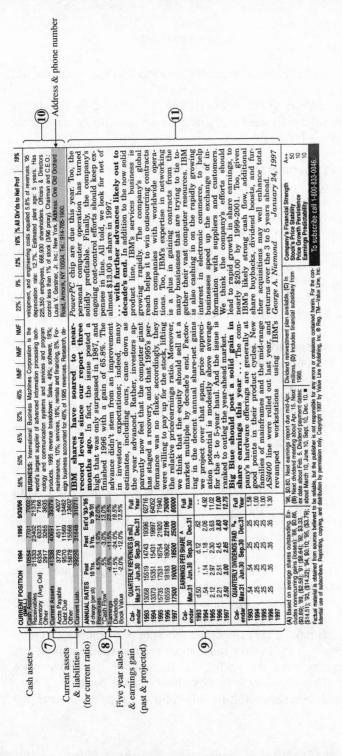

Cash assets — ⑦

Current assets & liabilities (for current ratio)

Five year sales & earnings gain (past & projected) — ⑧ ⑨

Address & phone number — ⑩ ⑪

| | 56% | 50% | 45% | 52% | 45% | 46% | NMF | NMF | NMF | 22% | 9% | 12% | 16% % All Div'ds to Net Prof | 19% |

CURRENT POSITION (\$MILL.)

	1994	1995	9/30/96
Cash Assets	10554	7701	7702
Receivables	21533	24043	21376
Inventory (Avg Cst)	6334	6323	7166
Other	2917	3265	3835
Current Assets	**41338**	**40691**	**39979**
Accts Payable	3778	4511	4007
Debt Due	9570	11569	13462
Other	15878	15568	13602
Current Liab.	**29226**	**31648**	**31071**

ANNUAL RATES	Past 10 Yrs.	Past 5 Yrs.	Est'd '93-'95 to '99-'01
of change (per sh)			
Revenues	4.5%	-3.0%	12.0%
"Cash Flow"	-6.5%	-11.5%	23.5%
Earnings	-11.5%	-24.0%	19.5%
Dividends			
Book Value	-2.0%	-12.0%	13.5%

Cal- endar	QUARTERLY REVENUES (\$ mill.)				Full Year
	Mar.31	Jun.30	Sep.30	Dec.31	
1993	13058	15519	14743	19396	62716
1994	13373	15351	15431	19897	64052
1995	15735	17531	16754	21920	71940
1996	16559	18103	18062	22196	75000
1997	17500	19000	18500	25000	80000

Cal- endar	EARNINGS PER SHARE A				Full Year
	Mar.31	Jun.30	Sep.30	Dec.31	
1993	d.50	..	d.12	..	d.62
1994	.54	1.14	1.18	2.06	4.92
1995	2.12	2.97	2.30	3.63	11.02
1996	2.21	3.04	2.45	3.63	11.00
1997	2.50	3.00	2.85	4.40	12.75

Cal- endar	QUARTERLY DIVIDENDS PAID B				Full Year
	Mar.31	Jun.30	Sep.30	Dec.31	
1993	.54	.54	.25	.25	1.58
1994	.25	.25	.25	.25	1.00
1995	.25	.25	.25	.25	1.00
1996	.25	.35	.25	.25	1.30
1997	.35				

(A) Based on average shares outstanding. Excludes nonrecurring (gains (losses): '88, \$.30; '89, \$.99; ('92.56); '94, (\$14.22); '94, \$0.10; '95, (\$3.79); (\$14.51); '93, (\$14.22); '94, \$0.10; '95, (\$3.79);
Factual material is obtained from sources believed to be reliable, but the publisher is not responsible for any errors or omissions contained herein, Confidential use of subscribers. Reprinting, copying, and distribution by permission only. Copyright 1997 by Value Line Publishing, Inc.

(B) Next earnings report due mid-Apr.
(C) Next dividend meeting about Apr. 15. Next ex-dividend date about Feb. 5. Dividend payment dates: about March 10, June 10, Sept. 10, Dec. 10. ■ '96, \$0.80. Next earnings report due mid-Apr.

Dividend reinvestment plan available. (C) In millions. (D) Includes financial subsidiary from 1988.

BUSINESS: International Business Machines Corporation is the world's largest supplier of advanced information processing technology and communication systems and services and program products. 1995 revenue breakdown: Sales, 49%; software, 18%; maintenance, 10%; services, 18%; rentals and financing, 5%. Foreign business accounted for 48% of 1995 revenues. Research, development, and engineering costs equaled 5.8% of revenues. '95 depreciation rate: 12.7%. Estimated plant age: 5 years. Has 225,350 employees, 668,930 shareholders. Officers & Directors control less than 1% of stock (396 proxy). Chairman and C.E.O.: Louis V. Gerstner, Jr. Inc.: New York. Address: One Old Orchard Road, Armonk, NY 10504. Tel.: 914-765-1900.

IBM shares have soared to near-record levels since our report three months ago. In fact, the issue posted a high that was only surpassed in 1987, and finished 1996 with a gain of 65.8%. The advance didn't stem from an improvement in investors' expectations; indeed, many estimates, including ours, came down as the year advanced. Rather, investors apparently now feel that the computer giant has staged a recovery, and that 1996's performance was no fluke; accordingly, they were willing to pay up for the stock, lifting the relative price/earnings ratio. Moreover, we think that the equity should sell at a market multiple by decade's end. Factoring in the decent annual share-net gains we project over that span, price appreciation potential is modestly above average for the 3- to 5-year haul. And the issue is ranked to outleg the year-ahead market.

Big Blue should post a solid gain in share earnings this year ... The company's hardware offerings are generally at good points in their product cycles. New families of mainframes and the mid-range AS/400 line were rolled out last year, and IBM's revamped workstations using IBM's PowerPC chip are due this year. Too, the personal computer operation has turned solidly profitable. Finally, the company's ongoing cost-control efforts should keep expenses in line. All told, we look for net of almost \$13.00 a share in 1997.

... with further advances likely out to decade's end. In addition to the now solid product line, IBM's services business is growing rapidly. The company's global reach helps it to win outsourcing contracts from companies with worldwide operations. Too, IBM's expertise in networking is a plus in gaining contracts from the many businesses that are trying to tie together their vast computer resources. IBM is also cashing in on the rapidly growing interest in electronic commerce, to help businesses speed up the exchange of information with suppliers and customers. We think the company's efforts should lead to rapid growth in share earnings, to nearly \$20.00 by 1999-2001. Too, given IBM's likely strong cash flow, additional share buybacks, dividend boosts, and further acquisitions may well enhance total returns over the 3 to 5 years ahead.
George A. Niemond   January 24, 1997

Company's Financial Strength	A++
Stock's Price Stability	50
Price Growth Persistence	70
Earnings Predictability	10

To subscribe call 1-800-833-0046.

almost does better at signaling the poor stocks than at picking out the winners."

You can see on the sheet that IBM is ranked 2 for timeliness and 3 for safety. Evidently, Value Line agrees with your neighbor about IBM's bright future.

2. Price Projections and Insider Decisions   Here you read Value Line's projections for the stock price over the next 3 to 5 years, and the annual percentage return that it translates to. You'll record the projected price high and low on your worksheet.

Below the projections is a box for insider decisions. It lists the buy and sell activity of company insiders for each of the past nine months. You'll write the buys on your worksheet.

IBM is projected to gain as much as 80 percent in the next 3 to 5 years. The worst-case expectation is a 20 percent gain. In the last nine months, three insiders chose to buy stock.

3. P/E Ratio and Dividend Yield   Because P/E and dividend yield are so commonly used, Value Line prints the current measurements boldly at the top of the page. You see on your sheet that IBM is currently trading with a P/E of 14 and a dividend yield of .8 percent. To give you a barometer reading of IBM's typical P/E, Value Line prints the median P/E from the past ten years. IBM's is 15, thus the stock is justly slightly cheaper than usual.

Value Line **Helps You Cover Slippery Ground**

4. Price History Chart   The chart plots stock price over the past decade or so. The overall trend line is comprised of little vertical lines for each month. The top of each vertical line indicates the month's price high; the bottom indicates the month's price low. The price highs and lows for each year are printed at the top of the graph.

In addition to the price history, there are two other lines on the graph. The solid black line is cash flow, a very important measure of a company's financial strength. It shows how much money was actually coming into the company over the years. The dotted line is relative price strength. That line shows you how the stock was performing compared to all other stocks. It usually follows roughly the same pattern as the stock price itself. That is, when the stock is falling it is performing poorly compared to other stocks. Makes sense, right?

Looking at IBM's chart, you can see that your friend is right about another thing. The stock has definitely roared back from its dismal 1993.

5. Historic Financial Measurements Here's the data dump. Value Line prints a company's financial measurements for the past 16 years or so. There's something for everybody such as earnings per share, dividends per share, average annual dividend yield, and net profit margin. I've put arrows next to the measurements that show up on your stocks to watch worksheet.

This section is excellent for spotting trends. For instance, if the company's net profit margin is slipping from year to year, that's a bad sign. If working capital is decreasing and debt is increasing, that's another bad sign. If earnings are growing steadily from year to year, that's a great sign.

As for IBM, it looks pretty good. Its 1996 earnings per share are just 2 cents below 1995, which is the best year on the chart. Both years are a far cry from 1993's loss and 1994's measly 4.92. The net profit margin was 8.1 percent in 1996, a gain from the year before and one of the best over the previous 5 years. It's always nice to see an improving profit margin. Also, 1996 debt is $8500 million, down from $9000 million in 1995 and the latest in a steady debt decrease from 1993's $15245 million. Hmm, perhaps your neighbor is on to something.

6. Capital Structure This is where you see how much debt the company carries and how much stock is outstanding. Debt is critical in evaluating a company, as you should know by now. Every one of the master investors in Chapter 2 says to avoid companies with excessive debt. You'll write the company's total debt on your worksheet.

Now you can write down IBM's actual long-term debt: $9669 million.

7. Current Position A company's current position shows its short-term health. It looks at assets that can be quickly turned into cash and liabilities that are due within a year. You'll use information from this section to compute the current ratio and quick ratio on your worksheet. Both are simple evaluations of a company's short-term health.

IBM has current cash of $7002 million, current assets of $39379 million, and current liabilities of $31071 million. Those numbers translate into a current ratio of 1.27 (current assets divided by current liabilities) and a quick ratio of .23 (current cash divided by current liabilities). Those numbers are adequate, I suppose, but nothing to sound trumpets about. I like to see current ratios of at least 2 and quick ratios of at least .5. What's most disturbing to me about IBM's 1996 numbers is that they're worse than 1994 and 1995. In both prior years, cash and current assets were higher, and current liabilities were lower. Overall debt is coming down, however, so maybe some of those current assets are going to good stuff. Still, this is a tarnish on IBM's otherwise sterling report.

8. Annual Rates   In this handy box Value Line computes rates of change for important measures like revenues, cash flow, and earnings. Included are the rates of change over the past ten years, past five years, and projected rates for the next five years. You'll write projected revenue and earnings on your worksheet.

IBM has definitely turned itself around, judging from the annual rates. Its earnings have fallen over the past 10 and 5 years. However, they're projected to increase by 23.5 percent over the next 3 to 5 years. That's excellent.

9. Quarterly Financials   For the last five years Value Line prints quarterly figures for sales, earnings, and dividends. You can look over these tables to see if a company's business is seasonal or steady all year long. IBM's numbers are consistent from quarter to quarter. I guess people buy computers all year long.

10. Business   This humble little box in the center of the page summarizes the basics about a company. You read about its main business, sideline businesses, how much of the company is owned by its directors, and where to contact the company.

From reading this information, you learn that IBM is the world's largest supplier of big-time computer equipment. It also makes 18 percent of its money from software and 10 percent from services. A full 48 percent of its business comes from overseas. That's great to know if you're worried about the U.S. economy.

Finally, directors own less than 1 percent of the stock. That's not good to hear. You want directors to own a lot of the stock because then they act in its best interest. If your investment ship sinks, you want the people in charge of the company to get wet too.

11. Analysis   One of Value Line's securities analysts follows every stock. In this section the analyst gives his opinion on the company's current status and future prospects.

IBM's Value Line analyst, George Niemond, says the company is doing better than he expected. He says IBM will post solid earnings in 1997 and should continue doing so through the end of the decade. One thing he didn't mention directly but you can infer from the last paragraph is that IBM is well positioned to exploit the growing popularity of the World Wide Web. Niemond points out that IBM already has a powerful global business network in place, he acknowledges the company's expertise in networking, and he highlights IBM's interest in electronic commerce. All three of those strengths are going to help IBM own some of the Web. If you think the Web has a future, perhaps IBM is a good investment for you.

At the very least, your time spent with *Value Line* gives you some real meat to chew with your neighbor. Your opinions are now based on hard evidence, not just tips whispered over your fence while the lawn mower idles.

Where to Find *Value Line*

You could find Value Line reports in your mailbox every week. An annual subscription costs $533. With that you receive a large binder containing all 1,700 reports in 13 sections. Each week a new section arrives to replace one of the existing 13. As you can see, the entire binder is updated every 13 weeks, or 4 times a year.

If you want to give it a whirl but aren't ready to part with $533, consider a trial subscription. For a mere $63, you get the initial binder with all 1,700 reports and you get the next 10 weeks of updates. After the trial runs out, you can assess whether you use the reports enough to justify a full subscription. You can buy a trial subscription once every three years.

Perhaps you don't want all 1,700 reports taking up space on your bookshelf. Instead, you just want reports for the companies

 that interest you at any given time. Then turn to your local library. Nearly every decent library I've been to has a copy of *Value Line* available. You can stop by with a list of companies that interest you, look them up, photocopy each page, and be on your way.

Contact Information: 800-634-3583. Annual subscriptions cost $533.

Limited Coverage in *Value Line*

One drawback to *The Value Line Investment Survey* is that it covers only 1,700 stocks. They're the big, well-established companies. I personally like investing in smaller companies and can rarely find them in the standard volume. Value Line does publish an expanded volume that reports on 1,800 additional smaller companies. The expanded reports lack analyst commentary and projections. Combined, the Value Line standard and expanded editions still cover only 3,500 stocks. That leaves about 17,000 companies without Value Line reports.

Thus, for small companies that you truly discover, you'll need to turn elsewhere for critical information. Such alternate sources include everything in this chapter, most notably information from the companies themselves. Financial statements tell you a lot of critical information about a company. Also, custom software packages such as *Power Investor* (page 167) provide almost everything contained in Value Line's publications.

Standard & Poor's Stock Guide

Another professional publication similar in spirit to *Value Line* is *Standard & Poor's Stock Guide*. It lists vital information about each stock in a single row spanning two pages. You'll find a description of the company's business, its stock-price range in several time periods, its dividend yield, P/E ratio, 5-year earnings per share growth, annualized total returns, current position, long-term debt, and earnings for the past 5 years and past 6 months.

The guide is considerably smaller than *Value Line*. It contains everything in a single softbound volume. It's updated monthly.

You can find *Standard & Poor's Stock Guide* at most

libraries, or you can subscribe to receive monthly updates in your mailbox.

Contact Information: 800-221-5277. Annual subscriptions cost $145.

Companies Themselves

Before I invest in any company, I insist on seeing an investor's packet from headquarters. In there you'll find an annual report containing a happy look at the company's future and financial statements that may not be as happy, a recent 10-K and a recent 10-Q, press releases, analyst reports, and general information.

For many small companies that interest you, the company investment packet will form the bulk of your research. Value Line and Standard & Poor's don't cover most small companies. The whole idea of discovering small companies is, well, discovering them. If Value Line and Standard & Poor's and everybody else already knows about them, they've been discovered.

This section shows how to request an investor's packet and how to use it.

Request an Investor's Packet

Get the company's phone number somewhere. You might get it from *Value Line*, a magazine article, the Internet, a custom software package, or directory assistance. On the World Wide Web, try typing www.NAME.com to find the company's site. For instance, you'll find Microsoft at www.microsoft.com, IBM at www.ibm.com, Federal Express at www.fedex.com, and Chrysler at www.chrysler.com. The company site should contain investor information and might include a button to request a complete packet. At the very least, you should find the phone number. If the company name isn't its Web address, search on the company name at a site like HotBot (www.hotbot.com). It will probably return lots of site links for you to explore for the phone number.

"Investor Relations, May I Help You?"

Once you have the number, call it and ask

to speak with the investor-relations department. The receptionist might ask if you need an investor's packet and just take your address on the spot. Otherwise, you'll be transferred to investor relations. Tell the friendly voice that you want a kit that includes:

- The annual report
- The 10-K and 10-Q
- Analyst reports
- Recent press releases
- Any free product samples

While the free samples are a long shot—especially if you're investing in Chrysler or Boeing—the rest is pretty standard. A week to ten days later, your very own investor's packet will arrive free of charge. What a joy, capitalism!

If you absolutely can't find the company's phone number, call the Public Register Annual Report Service to obtain a free current annual report for any public company. The phone number is 800-4-ANNUAL. You can order up to eight annual reports at a time. You won't get a packet as complete as the one from investor relations, but the annual report is better than nothing.

Tear open the envelope and . . .

Read the Investor's Packet

Clear a space on your kitchen table or desk and spread the contents of the investor's packet in front of you.

Annual Report

Start with the annual report. It's probably very attractive because it's as much marketing collateral as it is informative. Sometimes, if you're researching very young companies, the annual report will be little fancier than a student term paper. I personally like that. The money can be put toward something that will earn a profit. That's what we're all in this for, darn it!

Opening the report, you'll probably be greeted with a letter from the chief executive officer. Next, you'll page through photos of company headquarters, happy customers, select employees and lots of product displays. Following the photo gallery is usually an article about the company's roots, its recent accomplishments, its mission statement, and how well equipped it is for the future. The easygoing stuff generally concludes with a reprinted advertisement or one that was created specifically for the annual report.

They're all a bit different, but that's the general idea. Read over the fun stuff, then move along to the financial statements. They're almost always contained in the back half of the annual report, but occasionally they're separate.

Let's learn about the financial statements by looking at real-life numbers from IBM's 1996 annual report. We also examined IBM on the Value Line report earlier.

Balance Sheet

A balance sheet is a quick look at what a company owns and what it owes, also known as assets and liabilities. The difference between the two is called stockholders' equity and is what causes the balance sheet to balance. Rather than drag you through Accounting 101, I'm going to highlight just the important parts of the sheet. Here's IBM's:

IBM 1996 Balance Sheet

(Dollars in millions)	1996	1995
Assets		
Cash and cash equivalents	$ 7,687	$ 7,259
Notes and accounts receivable	16,515	16,450
(a bunch of other stuff I won't list)	56,930	56,583
Total assets	81,132	80,292
Liabilities		
Current liabilities		
Taxes	$ 3,029	$ 2,694
Short-term debt	12,957	11,569
Accounts payable	4,767	4,511
(other current liabilities)	13,247	12,874
Total current liabilities	34,000	31,648
Long-term debt	9,872	10,060
Deferred income taxes	1,627	1,807

(Dollars in millions)	1996	1995
(other long-term liabilities)	14,005	14,354
Total liabilities	59,504	57,876
Stockholders' Equity		
Preferred and common stock	8,005	7,741
(other stockholders' equity)	13,623	14,682
Total stockholders' equity	21,628	22,423
Total liabilities and stockholders' equity	81,132	80,292

Assets

Asset are divided into current and long-term. Current assets are things like money in the bank and uncollected invoices. Long-term assets are things like buildings. I spared you the tedious divisions on my excerpt and just showed a couple important items along with the total.

Cash is exactly what you think it is. At the end of 1996, IBM had $7.7 billion in its bank account—nearly twice what I had at the time. You want a company to have plenty of cash so it can pay its debts and take advantage of opportunities, such as buying smaller companies.

Notes and accounts receivable is money that IBM is owed by customers for computer hardware, software, and services. Whereas your drinking buddy might owe you a ten spot for last Friday, IBM's buddies owed the company $16.5 billion at the end of 1996. On the one hand, it's good to see a lot of money coming to IBM in the future. On the other hand, you don't want receivables to grow faster than sales. You'll find sales on the income statement.

The rest of the asset section shows things like marketable securities, inventory, plant and property, and other things that IBM owns. I've added it all together as "a bunch of other stuff I won't list."

Liabilities

Liabilities are also divided into current and long-term. Current liabilities are due within a year while long-term liabilities are due farther in the future.

The liabilities section is pretty straightforward. Taxes are what the company owes to the IRS just like you need to pay every year. Some tax is due soon and some is deferred.

Debt is bad. You would like to see as little debt on the balance sheet as possible, both current and long-term. You'd love to invest in companies that don't have any debt. As Peter Lynch points out, a company can't go bankrupt if it doesn't owe any money. IBM owed a staggering $22.8 billion at the end of 1996.

The last item is accounts payable. That's the money IBM needs to pay its suppliers for items purchased on credit.

Stockholders' Equity

Stockholders' equity is the difference between assets and liabilities. It consists of outstanding shares of stock and other things like retained earnings and unrealized gains. Added to liabilities, stockholders' equity causes the balance sheet to balance.

Income Statement

An income statement shows the company's earnings and expenses. It's where you can figure the all-important profit margin, the difference between what a company earns and what it spends. Here's an abbreviated version of IBM's income statement:

IBM 1996 Balance Sheet

(Dollars in millions except per share amounts)	1996	1995
Revenue		
Hardware sales	$ 36,316	$ 35,600
Services	15,873	12,714
(revenue from other divisions)	23,758	23,626
Total revenue	75,947	71,940
Cost		
Hardware sales	23,396	21,862
Services	12,647	10,042
(cost from other divisions)	9,365	9,669
Total cost	45,408	41,573
Gross profit	30,539	30,367
Operating expenses	21,943	22,776

(Dollars in millions except per share amounts)	1996	1995
Net earnings applicable to common shareholders (after taxes and preferred dividends)	5,409	4,116
Net earnings per share of common stock	$ 10.24	$ 7.23

Average number of common shares outstanding:

1996—528,352,094   1995—569,384,029

There's not a lot to it, really. Revenue shows you what IBM sold in each division of its business. Cost shows you what it cost IBM to achieve those sales in each division. Then the statement breaks the numbers down into investor-centric stuff like gross profit and earnings per share.

You can see that IBM increased both its revenue and its cost from 1995 to 1996, both by around $4 billion. However, the gross profit was higher in 1996 by $172 million. That's a good sign. You want gross profit to grow from year to year.

While gross profit increased by a small amount, notice how much earnings per share increased. Each share of stock earned only $7.23 in 1995 but earned $10.24 in 1996. That's a 42 percent increase! Current shareholders love to see that. The bottom of the income statement explains the jump in earnings per share: there were 41 million fewer shares in 1996 than in 1995. IBM bought back a lot of its stock, another plus for current investors.

10-K and 10-Q

If you want hard numbers without all the fancy marketing copy in the annual report, you're going to love the 10-K and 10-Q. Each is a meatier version of the financial information found in the annual report. 10-Ks come out yearly while 10-Qs come out quarterly. 10-Qs include management discussion of current issues facing the company. 10-Ks are audited, 10-Qs are not. As for the numbers on these sheets, you'll find revenues, costs, expenses, operating profits, net income or loss, and other items.

Stock Databases

Computers have revolutionized a lot of things, but few as much as investing. You've seen how detailed a Value Line report is and how intricate financial statements are. It takes a long time to research all the companies out there for the ten or twenty that are worth buying. Plus, many small companies aren't covered by print publications. That means you must contact investor relations at each one and slog your way through their financial statements, manually computing most of the information for your worksheet.

Custom software is here to save the day. Now the information you need for thousands and thousands of stocks is only a mouse click away. Instead of searching Value Line reports and waiting for the mail to deliver investor packets from every company you've heard of, you can simply specify the measurements you want for a company and have the computer search for those that meet your standards. Seconds later, a short list appears for you to read.

There are hundreds of high-priced stock databases out there. Some boast technical analysis as their forte, claiming to include technical indicators that will show you when to buy and sell. Others conduct an extensive interview with you and then search the database themselves for appropriate investments.

All that automation is interesting, but I would never, ever allow a software package to determine where I invest. All I want is quick, easy research that allows me to make my own best decisions. With that directive in mind, here are two excellent stock databases.

Software Here, There, Everywhere!

Although I profile only two stock databases, there are many more available. If you'd like to spend time finding just the right one for you, here's a good list of companies to check into:

- Equis International: 800-882-3040, www.equis.com. Produces popular programs such as <u>MetaStock</u>, a technical analysis tool.

- Omega Research: 800-871-3563, www.omegaresearch.com. Produces some of the best market-monitoring programs including <u>TradeStation,</u> a tool that helps you back-test your own stock strategies.

- Telescan: 800-324-8246, www.telescan.com. Produces a package of investment tools and boasts more than 100,000 users.

- Value Line: 800-535-9648. Produces its legendary investment survey on CD-ROM complete with query tools and sort filters.

- Window on Wall Street: 800-998-8439, www.wallstreet.net. Produces <u>Window on WallStreet,</u> a stock-selection program hailed as the "master of the financial universe" by <u>PC Magazine.</u>

Morningstar *U.S. Equities OnFloppy*

Morningstar's name is second to none in the mutual fund industry. It has earned a solid reputation for the best fund reports anywhere. Recently, it has turned its resources toward stocks. *U.S. Equities OnFloppy* is its software for personal investors. When you start reading investment magazines, you'll frequently see the program used by editors for stock screening.

U.S. Equities OnFloppy covers information on 7,500 stocks. You can find a company's competitors by searching on all companies with the same SIC code, the federal standard industry classification. Once there you can find all the companies with the lowest price-to-sales ratios, highest earnings growth, lowest long-term debt, highest cash flow, and best return on equity.

As its name implies, *U.S. Equities OnFloppy* ships on floppy disks and is updated via priority mail weekly, monthly, or quarterly depending on which plan you purchase. It's not cheap, though. Annual subscriptions are priced as follows: weekly updates for $995, monthly updates for $295, quarterly updates for $145. There's also a one-time trial for $55.

Contact Information: 800-735-0700. Annual monthly updates cost $295.

Power Investor

This is the software I use, and I love it. It's from the Investors Alliance, a nonprofit investment organization. A full year membership includes *Power Investor*, which alone justifies the cost of joining. You'll read more about Investors Alliance on page 179.

Just Don't Let the Computer Take Over Too Much of Your Life

Power Investor covers 9,000 stocks, provides more information on each one than you'll find in *U.S. Equities OnFloppy*, ships on a single CD-ROM, and gives free unlimited updates over the modem. The cost? A mere $92 for a full year. When I first read about this deal, I didn't believe it. I assumed the software would be garbage. But the screen captures on the flier looked good, so I gave it a shot and it turned out to be the best stock database I've ever used. Its interface is more elegant than any other, its data more comprehensive, and its updates the most convenient. All I do is click a button, and the program dials over the modem, grabs the latest numbers, and hangs up. I can even schedule updates to happen unattended in the middle of the night when I'm in bed and phone rates are low. Whether I update the information every day, once a week, or once a month, I'm never charged extra. Turn the page to see what *Power Investor* looks like.

The scenario I described for *U.S. Equities OnFloppy* is even better with *Power Investor*. You can still group companies by SIC code, still screen by price-to-sales, earnings, debt, cash flow, and return on equity. In addition, you can screen by any of the 1,600 measurements for each company including mainstays like net profit margin, but also obscure things like accounts-receivable turnover. Once you've concocted a recipe for winning stocks, you simply save it as a "document." Thereafter, whenever you update your data by simply clicking a button, switch to your saved document and it runs your filter to find new companies matching your criteria.

After a while you'll have several such documents saved with different names like "Fast Growing Companies," "Undervalued Companies," "Companies That I Like in My Home State," and so on. The program even ships with predefined documents, one of

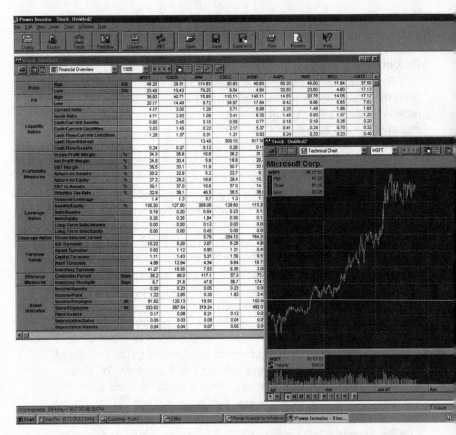

Screen Capture from *Power Investor*.

which is called "Benjamin Graham Values." Graham is one of our master investors that you read about on page 45. *Power Investor* interprets his values as a search for companies with a positive net income, a P/E less than 5, a debt-to-assets ratio less than .6, and a current price between 0 and the company's quick assets per share. Whether or not you agree with *Power Investor*'s interpretation of Graham's criteria, you can certainly appreciate the power of being able to search 9,000 stocks for such specific information. Imagine how long it would take to find every company's quick assets per share using annual reports. Ugh.

When you finally locate companies that are worth further investigation, you'll know how to reach them. *Power Investor* includes company addresses and phone numbers for your convenience.

Believe it or not, *Power Investor* also covers 5,000 mutual funds with charts and data going back 20 years. I won't detail all the capabilities available for funds, but it sure is convenient to monitor your entire portfolio from within one software package.

Power Investor Turns Your Computer into a Research Analyst

Bottom line, folks, if you're looking for a great stock database, then look no further than *Power Investor*. No, I am not paid to endorse this program. But I am thrilled to have found it and pained to know that some people still pay hundreds more for inferior programs. Products prosper from marketing, not quality. This one, however, won't need much marketing once the world discovers it. I'm doing my part.

Contact Information: 888-683-1181. Annual computer membership in Investors Alliance costs $92 and includes *Power Investor* with free daily modem updates for one year. See page 179 for more information about Investors Alliance.

The Internet

What started as a gathering of investors under a buttonwood tree in lower Manhattan turned into the New York Stock Exchange. To trade, you had to be there. Then the telephone came around and people could call their orders in. Now a successful investor can go her entire life without ever seeing Wall Street. Nothing represents everyman's worldwide access to the markets better than the Internet.

"Get Connected"

Cisco Systems, a premier networking company, described the Internet in its 1996 annual report:

> It stretches everywhere. From China to Chile, New Zealand to New Jersey, England to Egypt. From India to Iceland to Israel to Illinois. It touches us all, and it changes us daily. It is continuing to advance the frontiers of global communications in ways that

were incomprehensible to even the most forward-looking among us just a few years ago.

It's possible to cover the entire process of investing right from the keyboard in your den. You hear about a company on a chat forum. Curious, you visit the company's Web site and print out analyst opinions, press releases, and financial statements. While there you click on a button and order the annual report. While that's coming through the mail, you find other chat rooms that discuss the company you're interested in. You keep a few notes in a word processing file with excerpts from your various chats. By the time the annual report arrives, you've got a sizable file of research on the company. You read the annual report and make a final decision to buy the stock. So you log on to your broker's Web site, place the order, and buy 200 shares. Then you monitor the stock price and company progress all on the Internet with free quotes and periodic company information updates. A few months later, the stock has doubled. You log on to your broker's Web site and sell 100 shares. A few months after that, the stock has doubled again and you sell the remaining shares to go in search of a new stock in a different chat room.

Seem space age? It's not. It's going on right now.

You Never Know Who You'll Find Online

Great as the Internet seems, however, it's rife with misinformation and weirdness. There are 14-year-olds posing as experts, morons being themselves, and crooks trying to swindle you. It's a lot like the shopping mall, actually. If you can survive there, you can survive on the Internet. Just remember that there are no requirements for entry. Anybody with fingers and a keyboard can show up everywhere you go.

Commercial Services

Perhaps the best way to start is on a commercial online service. These are paid services that have their own dial-in numbers around the country and provide controlled content. That is, to create a site on one of them, you must apply and pass their scrutiny. After all, people are paying for the content. It better be good.

This section presents my two favorite commercial online services for investors.

America Online

America Online is the biggest commercial information service. It has millions of users, all with unique log-on names, that dial in every day to browse categories like shopping, travel, sports, and investing. You move around AOL by searching among different sites and their subsites, or by knowing the keyword of a site you want to visit. For instance, to check out stock quotes enter keyword QUOTES.

AOL is enormous. If you subscribe to the service, you'll spend weeks just cruising around finding how much it has to offer. For investment information, begin at keyword FINANCE. To get you started, this section lists three sites you'll find helpful for investment research.

Contact Information: 888-265-8001. Unlimited access costs $19.95 per month.

The Motley Fool

The Motley Fool is one of the most popular stock forums around. Named for a line in Shakespeare's *As You Like It*, the site is not for fools at all but rather for everybody who stands apart from Wall Street's so-called wise men. You know who I mean: the full-commission brokers, market prognosticators, and gurus. Shakespeare wrote, "I met a fool i' the forest, a motley fool." At this site, Wall Street's wise men are foolish and the Motley Fools are wise. That's why they're labeled Fools with a capital F.

The Fools hate mutual funds, love the Dow Dividend strategy which you read about on page 108, and adore small-cap stocks. Those three pillars support their entire investment approach. Most of their site focuses on choosing the right small companies. They espouse a set of criteria that they tell you about at the site and in their book, *The Motley Fool Investment Guide.*

All in all, I like The Motley Fool. My portfolio *does* include mutual funds for the reasons I explained in *The Neatest Little Guide to Mutual Fund Investing*, and I often buy large company stocks that I consider undervalued. But when it comes to buying small, growing companies, I think the Fools have a good approach. So put on a jingle-belled hat, tap your pointy shoes, and click your mouse to The Motley Fool.

Contact Information: America Online keyword FOOL. Website www.fool.com.

Morningstar

For unbiased stock and mutual fund information, stop by the Morningstar site. There you'll find complete coverage of both topics along with the usual message boards, chat rooms, and links to other sites. If you're so inclined, stop by the Morningstar store. You won't find commemorative coffee mugs or T-shirts, but you will find a complete list of investment products.

Contact Information: America Online keyword MORN-INGSTAR. Website: www.morningstar.net

Company Research

For quick access to almost everything you need to know about a company, stop by the company research site. There you can click your way to stock reports, financial statements, earnings and estimates, 10-Ks and 10-Qs, and historic price quotes with charts.

Contact Information: America Online keyword COMPANY RESEARCH.

CompuServe

CompuServe's parent company is H&R Block, so its information is more business-oriented than America Online's. *Worth* wrote in February 1997, "CompuServe still caters primarily to business users. Its investment forums remain the most wide-ranging and have the most informed, dedicated participants of any online discussion group around (the relatively high fees probably screen out yappers and gadflies)." Some people like the influence of yappers and gadflies. The choice is yours.

I read one study that estimated a full 24 percent of Compu-Serve's users are executives making more than $90,000 per year. Clearly, this is a place for exchanging serious information.

In place of America Online's keyword system, CompuServe

uses a "go" system. That is, you type the word go and then the search phrase you want or click your way through a menu.

On CompuServe you'll find a custom news-screening service that scans the major news services for stories on topics you specify. Such scans cover AP, UPI, Dow Jones, Reuters, and others. CompuServe has an excellent newsletter section where you can read the opinions of experts in hundreds of fields. There's also a ton of information on mutual funds and stocks, with mutual fund information provided by *Money Magazine*'s FundWatch system.

Contact Information: 800-848-8199. Five hours per month costs $9.95.

The World Wide Web

This is the first stage of becoming the Jet-sons. People are already ordering groceries from the Web, watching television there, buying concert tickets, and researching invest-ments. You've encountered Web addresses sprinkled throughout this book. They usually start with "www."

You Never Know Who You'll Find— or Who'll Find You—on the Web

The Web's biggest strength and biggest weakness are the same thing: anybody can put a site there. That means Standard & Poor's, Nike, Dow Jones, and Fidelity Investments. It also means Cousin Harvey, Charles Keating, your noisy neighbor, and the stripper on the freeway billboard. Don't laugh about that last one. I live in L.A. and have seen it with my own eyes. Right below her rather revealing pink negligee was her Web address: www.do-you-really-think-I'd-print-this.com. Without a doubt, the Web has gone mainstream. I'm expecting signs on the corner to read "Will work for Internet access."

To browse the Internet, you'll need to sign up with an Internet service provider (ISP). If you sign up with America Online or CompuServe, you have access to the Web through their bundled browsers. However, for direct Web access many people prefer a dedicated ISP. Two of the best are IBM Internet Connection (800-455-5056, www.ibm.net) and MindSpring

(800-719-4332, www.mindspring.com). After you're signed up with an ISP, you need to choose a Web browser. The only two worth considering are Netscape Navigator and Microsoft Internet Explorer, both of which are available at any software store. Oh, I almost forgot, you'll also need a computer.

This section presents search tools to find your own favorite investment sites, then covers some of my favorites for stock research and one-stop research, where you can check on more than just your stock.

Search Tools

The Web changes constantly. By the time you read this, half of the sites I recommend will have changed dramatically and hundreds of new ones will have appeared. You need search tools to keep on top of the ever changing Web universe. Here are some winners:

AltaVista

This is a comprehensive search page run by Digital Equipment Corporation. It's fast and provides the underlying capabilities of many other search sites.

Contact Information: www.altavista.digital.com.

Excite

This is a concept-based search engine, which doesn't seem to mean much. I don't think it keeps results any more relevant than any other engine. Nonetheless, it's a fast search site and worth a try.

Contact Information: www.excite.com

HotBot

Everybody's talking about this site. It's a sparse interface, but boy, does it spit out the sites. It's fast too. If HotBot can't find it, it probably doesn't exist.

Contact Information: www.hotbot.com.

Lycos

This is a search demon that returns tons of information, second only to HotBot.

Contact Information: www.lycos. com.

Webcrawler

One of the most popular Web sites, Webcrawler is a good all-purpose search engine. It's fast and well organized.

Contact Information: www.webcrawler.com.

Yahoo!

This is the best Web directory. It's not a search engine like every other listing in this section, but a directory similar to your yellow pages. It groups sites by category. You can still search for specific topics, of course, but you can also go to entire category listings and look over the contents. If something catches your eye, just click on it and you'll jump to that site.

Contact Information: www.yahoo.com.

Stock Research

Because stock information changes so quickly, the Web is a perfect place to keep on top of it all. Here are a bunch of helpful stock sites in different categories:

Quotes and Earnings

I've read several market studies that claim more people turn to the Web for stock quotes than for any other type of information. There are hundreds of places to go for quotes. Two of my favorites are **www.quote.com** and **quote.yahoo.com**. Each offers free quotes, price charts, and news headlines. For $9.95 per month at Quote.com, you can set up portfolios that are automatically tracked. At the end of each day Quote.com delivers a detailed report to your e-mail address. You can even customize the content of the report. For $19.95 per month, your daily reports include pertinent news, insider-trading activity, and earnings estimates. All of Yahoo's information is free. Its quotes come with links to company information—phone number and address included—and current news.

For beefier information, turn to Zacks Analyst Watch at **www.zacks.com**, where you'll find an array of services. For $150 per year you get a report e-mailed to you that tracks your portfolios and includes earnings revisions, changes in brokerage recommendations, earnings surprises, dates of upcoming earnings reports, and comparisons of each company's forecasted and actual earnings to those of its industry. Take advantage of a free trial period to see if Zacks information is right for you.

Fundamental Data

There's a lot of fundamental data besides earnings on the Web. A good place to start is Thompson MarketEdge at **www.marketedge.com**. For $7.95 per month you get all the usual quotes, price charts, and news. You also get company-screening tools, detailed industry reports, and individual company profiles. The three-page company profiles cover the most recent full-year and quarterly financial statements, stock-performance measurements like return on sales and three-year EPS growth, and insider-trading data.

Another good site for company reports is Market Guide at **www.marketguide.com**. It's a little rough around the edges, but serves up good information. A free company snapshot covers items like book value, P/E, sales-per-share, return on equity, and current ratio. More detailed reports are priced individually, but $9.95 per month gets you unlimited access.

Two of the most comprehensive free sites are Wall Street  Research Net at **www.wsrn.com** and Daily Stocks at **www.dailystocks.com**. In the company-research section, you enter a company's name or ticker symbol. The site returns a page with links to SEC filings, current news, quotes, charts, and great *Quick*Source reports. One report covers the basic company information such as telephone number, address, and a description of the company's business. Another report presents five-year historic data for almost every measurement that would interest you: return on equity, P/E, price-to-sales, profit margin, EPS, current assets and liabilities, long-term debt, and even a comparison of the company's key measurements to its industry averages.

For pay-as-you-go pricing, check out INVESTools at **www.investools.com**. It gathers information from dozens of sources including subscription newsletters, *Standard & Poor's,*

Zacks, and news services. You enter a company name or ticker symbol, and the site returns a list of information units that you can purchase individually. Prices range from 25 cents for a headline story to $7 for a newsletter article.

Finally, stop by Hoover's at **www.hoovers.com**. For $9.95 per month you have access to full Hoover's reports on thousands of companies. The reports cover basic company information, historic financial measurements, and major competitors.

Small Companies

The Stock Research Group at **www.stockgroup.com** offers an extensive collection of information about small companies. See who's hot, who's new, what's happened recently, and how the market is coming along.

Another good site for researching small companies is The SmallCap Investor at **financial.spiders.com**. You'll find an index of 50 microcaps, links to company home pages, and other investor information.

Government and Stock Exchanges

The Securities and Exchange Commission maintains a site at **www.sec.gov**. You can search for a company's EDGAR filings and other documents. The New York Stock Exchange maintains a site at **www.nyse.com**. NASDAQ maintains a site at **www. nasdaq.com** that shows how its market is performing and tracks a great index called the NASDAQ 100. The American Stock Exchange maintains a site at **www.amex.com**.

Discussion Forums

Stock Club at **www.stockclub.com** offers more than 500 forums discussing individual stocks of all types. You can add a new forum by submitting an electronic request. Silicon Investor at **www.techstocks.com** is the best place to talk technology stocks. Its forums contain useful commentary from people in the know, such as engineers, managers, and designers. Finally, don't forget The Motley Fool at **www.fool.com**. Nearly every online investor stops by for an occasional glance at the Fool's forums. They're some of the best around.

One-Stop Research

Now that you've seen a tiny glimpse of what's available on the Web, you'll be glad to know about two sites that pull it all together. Each provides unique information about stock and mutual fund investing combined with pointers to information kept at other sites.

I Do My Best to Keep NeatMoney Bursting with Good Info

NeatMoney at **www.neatmoney.com** is my Web site. It's divided evenly between stock information and mutual fund information. Access to the entire site is free. You'll find links to every Web resource mentioned in this book and lots more. They're grouped by type, so it's easy to find what you're looking for. NeatMoney provides quotes, charts, and news headlines. Participate in discussion forums and submit questions to be answered in a Frequently Asked Questions page for either stocks or mutual funds. When you're finished with that, view the performance of every portfolio covered in *The Neatest Little FundLetter* and *The NeatSheet*, and also read sample articles from each publication. Finally, stop by the NeatMoney store to browse a variety of tools and books that you can purchase if you'd like. NeatMoney is a great investment resource, if I do say so myself!

NETworth at **www.networth.galt.com** is an exquisite investment site. The format is easy on your eyes, the layout is simple to navigate, and the information is timely. Like NeatMoney, NETworth is divided evenly between stocks and mutual funds. It features quotes, charts, and news in addition to a searchable list of company Web sites and access to SEC filings. Its charting feature is one of the best on the Web, sporting customizable colors, ranges, and styles. You can view Morningstar mutual fund profiles, track your own personal stock portfolio, and search different Web site categories for information pertaining to you. NETworth is another great investment resource.

Investment Organizations

Joining an investment organization has a lot of benefits. It's a type of research because you'll be exposed to new ideas and helpful information along the way. You'll also meet other investors through publications, conferences, and possibly even regular meetings.

This section presents three dependable investment organizations.

American Association of Individual Investors

The American Association of Individual Investors (AAII) is a nonprofit group dedicated to helping individuals invest their own money. The group accomplishes its aim through educational materials, investment plans, and helpful tools.

A membership in AAII entitles you to several benefits. Actually, there are 21 benefits outlined in the most recent letter sent to me. A few of the neater ones include a subscription to the *AAII Journal*, published 10 times per year, an annual guide to low-load mutual funds, membership in a local chapter, an annual tax-strategy guide, a free quote phone number, access to AAII's computer bulletin board and Internet sites, and a dividend-reinvestment plan that includes hundreds of public companies.

Contact Information: AAII, 625 North Michigan Avenue, Chicago, IL 60611. Annual membership costs $49.

Investors Alliance

Investors Alliance is another nonprofit investment group. It formed in 1987 around the philosophy: "No one will ever care about your money as much as you do." True enough. My latest sales letter claims that membership is for self-reliant investors who want to be able to discover profitable investment opportunities that average investors overlook.

The Alliance Helps You Jump Right into the World of Investing

The best benefit to joining Investors Alliance is its awesome software, *Power Investor,* which you read about on page 167. There are other benefits too, such as a monthly subscription to *Investors Alliance Investor Journal.*

Investors Alliance also offers three telephone hotlines. One alerts you to stock market developments, another to mutual fund developments. The third line is a toll-free number where you can order annual reports for free. That's right, if you've heard of a company and don't have time to go to your library for a Value Line Report, you can just call the Investors Alliance number for a copy of the company's annual report. Of course, you'll already have *Power Investor* on your computer and could get the company's direct number from there.

Finally, your membership includes an investment self-study course. It covers 10 important topics including how to analyze mutual funds and stocks, how to read the financial pages, and how to protect against bear markets.

It's quite a bargain, really. I enrolled just to receive *Power Investor* but I find myself reading the journal and calling the hotlines too. What the heck, I paid for them!

Contact Information: 888-683-1181, www.freequote.com. Annual computer membership costs $92.

National Association of Investors Corporation

The National Association of Investors Corporation (NAIC) is a nonprofit organization that educates investors and tracks the performance of investment clubs.

Members receive an annual subscription to *Better Investing Magazine*, a slew of investment charts and worksheets, invitations to investment conferences around the world, a chance to participate in a dividend-reinvestment program, and access to a network of investment clubs.

I called to see how you can find a local investment club. I learned that the NAIC does not match individuals with clubs. So, you join as an individual and find out about an existing club by attending a conference, or you can join and start your own club. The NAIC's official guide, *Starting and Running a Profitable Investment Club,* is available in most bookstores.

Contact Information: 810-583-NAIC. Annual individual membership costs $39.

7 This Book's Strategy

You've come a long way, my friend. You speak the language of stocks, you've studied master investors and the lessons of history, you know how to use the Dow Dividend strategies, you're all set up with your discount broker, and you know both how and where to conduct research. After all that preparation, it's time to assemble a strategy of your own. That's the focus of this chapter.

To make the strategy simple for you to implement, I've divided the chapter into steps. Within each step I provide background information and conclude with one or more actions for you to complete. At the end of the chapter I group all the actions together for quick future reference.

The strategy has three parts. First you'll build a core portfolio using the Dow Dividend strategy; next you'll assemble and track a list of potential investments; then you'll manage a portfolio of individual stocks from your list to enhance the returns of your core portfolio.

I'm trembling as I write. Profits are near. Years from now you'll look back and write in your personal journal the words of John Keats: "Much have I travel'd in the realms of gold . . ."

Build a Core Portfolio

Before you travel the realms of gold in search of riches, you need a strong fortress from which to base your searches. You can retreat to the fortress when your search party turns up nothing or is attacked by marauding bears. Your fortress will probably start small, but will grow in size as your search party returns with riches.

You're going to combine growth and value in your fortress and your search party. Some of the best investors combine these two approaches, and history shows that they coexist well. Often, when growth investing is struggling in the market, value investing is soaring and vice versa. By combining the two, you should come closer to steady superior returns.

You're going to build your fortress with a proven material: the Dow Dividend strategy.

Off to the Realm of Riches

Choose two girders for your fortress with the Dow 2 strategy. I provide background for all the Dow strategies in Chapter 4 and explain the Dow 2 specifically on page 120.

To get these two companies—one in some years—you will conduct a mere 15 minutes of research annually and make two trades a year at most. These stocks will be the two lowest-priced of the high-yielding Dow stocks. They are powerful companies with broad influence and will add considerable strength to your fortress. When the Hun attacks with his army of bears, you'll be glad to have Dow companies holding up the walls.

Maintain Your Stocks to Watch Worksheet

Once you've built a core portfolio, you've got a strong fortress from which to base your searches for wealth. The fortress should stand through good times and bad, held up by powerful Dow companies. Now it's time to enter the wild world of individual stock picking. You'll rely on the advice you received from the six master investors in Chapter 2 and history's lessons in Chapter 3.

Some Stocks May Never Return

To shield yourself from the influence of rumors, great stories from your neighbors, catchy headlines, and cool-sounding company names, you're going to keep a personalized list of 20 companies to watch. That's right, just 20 companies. In order for a new company to get a space on the list, it must be better than one of the current 20. By structuring your list in this fashion, you force it to improve over time.

Continuing the realm of riches metaphor, this list is your roster of henchmen that you use to assemble search parties. When you actually invest in one or more of the stocks, you send them out of your fortress to find riches. When you sell, they return to the fortress, where you store the money either in your Dow 2 stocks or cash coffers. The realm is a nasty place outside the fortress. Some of your henchmen may never return. In other words, some stocks might go to zero and you'll strike them from your list. Sometimes you'll sell a stock but still keep an eye on it. It stays on your list until something better comes along to bump it off.

I love this system. When I first started looking for good investments on my own, my life piled high with company reports, *Value Line* pages, *Standard & Poor's* profiles, magazine articles, and so on. It became so ridiculous that at one point I thought my portfolio was coming together based on which papers beat their way to the top of the pile that day. That's not a neat way to invest.

So I stole a blank sheet of paper from my laser printer and scribbled across the top, "Stocks I Like." Then I went through every stack of paper, writing down the name of each company and a few measurements that were easily obtained from the paperwork. When the last piece of paper hit the floor, I had a list of 58 company profiles in front of me. Picture me looking at the sheet of paper as fairy dust sprinkled the air. What a revelation! Putting every company in the same place with the same measurements allowed me to see instantly which companies were most attractive. I scratched out the duds and gleefully whittled my list to a tidy group of 20 stocks. I've never looked back since. Now whenever I encounter a stock tip in an article, a conversation, or on a bathroom wall, I simply find its worksheet measurements, compare it to the 20 stocks I'm watching, and see if it beats out any of the current 20. If not, I forget about it. If so, I strike the weakest of the 20 and replace it with the new stock. In the course of this simple process, I either save myself the hassle of reading a lot of material on a new company or I strengthen my list of potential investments.

Constant scrutiny of your list is healthy. Call it investment Darwinism, survival of the neatest, or natural stock selection. I've evolved alongside my list since that first glorious day with the fairy dust. I now call the process "Stockwatch" and list my companies on the "Stocks to Watch Worksheet." There's a copy for you in the back of this book. Let's explore how to use it.

Find Companies to Watch

First, you need companies to watch. There are four idea sources to help you find companies worth examining: personal experience, the investment grapevine, investment publications, and the Internet. Each has shown me to some great investments. Few companies from any of the four sources will ever make your stocks to watch worksheet. You'll be able to rule out most of them with a few criteria. But every once in a while a company passes your first tests and then the second. Your excitement builds. You dig a little deeper and the sparkle grows brighter. Finally, you go full-tilt, gathering information from the company and visiting its customers or stores that sell its product. Those times are going to be your big stories, and each one of them will start as a remote possibility from one of the four sources. I explain each source in this section.

Personal Experience

Follow your money to find great companies. It works for Peter Lynch, and it can work for you too. If you need to jog your memory, take a look at your last few credit card statements or your checkbook register. Where do you repeatedly spend money? Life's necessities can turn up great companies. Take food, for example. You might not want to invest in your local grocery chain, but what about that restaurant chain you keep visiting? All your friends like it, the paper gave it a four-star rating, it's always packed, the food is wonderful and reasonably priced. It's worth checking into. That's how an investor friend of mine found Starbucks Coffee when it sold at $6.50 in August 1992. At the end of 1996, it traded at $28.

How about clothing? Like me, you might enjoy watching people in public places such as a shopping mall. What are they wearing? One year I noticed kids wearing Tommy Hilfiger clothes more and more frequently. It didn't take a genius to know the clothing was from Hilfiger because the name was emblazoned across the front of every T-shirt and sweatshirt. I went into the department stores and looked for racks of Hilfiger clothing. Much to my intrigue, I found entire sections of the stores devoted to Hilfiger. In a local Macy's, "Hilfiger" hung in huge gold letters against the wood paneling, and throngs of kids stood under the sign holding shirts up

Life Is Full of Investment Ideas

to each other for first looks. That's darned interesting to an investor, wouldn't you say? I checked out the company's numbers and recommended Hilfiger to friends in Spring 1993. A buddy picked up shares at $10.50 in July. At the end of 1996, he could have sold them for $48.

Food, clothing, and other necessities are good places to start looking for companies. Once you've exhausted them, think about where you spend your discretionary dollars, that is, for things you don't absolutely need. Perhaps you buy home movies and notice that one company just won't go away. That company might be the place you buy videos, Blockbuster. It might be the movie company, Disney. If you decided back in October 1990 to get more out of Disney than a mouse cartoon and a few roller coasters, you could have purchased its stock at $22 and sold it at the end of 1996 for $69. That's a

Home Movie Buffs Could Invest in Disney

214 percent gain in six years that you would have found by just vegging out on home movies. Who says couch potatoes can't get ahead?

If your company is making an office-wide computer upgrade, somebody is going to research which computers to buy. Ask that person why he chose Gateway 2000, or Apple, or Dell, or Compaq, or IBM, or Micron. Maybe your friends use the same brand. If your family needs a personal computer, conduct research yourself and pay attention to the things that are important to you. What matters to you and your family probably matters to millions of others. If one company meets your every need, check it out. You might find a kaleidoscope of big-name players and decide to research all of them. One will probably surface as a clear leader. If not, consider investing in more than one.

Getting investment ideas from your personal experience is an easy way to start your stocks to watch list. Keep buying what you buy, but observe what you buy and who else is buying it with you. Your tendencies will often prove to be the tendencies of a lot of people. If you love a product, so will others. Of course, you need to keep your wits about you and always conduct further research before investing. Don't buy stock in every company you ever patronize. Even companies you love can lose money, and not every successful product will produce a soaring stock. As Peter Lynch points out, a product that is a tiny part of a company's business can't move the stock very much. So no matter how much your kids love the lunar ball you bought for them, if it's one of only 800 toys made by Whacky Whimsicals, you don't have much reason to invest. Maybe the company's Mars mittens are causing hives to break out on little hands everywhere and little lawyers are filing little papers. Always, always look beyond your first impressions.

The Investment Grapevine

Just past your personal experience lies the investment grapevine. After I noticed everybody packed into the Hilfiger clothing section, I conducted further research and decided Hilfiger was a stock worth buying. Notice that I didn't actually buy it myself, but I did tell a friend. He bought it and made a killing. I guess I was content to provide free advice on that one. I'm still kicking myself for not investing, but we all make mistakes.

But forget about me and focus on my lucky friend. Where did he learn about Hilfiger? From *my* personal experience. He harvested the investment grapevine to find a great company.

Always be careful of stories that are too good. It's human nature to talk about our triumphs and usually to build them up bigger than they really are. Remember those fishing stories your grandpa used to tell every Christmas while your grandma rolled her eyes? They were probably a lot closer to the truth than his investment stories. Always remember that any company you hear about is only a lead. That is, something to look into further. You probably wouldn't hire a baby-sitter at the advice of a friend who heard about her from his manager who talked to his brother who saw an ad tacked to a telephone pole. Don't invest on that kind of reference either. Best friends, colleagues, and especially relatives are notorious for their hot tips that freeze over the moment after you buy. Be warned and conduct your own due diligence.

Beware the Stories of Politicians and Investors

Instead of tuning into somebody else's success, listen for people lamenting an investment gone bad. If somebody conducted thorough research on a company, decided it was a great investment and happened to buy at the wrong time, you can take advantage of the situation to buy that great company at a discount. Unfortunately, most people prefer telling others about their winners. Too bad for the listener because knowing somebody's runaway, high-flying stock isn't nearly as useful as knowing which of their holdings are down. My friends and I have made a point of disclosing everything in our portfolios to each other. That way, when one of us gets in at the wrong time, others can use that information to buy a good stock at a bargain price. And, of course, the person who got in at the wrong time can always buy additional shares to profit on the way back up.

It pays to listen to tales of woe. The next time somebody comes up to you and starts bragging about their latest triumph, ask about their most disappointing stock. Ask if they're planning to buy additional shares at the lower price. Let other people make mistakes with their money while you show up in time for the recovery. If you keep investing long enough, I guarantee you'll have an opportunity to return the favor.

Investment Publications

Reading investment publications will provide you with a constant stream of investment ideas. This source is as close as your nearest grocery store and won't run you more than $3 for a magazine. Picking up today's copy of the *Wall Street Journal* or *Investor's Business Daily* will run you only a buck, *Barron's* only

$3. In this section I present investment publications that you can use to generate investment ideas.

Magazines   My three favorite investment magazines are *Smart-Money*, *Worth*, and *Kiplinger's*. Watching magazine recommendations over the years has shown me that great company earnings do not always make a great stock, that few companies are as down and out as the world thinks, and that doing nothing has its merits. I remember one instance when I encountered a list of best buys in one of the magazines. Every company on the list had already been on my mind as a possible investment, and the list confirmed their worthiness. I was ready to take the plunge when a series of catastrophes left me with no money to invest for a while. Disappointed as I was, it ended up working in my favor. Every company on the list fell in price by at least 20 percent. By the time I accumulated enough cash to buy a few shares, I picked my three favorites off the list at a 25 percent discount from their recommended price. Months later I read in the magazine, "After suffering an initial setback, our ten stocks are well on their way to substantial profits." They sure were, and life's little curve ball helped me add to the loot.

To read more about my favorite magazines, including subscription information, turn back to page 142.

Newspapers   The reigning champs among investment newspapers are the *Wall Street Journal*, *Investor's Business Daily*, and *Barron's*. Every investment newspaper runs stories on winning companies, losing companies, and general business happenings. They are *news*papers, after all! News can tip you off to potential investments as much as the hard numbers. The stories usually pop up in response to hard numbers worth examining.

WSJ and *IBD* both provide news clips on their front page that make it easy to scan for items of interest. In the area of company profiles, *IBD* is great. Its front-page detail stories are continued on the back of the front page. Thus, you can tear off the page and get the entire story for your files without messing with remotely continued stories. That one

**Back to the
Newspapers Again**

design component is so simple, yet goes so far in simplifying your research. I hate flipping through papers for continued stories.

Although *WSJ*, *IBD*, and *Barron's* are the nation's best investment newspapers, don't overlook your local newspapers—especially if you live in a major city like New York, Los Angeles, or Chicago. Local papers have business sections that do a good job covering local companies. Also, they typically run syndicated columns with a national scope where you can find good companies to research.

To read more about the big three investment newspapers, including subscription information, turn back to page 143.

Professional Publications If you've got some extra dough to spend on subscriptions or time to research at your library, professional publications are excellent places to find investment ideas. Value Line and Standard & Poor's are the leading providers of stock information and publish materials helpful to anybody. Value Line's list of timely companies and Standard & Poor's list of 5-STAR companies are quick paths to new ideas. To read more about Value Line, turn back to page 150. For Standard & Poor's, turn back to page 158.

Subscription newsletters are another place to find potential investments. Quality among stock-picking newsletters varies widely, and a lot of investors I know say that if you need to rely on a newsletter, then you shouldn't be picking stocks yourself. I disagree with that extreme position, but the point is well taken. You shouldn't rely exclusively on leads you find in newsletters. If that becomes your strategy, you might as well place your money in a full-service account and let your broker invest for you. Treat leads from newsletters the same way you treat all investment leads: cautiously. At the risk of flogging an expired equine, I must tell you again to always research everything yourself before you invest. For more newsletter information, see page 147.

The Internet

Going online is quickly becoming the easiest way to find investment ideas. It's so darned convenient because you can do it from home and get other things done while you're online. If you have an online discount broker, you can check your account balances, see current quotes, place trades, and get new investment ideas all with one local phone call and without standing up.

The Internet doesn't offer any new information to investors; it simply offers a new way to get the same information investors have always gotten one way or another. For example, the Internet is rife with investment discussion forums and live chat rooms.

You May Never Know the People You Deal with Online

Both let you see what others think about a stock and let you offer your own two cents worth of info or ask a question. Discussing investments with other investors online is a way to extend your investment grapevine. However, it's no better than calling up your pal Joe who works in the industry you're considering. In fact, it's less reliable than ol' Joe because the people with whom you're discussing stocks online are usually complete strangers whose identity you'll never know. They might be more ignorant than you are. To paraphrase Ernest Hemingway's advice to aspiring novelists, going online requires a built-in, shock-proof crap detector. Keep it humming at all times.

The Internet offers hard data in addition to discussion opportunities. Again, investors have been getting the hard data through printed publications and local computer programs for years. Now it's available to everybody online, sometimes free and sometimes for a price.

On page 169, you learned all about using the Internet for investment research.

Gather the Worksheet Criteria

You should be bursting with investment ideas after spending time with the four sources explained in the previous section. If you're like me, there will be too many great investments and not enough money. The trick now is to pare your satchel of stocks down to the best twenty for placement on your stocks to watch worksheet. That's what this section is all about. It's the heart of our strategy.

We've reached the point of your investment journey where it's time to discover specific measurements that capture the advice of our six master investors, reflect the lessons of history, and are easy enough for you to actually use. Too many books list hundreds of ideal measurements for your stocks to possess, but fail to note that it takes hours just to find them all—if you ever do. I don't have the patience for such approaches and assume that you don't either.

For convenience, I group all measurements on the stocks to watch worksheet. To pack in all the information I like to know about a company, I needed to break the worksheet into two sets of column headings and put only ten companies on a page. Thus, to track 20 companies, you'll have two stocks to watch worksheets. Your 20 stocks might contain 5 large-cap value companies, 5 medium-cap growth companies, and 10 small-cap growth companies in one place. The combination will be unique to your interests, of course, but you don't need to juggle multiple criteria for different types of companies. I designed the worksheet to be flexible enough to follow any stock you like.

I toyed with the idea of creating two worksheets: one for growth investors and one for value. Based on my own lazy habits, I decided we'd all be happier with one worksheet that tracked a lot of criteria. Growth investors will pay more attention to certain items while value investors will focus on other items. By blending all information on one sheet, you are better able to see opportunity in growth and value, and compare how the two styles are performing among the companies you watch.

If you're scouring stocks for the first time, your goal is to build your initial list with the 20 best stocks you can find. Thereafter, you will scrutinize every stock you encounter against the 20 already on your list.

Your worksheet is in the back of the book. But before turning to the back of the book, follow along as I explain each measurement and where to find it. The worksheet looks something like this. . . .

Company Name	Current Price	52 wk Hi/Lo	Market Cap	Day Dol Volume	Sales	Net Prof	Cash	Total Debt	Sales /Share	Cash Fl /Share	Earning /Share	Div Yield	ROE	Insider buy/own	Stock buyback
		/				▲▼			▲▼	▲▼	▲▼	▲▲▼▼		/	

Company Name	EPS Rank	RPS Rank	5 yr Sales	5 yr Price	Proj Sales	Proj Hi/Lo	Time Safe	STARS Fair Val	Current P/E	Avg P/E	P/S	P/B	Current Ratio	Quick Ratio	Max Min
						/	/	/							/

For each measurement, I explain what it is, the requirement to make your list, the ideal direction of the measurement, and where to find it. In some cases, not all of the items apply, so I leave some out. Also, rather than reprint sample pages from information sources such as Value Line, I point you to the resources section where I reprint a sample page one time and identify each pertinent piece of information on it. You'll eventually know by heart where to look for the information you need.

Company Basics

These are the essential measurements of a company. They tell you who the company is, its stock price, and how big the company is.

Company Name, Symbol, and Phone
Company Name, Symbol, and Phone

We'll start out easily enough. Simply fill in the name of companies that make your list, their ticker symbols, and their phone numbers. Make sure you get them right. That sounds silly, but I know a guy who bought a ton of MFS Communications stock (NASDAQ: MFST) thinking he was buying Microsoft (NASDAQ: MSFT). Switching the F and S leads to a world of difference.

Where to Find It: If you encounter a stock in an article, its symbol is usually provided in parenthesis after the first appearance of the company name. You'll find abbreviated company names and ticker symbols in almost every newspaper's stock tables. You can also look up names and symbols on the Internet.

Better than all these, however, is to buy a copy of Standard & Poor's *The Ticker Symbol Book*. It's updated every year and arranges companies alphabetically by symbol in the first half of the book and by name in the last half. It also shows which exchange each stock trades on. The book costs less than $10 and is great to have sitting in your briefcase or next to your computer. Interestingly enough, the confusion my friend had between MFS Communications and Microsoft must be common because that very problem was mentioned in the foreword of *The Ticker Symbol Book*, 1997 edition.

For company phone numbers, consult *Value Line*. It prints the address and phone number in the middle of each company's profile page.

Current Stock Price and 52-Week High/Low	Current Price	52 wk Hi/Lo

This is simply the stock's recent trading price along with its high and low over the past 52 weeks. It's always good to know the current price because that's what you'll be paying if you buy now. The high and low are good to know because they'll give you an idea if the current price is near the top or bottom of the range. Lots of growth investors prefer to buy near the top of the range, hoping that the stock will continue pushing the upper limit. Many value investors prefer to buy near the bottom of the range, hoping that the stock recovers to its previous highs.

While there is technically no such thing as an ideal stock price, I have a range that I prefer. Between $5 and $50 per share is my sweet spot. Anything under $5 is too crummy. While there are a lot of good buys above $50, they seem to grow so much slower than lower-priced issues that I get antsy. One glaring exception occurs when buying additional shares of a stock that is rising. If I bought in at $15 and it has risen to $75 with no end in sight, I have no qualms about buying more. But for initial investments I try to stay in the $5 to $50 range. A $20 stock gaining $10 returns 50 percent. An $80 stock gaining $10 returns only 12.5 percent. Low stock prices multiply faster than high ones.

**A Lower Price
Is Better**

Small-cap investors take note: a low stock price is often a trait of small companies with modest sales figures. That's good, because small sales figures double and quadruple easier than large ones, and when they do they usually take share prices with them. Is it more likely for IBM to double its $70 billion annual sales or for Mister Magazine to double its $5 million? Mister Magazine to double its $5 million, naturally. When sales and earnings double, share prices should follow. Peter Lynch confirms this correlation between earnings growth and share price in *One Up on Wall Street.* The Gardner brothers also underscore it in their book, *The Motley Fool Investment Guide,* then recommend that small-cap investors search for stocks trading between $5 and $20.

Where to Find It: Any newspaper's stock table lists yesterday's trading price and the 52-week high and low. The Internet is also a convenient place to find stock-price information. Stock quotes are one of the most common reasons people go online.

**Market
Capitalization**

This shows you how big the company is. To refresh your memory, determine market capitalization by multiplying the number of outstanding shares of stock by the current stock price. The number you get will reveal whether the company you're considering is large, medium, or small. For example, at the end of 1995 First Team Sports, an inline skate manufactur r, had 5.7 million shares outstanding at a price of $15.25 per share. Multiplying the two showed me that the company's market cap was $86.9 million. That's a micro-cap stock. At the end of 1995, IBM's market cap was around $51 billion, Cisco Systems' was around $23 billion, and Gateway 2000's was around $2 billion. Know the size of companies you're considering so you have an idea whether your portfolio is weighted too heavily toward one size or another.

You are already investing in larger, established companies through the Dow 2 Dividend strategy. Remember that the 30 Dow stocks contain names like 3M, McDonald's, Boeing, Merck, and Disney. They're the hugest of the huge.

Because you're already in larger companies through the Dow Dividend strategy, consider focusing your individual stock-picking efforts on smaller companies. They'll add some spice to your portfolio and allow you to capture a truer picture of the marketplace. I'm not suggesting you ignore household names just because they're big, I'm suggesting you make a concerted effort to find undiscovered companies that will be tomorrow's household names. Referring back to the Morningstar capitalization table on page 41, you'll see that small companies have market caps below $1 billion. Those with market caps below $250 million are considered micro cap.

Look for Smaller Companies

I can't list an ideal market cap for a company because there is no such thing. I quadrupled my money in IBM while friends lost 60 percent in Diamond Multimedia, a small company. Opportunity and danger lurk everywhere.

Where to Find It: You can find the total number of shares outstanding listed in several places. The easiest is probably on the Value Line page you'll be using for gobs of other stock information. There you can see the number of shares over the past 15 years in addition to the current number. Another good source is *Standard & Poor's Stock Guide*. Shares outstanding is also printed with quarterly earnings in financial newspapers such as *Investor's Business Daily*. Finally, several Internet sites list market cap itself, saving you the time of calculating it.

Daily Dollar
Volume

While market cap tells you a company's size, dollar volume tells you how much money trades in the stock on a given day. That information determines how liquid the stock is—that is, how easily it is bought and sold. It's easy to figure daily dollar volume: multiply a stock's average daily trading volume by its share price. For example, on October 25, 1996, Exxon's daily trading volume was 851,800 and its price was 87\frac{1}{4}$. Multiplying the two, you see that on that day the stock traded a dollar volume of $74,319,550.

Most mutual funds won't touch stocks with low dollar volumes because it might be difficult for them to sell the stock in the future. If nobody's buying, the price will drop and the spread will be big. If you try selling shares of Mister Magazine, people won't even know what the company does, much less be interested in buying it. If you try selling shares of Exxon, there's a buyer at every turn. Mister Magazine is an illiquid stock; Exxon is very liquid.

Like market cap, there is no ideal number for daily dollar volume. The measure is of most interest to small-cap investors. If you're a small-cap investor, you'll look for low daily volume, say less than $3 million because that means mutual funds will stay away until the volume starts increasing. When it does, funds might buy in and drive the volume and price even higher. You will have been invested since the early days when you and ten other people followed the stock. Handsome profits should come your way. Large-cap investors don't pay much attention to daily volume because it's always big and everybody already knows about the company. You're not going to sneak up on the world with shares of Exxon.

**Small Caps Should
Have Low Volume**

By the way, don't get too illiquid no matter what your market-cap preference is. A widely accepted bare minimum trading volume is $50,000 a day. Much below that and you're going to be selling your stock on the street corner along with cheap pencils and windshield cleanings.

Where to Find It: The best place to locate volume information is *Investor's Business Daily*. Every day it prints the number of shares traded in a stock and the percentage that the number differs from the stock's usual volume. In *IBD* listings you'll find (along with other stuff) this information:

Stock	Vol. 100s	Vol.% Change	Closing Price
Exxon	8518	-42	87 1/4

8518 is the previous day's trading volume shown in hundreds. In this case Exxon traded 851,800 shares. -42 shows you the percentage difference that 851,800 is from Exxon's usual volume. To arrive at the average daily volume, just divide 851,800 by .58 (the difference between 1, which represents 100 percent volume, and Exxon's dip of 42 percent. 1 minus .42 equals .58) to get an average daily share volume of 1,468,620. Multiply that by the share price of $87¼ to get, ta-da, an average daily dollar volume of $128,137,155. Every day $128 million of Exxon stock changes hands.

You'll also find volume information on the Internet.

Sales

It's helpful to know how much business your companies are doing. Sales reveals that number to you. Market cap, daily dollar volume, and sales usually follow the same trend. That is, small companies tend to trade in low dollar volumes and have modest sales. Large companies tend to trade in large dollar volumes and have a lot of sales. In 1995 Koo Koo Roo, a chicken restaurant chain, had sales of $19.8 million; Anheuser-Busch of Budweiser fame had sales of $10.3 billion; and Coca-Cola had sales of $18 billion.

Once again, I can't tell you an ideal figure for this measure. Common sense screams, "BIGGER, OF COURSE!" However, that isn't always so. A lot of small-cap investors prefer sales to be little because it indicates that the company is still undiscovered. A high-tech junkie I know in Palo Alto limits herself to companies with sales under $100 million because she insists on getting in on the ground floor. Sometimes her investments sink to the sub-basement, but those that rise to the fifteenth floor more than make up for the sinkers. David and Tom Gardner at The Motley Fool limit themselves to companies with sales under $200 million. One reason they do so is that little sales can grow faster than big sales. It makes sense. Coke can't easily turn its $18 billion annual sales into $36 billion, but Mister Magazine can turn its $5 million annual sales to $10 million just by taking out a bigger yellow pages ad. When sales and earnings grow quickly, share price tends to follow—more on that in the discussion on stock price next.

Little Sales Grow Faster Than Big Sales

You won't pay too much attention to this figure for your large-cap stocks. In the price-to-sales ratio discussed later, sales per share becomes important. But there are few times that I look at the overall sales of my large-company investments for anything other than curiosity: "$10 billion? Wow, that's a lot of beer." It doesn't mean I want to invest, necessarily, but I might want to give serious thought to starting that microbrewery I've always dreamed of. People love a tall, frosty mug of amber. I'm getting thirsty just writing about it.

Where to Find It: The easiest place to get sales is on your handy *Value Line* sheet. It's right there along with nearly everything else you could ever want to know about a stock. By the time you're finished with this book, you'll want an "I ♥ Value Line" bumper sticker on your car.

Also, the earnings page of both *Investor's Business Daily* and the *Wall Street Journal* show sales in a format like this:

Anheuser-Bush

Qtr. Dec 29:   1995

Sales   2,585,125,000

Coca-Cola

12 mo Dec 29: 1995

Sales   18,018,000,000

Koo Koo Roo

12 mo Dec 29: 1995

Sales   19,800,000

When you get the numbers from a newspaper, make sure you know the time period reported. For instance, you can see above that Anheuser-Busch reported quarterly sales, while the other two reported sales for one year. The number you want on your worksheet is the one-year sales. Assuming that Anheuser-Busch posts similar sales reports for other quarters in the year, just multiply $2,585,125,000 by 4 to get $10,340,500,000 as the yearly sales. That should sound familiar: $10.3 billion.

Company Health

Now you know the basic information about your company. It's time to see how healthy it is. This section discusses measurements that will tell you.

Net Profit Margin

As you read in Chapter 2, a high net profit margin is one of Warren Buffett's requirements for investing in a company. On page 29, you learned that a company's net profit margin is determined by dividing the money left over after paying all its expenses by the amount of money it had before paying expenses. So, if a company makes $1 million and pays $900,000 in expenses, its net profit margin is 10 percent

($100,000 divided by $1,000,000). If a competing company also makes $1 million but pays only $700,000 in expenses, its net profit margin is 30 percent ($300,000 divided by $1,000,000). All other things being equal, which company's stock would you rather own? The company with a 30 percent profit margin, of course. It makes the same amount of money as its competitor but keeps more.

Net profit margin is the first measurement on your sheet that looks beyond a company's size to the effectiveness of its operation. A management team that can maintain a high net profit margin in the midst of increasing competition is every investor's dream. This one number answers the question that gets to the heart of a company's capabilities: how much of its earnings does it keep?

On your worksheet, record the net profit margin and circle the up or down arrow based on the trend over the past five years. If the numbers aren't consistently increasing or decreasing, look at the change from five years ago and the projected figures for this year and next.

Required: Any company making your sheet should have a net profit margin in the top 20 percent of its industry. These are the leaders in their fields and where you want your money.

The reason I go with a relative value instead of an absolute value is that typical net profit margins change from industry to industry. Airlines generally have negative profit margins—I'm not kidding—and put in their business plans guidelines for declaring bankruptcy. Most commodity retailers such as supermarkets, auto-parts stores, cheap clothing stores, and consumer

Companies with High Profit Margins Keep More of What They Earn

electronics stores have net profit margins below 5 percent. I've seen some around 1 percent. For every dollar they sell, they keep a penny.

Companies with the highest net profit margins are those with exclusive rights to something, such as a brand-new laser-printing technology. If nobody else makes it, the company can charge whatever they want. Less competition, or no competition at all, allows prices to rise and profit margins to expand. As a consumer, you love *low* profit margins because they mean less money out of your pocket. As an investor, you love *high* profit margins because they mean more money out of customer pockets into company coffers. Sometimes it doesn't mean more money out of customer pockets. If the company is truly clever, the high net profit margin will come from cutting costs everywhere possible. That leads to a low price for the customer but more money kept by the company. Yes, you cynic, win-win situations are possible even in the business world.

I've met investors who insist on absolute minimum net profit margins, say 15 percent. That immediately keeps them from investing in Wal-Mart (2.9 percent), Harley-Davidson (8.2 percent), and even Nike (8.5 percent). But Microsoft passes with a net profit margin of 25.3 percent. Usually, people insisting on absolute profit margins are small-cap investors. David and Tom Gardner recommend in *The Motley Fool Investment Guide* that small-cap investors insist on a 10 percent net profit margin.

If you decide in the course of your investment career that an absolute net profit margin makes sense among companies you consider, pencil it above the column heading on your worksheet. There's nothing wrong with that. I've personally found that my portfolio holds companies of all stripes, and I haven't been able to find a minimum net profit margin that fits them all. That's fine too. There are lots of ways to make money in stocks.

Ideal: With net profit margin, bigger is always better. If you have a company on your sheet and encounter another in the same industry equal in all regards but net profit margin, strike the old company and add the new one. Sure, you'll want to look at how big the difference is and if the new company consistently boasts a higher margin, but you get the picture. Bigger is better, and a big net profit margin getting bigger every year is heaven.

Where to Find It: Net profit margin is computed from a company's income statement. "Oh, no," I can hear you gasping, "I knew this was going to happen sooner or later. So much for the friendly little guide." Have no fear. First of all, company financial statements aren't that complicated. If you need a quick

Look for a High Net Profit Margin

refresher, turn back to "Read the Investor's Packet" on page 160. Second, *Value Line* prints a company's net profit margin for the past fifteen years along with projected figures for this year and next. If the company is covered by *Value Line*, you won't need to compute its profit margin or stare at columns of numbers on an income statement.

Unfortunately, software is the only easy way to find how a company's margin compares to its industry peers. I wish *Value Line* showed the average net profit margin for every industry and where each company's margin fell in the spectrum. But it doesn't. The next best thing is for you to be aware of a company's competitors and simply look up a few of them in *Value Line* to compare. This is quite unscientific because there's a good chance you'll miss a few competitors or won't know any, but it's better than nothing. From reading this book, you'll come to understand the importance of research. It doesn't take much research on a company to discover its major competitors. Keep them on a list and check their figures against the company you're considering. In so doing, you might find a company better than the one you set out to research.

With a stock database the story changes. *Power Investor* (page 167) allows you to group competitors by their SIC codes. You can then rank them by their net profit margins, seeing in seconds who's on top and who's not.

You can also get net profit margins off the Internet.

The master investors in Chapter 2 teach that good companies have strong financial statements: high net profit margins, lots of cash, and little or no debt. You just finished reading about net profit margin. Now it's time to discuss cash and debt.

A company with a lot of cash can respond to business needs better than one with little cash. All a business does is buy things and sell them for more than they cost. It takes cash to buy things whether they're qualified employees, new equipment, supplies, marketing material, or even other companies. A business cannot have too much cash.

Debt, on the other hand, sucks a company dry. It eats up money that could otherwise go toward those employees, equipment, and supplies. If a business is forced to spend its money satisfying debt, then it can't spend as much strengthening its operation.

Ideal: We've already discussed cash and debt extensively, so I won't belabor the points here. Your companies should have a lot of cash, and little or no debt. We'll use ratios later in the worksheet to make sure the levels of cash and debt are acceptable.

Look for Lots of Cash and Little or No Debt

Where to Find It: Cash and debt are reported on a company's balance sheet. As with net profit margin, however, you can get what you need from *Value Line* as well. It lists cash assets and total debt.

You can also find the figures in stock databases and on the Internet.

Stock Health

You've got a pretty good picture of the company's health at this point. Let's take a closer look at the stock's health specifically. This section looks at seven great vital signs for every stock.

Sales per Share

You already know the importance of a company's sales. Now it's time to see that figure per share to understand how much you're paying for a piece of those sales.

In the sales discussion on page 197, I said there is no ideal sales figure. Because sales per share is simply sales divided by shares outstanding, there is still no ideal figure for sales per share. Small-cap investors often prefer it small while large-cap investors usually don't care except as it relates to price. We'll discuss that later in the price-to-sales ratio. For comparison's sake, let's break down the sales figures for the three companies in the sales discussion.

In 1995, Koo Koo Roo had sales of $19.8 million, Anheuser-Busch had sales of $10.3 billion, and Coca-Cola had sales of $18 billion. Each company had shares outstanding of 11.7 million, 516 million, and 2.5 billion respectively. Dividing the sales by the number of shares outstanding gives us a sales per share of $1.69 for Koo Koo Roo, $19.96 for Anheuser-Busch, and $7.20 for Coca-Cola.

On your worksheet, fill in the sales-per-share number and circle either the up or down arrow based on the trend over the past five years. If some years are up and others are down, you'll need to exercise judgment to decide whether it's an up or down trend. Compare the current number to five years ago. Is it bigger or smaller? Finally, look at projections. Is the company expected to report higher sales per share next year?

Look for Increasing Sales per Share

Required: For growth companies, list only those that have increased sales per share in each of the past five years and are projected to increase them again this year and next.

Ideal: While you will insist on five years of increasing sales per share in your growth companies, you want this number to have increased in each of the past five years for all companies. Even stocks that have been hammered in price will occasionally show a history of increasing sales. Those are great bargains.

Where to Find It: *Value Line* prints sales per share for the past fifteen years and projects the figure for this year and next. If you enjoy using your calculator, you could figure the number yourself by dividing sales by the number of shares outstanding.

Sales per share is also available on the Internet and in stock databases.

Cash Flow per Share	

As its name suggests, cash flow is the stream of money through a company. You want it to be positive, and you'd love it to be big. A positive cash flow means the company is receiving in a timely fashion the profits that it's owed. It may come as a surprise to you that not every profitable company can boast a positive cash flow. Why? Because some companies sell their goods on credit. Let's say Mister Magazine, my stalwart subscription-selling company, came up with a promo that allowed people to try their new magazine subscriptions for six months before paying. That's great for business. Thousands of people would pile onto the Mister Magazine bandwagon, and the company's accountants could put those promised subscription dollars on the books under "accounts receivable." At first glance Mister Magazine appears to be flush with new profits.

And it will be—eventually. During the six-month lag time, lots of expenses need to be paid. There's the prizes to buy for the company's best sales reps, fliers to be printed, electricity bills, energy bars for the bicycle-based sales force, and so on. Where's the money going to come from? Not from the newly signed thousands of subscribers. They don't owe a dime for six months. If times get too tight, Mr. Mag might be swaggering its way to the local bank for a short-term loan. I won't even waste ink on how much you and I hate debt by now. The situation at Mister Magazine would be grim.

Expenses Always Need to Be Paid

That's why you want to invest in companies with positive cash flow. They get paid as they sell. When the electric bill comes in, they cut a check from their profits. They don't need no darned bank because their businesses generate cash. I like to see cash flow per share as opposed to cash flow for the whole company. Breaking this and other measures into their per-share figures makes for easy comparisons and easily computed ratios.

Let's look at some real-world cash flow per share figures for companies you know. In 1995, Ford's cash flow per share was $13.20, Nike's was $1.60, Microsoft's was $1.37, Pete's Brewing Company's was $0.28, and Netscape Communications' was $0.03. Let's add a 5-year perspective. In 1990, Ford's cash flow per share was $6.20, Nike's was $0.86, Microsoft's was $0.30, and neither Pete's nor Netscape was public yet. So, all three of the companies that were around at least five years improved their cash flow per share.

On your worksheet, fill in the cash flow per share and circle the up or down arrow based on the trend over the past five years. As with sales per share, use your own judgment to determine whether a company whose cash flow per share fluctuates up and down over the years is in an uptrend or a downtrend. Don't forget to look at projected cash flow per share when deciding on an arrow to circle.

Required: To make your list, a company must have a positive cash flow per share. For growth companies, list only those that have increased cash flow per share in each of the past five years and are projected to increase it again this year and next.

Ideal: For all companies, bigger is better, and you prefer it to have increased over each of the past five years.

Where to Find It: Cash flow is reported on, surprise of surprises, a company's statement of cash flows. It's one of the financial forms sent to you along with the balance sheet and income statement.

What we're searching for is cash flow per share. While you could figure it yourself by dividing the company's cash flow by the number of shares outstanding, it's easier to just get it from *Value Line*. Just below sales per share you'll find cash flow per share for the past fifteen years along with projections for this year and next.

Look for Increasing Cash Flow per Share

You'll also find the information in stock databases and on the Internet.

Earnings per Share

This is the most commonly cited per-share measurement. It's the "E" part of P/E ratio, the first yardstick almost every value investor examines to determine whether a stock is expensive or cheap. Before you can know P/E ratio, you need to see the earnings per share. Also, you want to know whether earnings per share have been increasing or decreasing over time. Growth investors insist on an increasing earnings per share. Gary Pilgrim, one of our master investors in Chapter 3, not only insists that earnings per share be increasing but that they be increasing faster than expected.

On your worksheet, fill in the earnings per share and circle the up or down arrow based on the past five years. For growth stocks, circle the up arrow only if earnings have increased in each of the past five years and are projected to increase this year and next. For value stocks, a super discount is often accompanied by a dip in earnings. Occasionally, however, something else hammers a stock's price and earnings remain constant or increase. In that case you're really getting a bargain. With value stocks, use your judgment to decide on an up or down arrow based on whether the current number is an overall increase from five years ago, whether the increase is large or small, and by the projected earnings per share for this year and next.

Required: For growth companies, list only those that have increased earnings per share in each of the past five years and are projected to increase them again this year and next. This requirement is by definition. A growth company *is* a company that has been increasing earnings and should continue doing so. Just to be safe, though, I wanted to spell it out. If you are a growth investor, you'll invest only in companies that have the up arrow circled on your worksheet. In fact, the only companies that ever make it to your worksheet are ones with up arrows. It's a basic requirement for growth investors.

Ideal: While earnings increases are required for growth stocks, they're still nice among value stocks. For every stock you prefer to see five years of earnings increases with projections for further increases this year and next.

Look for Increasing Earnings per Share

Where to Find It: Below cash flow per share and sales per share, *Value Line* prints earnings per share for the past fifteen years along with projections for this year and next. In two seconds you can get all three of these measurements from one place. That's the kind of research I like.

Once again, you can find this information in stock databases and on the Internet.

Dividend Yield　　　

You read a lot about this measure in Chapter 4. A high dividend yield is the deciding factor used in the Dow Dividend strategy and was proven to work among large companies in James O'Shaughnessy's study of stock market history. It's a very important figure to large-company investors.

Small-company investors ignore dividend yield because small companies don't usually declare dividends and therefore have yields of zero. The measure is neither a thumbs-up nor thumbs-down on a company that declares no dividend. It's a solid thumbs sideways, totally meaningless. Thus, if you're a small-company investor, you'll leave this column blank on your worksheet.

On your worksheet, record the dividend yield. You'll notice there are two sets of arrows in this column. Circle the up or down arrow on the left based on the past five years. As with the other measures in this section, use your judgment to decide on an arrow. If the current dividend yield is substantially larger than it was five years ago and is larger than it was last year, that's an uptrend. Dips along the way are common. Circle the up or down arrow on the right based only on whether the current dividend yield is larger or smaller than last year.

Ideal: In general, you want to buy large companies with high dividend yields.

To split hairs over this, you prefer to invest when the overall dividend yield has been decreasing but the change from last year to now has shown a remarkable increase. On your worksheet, this translates to the left down arrow circled and the right up arrow circled. Such a situation could indicate a stock that has been growing in price over the past few years, but took a quick fall recently. Notice that this is ideal, not required. I haven't tested this or confirmed it with anybody else. I merely read James O'Shaughnessy's findings in Chapter 3 and

Large Companies Should Have High Dividend Yields

looked at how the Dow Dividend strategy works. Judging from those two sources, this treatment of dividend yield among large companies makes sense. Keep it in mind, but don't let it cloud the tried-and-true technique of choosing large companies with high dividend yields.

Remember, ignore dividend yield among small companies.

Where to Find It: *Value Line* prints the average annual dividend yield for the past sixteen years along with projections for this year and next. The measure is of such importance to investors that *Value Line* prints the current dividend yield at the top of the page.

You will also find current dividend yield listed in the stock tables of most newspapers, in stock databases, and on the Internet.

Return on Equity

As you read on page 34, return on equity shows you what a company has earned with the money people have invested in it. You simply divide net income by total shareholders' equity to come up with a percentage. For example, if a company reports net income of $8 million and total shareholders' equity of

Look for a High Return on Equity

$40 million, its return on equity is 20 percent. For those who are very tired right now, 8 divided by 40 equals .20, or 20 percent. Warren Buffett likes this measurement because it gives a clear picture of what a company does with its profits. If a company gets bigger every year, it will probably earn more money. But investors should ask, does it earn enough additional money to support its larger size? Return on equity answers that. If a company can maintain a high return on equity as it grows, you know that management is directing profits wisely.

Although there is no requirement for ROE, I like to see ROEs of at least 20 percent maintained or improved over the years. Occasionally, value investors will accept low or negative ROEs in companies they think are about to make a change for the better.

Ideal: Twenty percent is a solid return on equity. Of course, bigger is better. If you're bargain hunting, you might accept a low or even negative ROE from time to time. That should be quite rare, however. For the most part, you want a company that continues returning substantial profits to investors. A steady ROE will reveal that.

Where to Find It: Net income is reported on a company's income statement; total shareholders' equity is reported on a company's balance sheet. You'll receive both of these financial statements in the investor kit mailed to you from the company. You would never invest in a company without seeing these statements first. Remember, you're a professional now.

Also, ROE is in most stock databases and on the Internet.

Insider Buys/Ownership   Insider buy/own

Remember that our master investors like to see insider ownership of a company. If the people who run the place have a material interest in its success, they're more likely to do a better job. To that end, you want to own companies that are owned by insiders.

It's worth repeating that you shouldn't pay attention to insider sells. People raise money all the time for needs ranging from housing down payments to exotic vacations. Sale of stock is not necessarily a comment on the seller's belief in the stock's future. It might just be a need for cash.

On your worksheet, write the number of insider buys over the past year and the percentage of insider ownership.

Ideal: The more insider ownership, the better. You can't have too many insiders buying shares of their own company. For small-cap investors, insider ownership is of particular importance because a lot of small companies are just starting out and management is a crucial factor in their success. The founder and president probably knows how to run the machines, answer the phones, and respond to customer complaints. You want that person to

Look for a Lot of Insider Ownership

own a stake in the company. David and Tom Gardner of The Motley Fool look for small companies to have at least 15 percent insider ownership.

Where to Find It: *Value Line* prints a chart of insider decisions to buy and sell. It lists the numbers for each month over the past year. Simply add up the buy decisions and write the number on your worksheet. In a business overview box in the middle of each company's page, *Value Line* often prints the percentage of the company that officers and directors own.

Insider ownership is also reported in the *Wall Street Journal*, *Investor's Business Daily*, and *Barron's*. However, it's rare for one of the publications to be covering a company you just happen to be interested in. To find insider ownership for a company you're researching, the quickest path is a call to the company itself. You'll be calling to request an investor packet anyway and can ask the representative about insider ownership.

Finally, don't forget to check the company Web site. If it's not at www.[name].com (i.e., www.ibm.com, www.chrysler.com), try searching for it on Yahoo (www.yahoo.com), or Hot-Bot (www.hotbot.com), or Daily Stocks (www.dailystocks.com). The investor section of the Web site might mention insider holdings.

Stock Buyback

It's great to see a company buying its stock back. There will be fewer shares outstanding, which will increase demand and should increase the share price eventually. You want to see your companies buying back shares of their stock. Simply write the word Yes or No in this column of your worksheet. Make sure if you write yes that it's a significant enough buyback program to earn a yes. If the company bought back a few token shares one time, that hardly qualifies as a stock-buyback program. Use your judgment.

Ideal: You want a Yes in this column.

Where to Find It: The best place to find out about a stock-buyback program is from the company itself. Contact the company by calling investor relations or browsing the company Web site.

Past Performance
After seeing the current health of the stock, it's a good idea to take a peek at how it's fared in the past. This section shows four measurements that tell you.

EPS Rank

A company's earnings per share drives just about everything related to the stock. By now you know that. EPS rank looks at a company's earnings record and compares it to the earnings record of all other companies to see how the company stacks up. It's a quick way to see which companies are earnings machines and which are earnings accidents.

EPS rank is printed every day in *Investor's Business Daily*. The paper takes each company's earnings per share for the two most recent quarters and computes their percentage change from the same two quarters a year ago. That result is combined and averaged with each company's five-year earnings growth record. The final figures for every company are compared with each other, giving each company a rank from 1 to 99, with 99 being the best. Thus, a company with an EPS rank of 95 has earnings figures in the top 5 percent of all companies in the tables.

Growth Investors: Look for High EPS

This measure is of most interest to growth investors because they look for consistently strong earnings and for the company to exceed expectations. Value investors like earnings too, but they'll often buy a company with struggling earnings if it means the stock is enough of a bargain.

Required: Growth investors should insist on companies that have an EPS rank of 85 or better. Value investors have no requirement for this measure because they'll accept lower earnings if it means a bargain stock with a chance of recovery.

Ideal: For growth investors, bigger is better.

Where to Find It: *Investor's Business Daily* prints every stock's EPS rank each day. How's that for convenient? Simply locate your stock in the tables and see its rank from 1 to 99 in the column titled "EPS." A stock with a rank of 85 has earnings results in the top 15 percent of all companies.

Relative Price Strength Rank

This measure looks at the stock's price performance in the latest 12 months. That's it. It doesn't look at stories, earnings, or price ratios. It simply reports the hard numbers and answers the question, how did this stock perform compared to all others?

Investor's Business Daily updates the numbers daily, compares all stocks to each other, and ranks them from 1 to 99, with 99 being

**Growth Investors:
Look for High RPS**

the best. That means a company with a relative price strength of 90 outperformed 90 percent of all other stocks in the past year.

As with EPS rank, relative price strength rank is of most interest to growth investors. Momentum investing, a strict growth discipline, requires investment in companies that have done well and should continue that momentum to do well in the future. So, a high EPS rank combined with a high relative strength rank could indicate a stock on a roll. Maybe even an ace in the hole.

Required: Growth investors should restrict themselves to stocks with a relative strength rank of at least 80. Value investors have no requirement for relative price strength because it would preclude bargain companies.

Ideal: For growth investors, bigger is better.

Where To Find It: Investor's Business Daily prints every stock's relative price strength each day. Just find your stock in the tables and record its rank from 1 to 99 on your worksheet. The column is titled "RelStr." A stock with a relative strength rank of 80 has outperformed 80 percent of all other stocks in the past year.

**Five-Year Sales
and Earnings Gain**

You've already found the company's sales per share in the "Stock Health" section of your worksheet. Now you're going to find its average annual gain for sales and earnings over the past five years. Our requirement for growth companies is to have increased sales and earnings in each of the past five years. Here we find out by how much.

With small companies especially, strong sales and earnings are essential. The Gardner brothers at The Motley Fool require their small company investments to have grown sales and earnings at least 25 percent over the past year. We are looking at five-year history here. I like small companies to have five-year average annual sales and earnings increases of at least 15 percent.

For larger companies I accept nothing lower than 10 percent.

Want some real-world perspective? In 1990, Ford's earnings per share were $0.65, Nike's were $0.50, and Microsoft's were $0.43. In 1995, Ford's were $2.71, Nike's were $1.89, and Microsoft's were $1.72. As with cash flow per share, all three of the companies improved.

Look for Increasing Sales and Earnings

Required: Look for companies that have grown both sales and earnings an average of at least 10 percent a year over the past five years. For small companies, require 15 percent.

Ideal: For those who like to see a strong history of sales and earnings, bigger is better. Count me and a lot of others in that camp. There are some who look for weak sales and earnings records in hopes of finding a turnaround, but that approach makes me queasy. It forces you to buy into an industry's worst competitors instead of the best. I say stick with strong sales and earnings even if you're a value investor.

Where to Find It: *Value Line* prints both sales and earnings growth per share for the past 5 and 10 years in a small box titled "Annual Rates" on the left side of each profile page.

You can also find the measure on the Internet and in stock databases.

Five-Year Price Appreciation

This one's simple enough. You just want to see how much the stock price has changed over the past five years. I take the high price from five years ago and compare with the current price. To compute the percentage change, you can use the % CHG button on your handy business calculator or just do it manually. For you manual types, divide the current price by the high price from five years ago. Subtract one from the difference to get the percentage change. For example, say Mister Magazine traded at a high of $22 five years ago and is trading at $95 today. Divide 95 by 22 to get 4.32. Subtract 1 to get 3.32, or a 332 percent increase.

There's no rule for this number. A lot of value investors prefer to see a decrease from five years ago. Growth investors won't touch a stock that has lost money in the past five years. Regardless of your preference, it's good to know what happened to a stock in the past five years.

Where to Find It: *Value Line* prints the high and low stock price for the past sixteen years at the top of each profile page. You can also get a recent trading price at the top of the *Value Line* page. For a stock's current trading price, check the stock tables in a newspaper or get a quote from the Internet. For historic quotes, use a stock database.

Projected Performance

After seeing the stock's current health and how it has fared in the past, take a look at projected performance. This section uses two measurements from Value Line: projected sales and earnings, and projected stock high/low price.

Sales and Earnings Proj Sales

It's our old friends again. Sales and earnings make up the lifeblood of a company and have more influence on a stock's price than any other measures. It makes sense to see how they're projected to grow in the next five years.

I look for companies that are expected to grow by double digits. I get stricter as company size gets smaller because small companies should be growing faster than large ones.

Look for High Projected Sales ***Required:*** Large companies should be expected to grow at least 10 percent a year, medium companies at least 15 percent, and small companies at least 20 percent.

Ideal: Bigger is better.

Where to Find It: *Value Line* prints the five-year projected rates of change for both sales and earnings in the same place you found results for the past five years. It's a box titled "Annual Rates" on the left side of the page.

There are lots of other places to find earnings projections, including publications from Standard and Poor's, information from companies themselves, subscription newsletters, and the Internet. Because you're already using *Value Line* for so much of your other information, it's convenient to rely on its projections.

**Projected Stock
High/Low**

Want to see just how much money you stand to gain? This is the measure. It relies on projections, of course, and those are never guaranteed. But analysts spend their lives trying to be accurate, and it never hurts to see what they expect to happen. This measure simply records the projected high and low stock price for the next three to five years. Later, in the max/min ratio, you'll compare the percentage gains for the projected high and low prices to see how much bigger the maximum is than the minimum.

Required: Both the high and low price projections must be bigger than the current price. Never invest in a stock that's expected to fall in price. It seemed silly even writing that last sentence, but repeating the basics never hurt anybody. Oh, by the way, make sure the low projection represents a worthwhile gain. If the stock is currently trading at

**Look for High
Projected Prices**

$50 and the three-to five-year projected low price is $55, why bother?

Ideal: Bigger is better for both the high and low.

Where to Find It: I'm sure it'll come as a shock to learn that *Value Line* prints a company's three- to five-year projected high and low price. The numbers are in a box titled "(Years) Projections" on the upper left of the page, where "years" is the three to five range. For instance, in 1996 the title would read "1999-01 Projections."

You'll also find projections on the Internet.

Rankings

Professional rankings are a quick way to see what others think of a company you're considering. The two grand Poobahs of stock rankings are Value Line and Standard and Poor's. You'll record rankings from each of the two on your worksheet.

Value Line
Timeliness/Safety

The folks at *Value Line* are nice enough to provide two rankings for every stock. Each is on a scale from 1 to 5, with 1 being the best. Timeliness is a prediction of how well the stock should perform relative to all other stocks in the next 12 months. Safety is a measure of a stock's volatility as compared to its own long-term record. If a stock continually trades in a tiny range, it is considered safe and receives a better rating, say a 1 or 2. If the stock fluctuates widely from its historic average, it receives a rating of 4 or 5.

Look for a
Timeliness of 1 or 2

Required: I pay a lot more attention to the timeliness rank than the safety. In many cases I actually prefer a wider trading history because it means there's a better chance the stock will rise. That translates into a poor safety rating, perhaps a 4 or 5. If a company is poised for tremendous things, I want it to break from its historic average. So take the safety rating with a grain of salt, unless you're looking for steady dividend payers and don't want much fluctuation in the stock value.

As for timeliness, limit yourself to stocks with ranks of 1 or 2. Nobody ever complains about a stock that rises in price!

Ideal: For timeliness, look for stocks ranked 1. There's no ideal for safety because some investors want volatility while others do not.

Where to Find It: *Value Line* prints timeliness and safety in a box at the upper left corner of each profile page. You can't miss them.

S&P STARS/
Fair Value

The Standard & Poor's STARS and fair-value rankings are used to select stocks for the S&P platinum portfolio, which consists of S&P's favorite stocks. Now you'll gather both measurements for individual stocks you select.

Standard & Poor's uses its STARS system to predict a stock's potential over the next 12 months. STARS stands for Stock Appreciation Ranking System, and classifies stocks from 1 to 5 with 5 being the best. I know, it's a bummer that *Value Line* makes 1 the best and S&P makes 5 the best. Try this: stars are in the sky and 5 is the highest number. Both are upward. That's a quick association to remember what S&P STARS strives for.

Fair value is a rank of the stock's recent trading price compared to what S&P considers its fair value. We'd all prefer to buy stocks at a price way below their fair value. Therefore, S&P ranks all stocks on the handy 1 to 5 scale with 5 again being the best. That means stocks with a fair-value rank of 5 are the most undervalued—bargains—and stocks with a fair value rank of 1 are overvalued—ripoffs. Well, they might not be ripoffs, but they are selling at a price considerably higher than S&P thinks they're

Look for S&P Rankings of 4 or 5

worth. In politically correct terms, they're value challenged.

Required: Limit yourself to stocks that are ranked 4 or 5 in each S&P ranking. That keeps you in stocks expected to be among the best performers and reduces your risk because you're buying in at a price below their estimated value. That's Graham's old margin of safety again. If the stock's already below its value, then it probably won't go much lower. That's the idea, at least.

Ideal: Best of all is a stock ranked 5 STARS and with a fair-value rank of 5. That combination, by the way, is what the platinum portfolio requires for a stock to enter. So, for a quick list of stocks that are ranked high in both categories, take a look at the S&P platinum portfolio list.

Where to Find It: The easiest place to find periodic lists of companies that are ranked high in both STARS and fair value is *The Outlook*, a weekly newsletter from Standard & Poor's. You can find it in most libraries.

Stock Ratios

Only now are we getting to the stuff you'll hear most often on a public bus, or at a lunch meeting, or in the bleachers at Little League. Here are seven stock ratios to give you all the ammunition you need to defend your stock portfolio.

Current Price-to-Earnings

Here it is at last—the grandaddy of valuation measures. Your reading in Chapter 3 should have convinced you that P/E is not the end-all, be-all of stock measures. In fact, P/S has proven itself more telling of a company's prospects. Nonetheless, P/E is so widely followed that you should know it for each of your stocks.

It's the easiest measure in the world to find, second only to the stock price itself.

To recap from page 31, P/E is simply the stock price divided by the earnings per share. It shows you how much you're paying for each dollar of the company's earnings. Value investors want to pay as little as they can for each dollar of earnings; growth investors don't care very much. Gary Pilgrim and William O'Neil don't even look at P/E for their portfolios. Peter Lynch does, however. In *One Up on Wall Street* he writes:

> The P/E ratio of any company that's fairly priced will equal its growth rate. I'm talking about growth rate of earnings here. . . . If the P/E of Coca-Cola is 15, you'd expect the company to be growing at about 15 percent a year, etc. But if the P/E ratio is less than the growth rate, you may have found yourself a bargain. A company, say, with a growth rate of 12 percent a year and a P/E ratio of 6 is a very attractive prospect. On the other hand, a company with a growth rate of 6 percent a year and a P/E ratio of 12 is an unattractive prospect and headed for a come-down.
>
> In general, a P/E ratio that's half the growth rate is very positive, and one that's twice the growth rate is very negative.

I'd like to toss in another popular filter for value companies. The current P/E should be at or below the five-year average P/E. That keeps you from buying in just after the company has broken into higher trading territory. Sometimes a company will steadily improve its position, however, and its P/E will rise along with its growth rate. That's a positive sign for the company, and you wouldn't want to overlook it simply because its current P/E is higher than its average. Therefore, we'll make this an ideal P/E condition instead of a required one.

For your value companies, keep a close eye on P/E. For your growth companies, write the P/E on your worksheet but don't let it affect your decision very much. There are more important measures for growth investing.

**Value Investors:
Look for a Low P/E**

Required: For value companies, P/E must equal the earnings-growth rate.

Ideal: For value companies, the lower the P/E the better. As Lynch points out, a P/E that's half the earnings growth is a very positive sign. A P/E that's below the five-year average P/E is another positive sign.

Where to Find It: P/E is listed in the stock tables of most newspapers. That's a handy place to find it if you're in a hurry. *Value Line* considers P/E important enough to print it at the top of each company page. You can also find P/E ratios all over the Internet and in stock databases.

Average Price-to-
Earnings   **Average P/E**

Just after you pencil in the current P/E, take a moment to compute the average P/E for the past five years. Simply add up the five average annual P/E ratios and divide by five. Write the figure on your worksheet.

Knowing this number will let you see how the current P/E measures up to the stock's recent trading levels. As I just mentioned in the discussion on P/E, it's nice to have a current P/E that's less than the average for the past five years.

Ideal: You'd like the average P/E to be higher than the current P/E.

Where to Find It: *Value Line* lists the average annual P/E ratio for the past sixteen years. You'll also find it in most stock databases.

Price-to-Sales   **P/S**

The price-to-sales ratio is catching on as investors recognize its superiority over P/E for valuing stocks. The most compelling evidence I've encountered is James O'Shaughnessy's study of stock market history, which you read about in Chapter 3. O'Shaughnessy found that P/S is a more accurate measure of a company's value because sales can't be manipulated as easily as earnings. Also, the measure helps even growth investors identify companies that are selling below their potential. Even growth companies are best purchased cheap.

At this point you have the information you need to compute P/S from your worksheet. Simply divide the current stock price by the sales per share. That's it. Write the figure on your worksheet. If one of your stocks is selling for $72 per share and is expected to report sales per share of $47.65 this year, its P/S ratio is 1.51 ($72 divided by $47.65).

Let's look at a few examples to give you a feel for P/S figures among different companies. In the discussions on sales and sales per share, we looked at three companies: Koo Koo Roo, Anheuser-Busch, and Coca-Cola. We found that in 1995 Koo Koo Roo had sales of $19.8 million, Anheuser-Busch had sales of $10.3 billion, and Coca-Cola had sales of $18 billion. Each company had shares outstanding of 11.7 million, 516 million, and 2.5 billion respectively. Dividing the sales by the number of shares outstanding gives us a sales per share of $1.69 for Koo Koo Roo, $19.96 for Anheuser-Busch, and $7.20 for Coca-Cola.

Now we introduce the component of share price. On December 29, 1995, Koo Koo Roo shares sold for $6.31, Anheuser-Busch for $33.44, and Coca-Cola for $37.13. Dividing these share prices by the respective sales per share number for each company gives us the following:

Company	Share Price	Sales per Share	P/S Ratio
Koo Koo Roo	6.31	1.69	3.73
Anheuser-Bush	33.44	19.96	1.68
Coca-Cola	37.13	7.2	5.16

What do the numbers mean to you? It means that if you bought each company, you'd be paying $5.16 for every $1 of Coke's sales, but only $1.68 for every $1 of Budweiser's sales. By this measure Anheuser-Busch is the better buy. For curiosity's sake, let's see how each company fared in 1996. On December 31, 1996, Anheuser-Busch closed at $40 and Coca-Cola closed at $52.63. That's a one-year gain of 19.62 percent for Bud and 41.75 percent for Coke. This isn't a conclusive study, but does demonstrate that better bargains don't always come through in the short term. The word *always* should never appear in a discussion about the behavior of stocks.

Look for Low Price-to-Sales

Ideal: For all companies except utilities, smaller is better. You want to be paying as little as possible for the sales the company generates. O'Shaughnessy looked for companies with P/S ratios below 1.5, which happens to be the figure for most companies. I like to stay with a ratio below 2, but this is an ideal, not a requirement. Microsoft's P/S in July 1996 was about 9. That seems outrageously high given my preference to stay below 2, but the stock split and gained more than 200 percent in the next six months. Insisting on a P/S below 2 would have kept you out of Microsoft. On the other hand, it would have given you the green light on IBM, which had a P/S around .76. IBM gained more than 60 percent. So, as with all investment rules, sometimes this one works and sometimes it doesn't. History suggests, however, that a low P/S is a good sign.

Where to Find It: Because you have share price and sales per share on your worksheet, you can figure P/S yourself with a calculator. Simply divide share price by sales per share.

The Internet is another source of share price and sales per share. Some sites even list a company's P/S ratio for you. You'll also find P/S in most stock databases.

Popular magazines, such as *SmartMoney* and *Worth*, sometimes list P/S in tables summarizing potential stocks.

Price-to-Book   P/B

As you read on page 30, price-to-book compares a stock's price to how much the stock is worth right now if somebody liquidated the company. It's the second most common valuation measure following price-to-earnings. It tells how much you're paying for the actual assets of the company.

In truth, P/B isn't worth much to me. I care a lot more about a company's use of its equipment to earn money than I do about the auction value of that equipment. If I really wanted to get the most equipment for my money, I'd go to the auction myself. I want the skill of human beings to turn the output of equipment into profit. That's the point of investing.

However, it is nice to see that if everything crumbles at the company, you'll still get your money back. Growth investors don't care at all about P/B, but value investors like to see it less than 1. That means they're paying less for the company than it would fetch at auction.

Ideal: Smaller is better. A P/B of 1 means you're paying the auction price for a company. A P/B less than 1 means you're paying less than auction price. Benjamin Graham recommended investing in companies with a P/B less than .66.

Where to Find It: Book value per share is computed from numbers on a company's balance sheet. Simply divide common stockholders' equity by the number of outstanding shares. Then divide the stock's current price by its book value.

**Look for Low
Price-to-Book**

If you'd rather pluck out all your eyelashes than compute P/B on your own, you're not alone. Luckily, *Value Line* prints book value per share for the past 16 years. You can also find P/B in stock databases and on the Internet.

Current Ratio   Current Ratio

As you read on page 26, the current ratio is the most popular gauge of a company's short-term liquidity. It's the current assets divided by the current liabilities. That's it. It's usually expressed in the number of "times," as in the current ratio is three times. That would mean the company has three times as many assets as liabilities, which is good news. Perhaps the company has $300,000 in assets and only $100,000 in liabilities. The more assets a company has in relation to its liabilities, the better it's able to handle ugly surprises.

Why? Simply because it owns more than it owes—a situation everybody prefers.

Run the numbers, then write the current ratio on your worksheet.

Look for High Current Ratios

Required: Every company on your sheet should have a current ratio of at least 2 (two times and 2-to-1 are other ways of saying the same measure).

Ideal: Bigger is better.

Where to Find It: Assets and liabilities are on a company's balance sheet. However, because we love *Value Line* so much by now, we'll just use the numbers printed there. Halfway down each profile on the left side of the page is a box called "current position." In there you'll find current assets and current liabilities. As usual, the current ratio is on the Internet and in most stock databases.

Quick Ratio

As you read on page 33, the quick ratio divides cash and cash assets by current liabilities. It's stricter than the current ratio when evaluating how prepared a company is to deal with short-term crises or opportunities. The current ratio compares current assets to liabilities, but we all know that it's difficult to convert a $5 million inventory into cold hard cash. Cold hard cash, on the other hand, is always ready for spending. No conversions required, no convincing people of its worth. That's why the quick ratio compares a company's cash assets to its liabilities. A solid quick ratio tells you that the company is very prepared for short-term obligations.

Run the numbers, then write the quick ratio on your worksheet.

Required: Every company on your sheet should have a quick ratio of at least .5. That is, the company should have half as much in cash as the liabilities on its balance sheet.

Ideal: Bigger is better.

Where to Find It: Cash assets and current liabilities are on a company's balance sheet. But, as with the current ratio's necessary numbers, *Value Line* prints cash assets and current liabilities in the "current position" box on every profile. You'll also find it on the Internet and in stock databases.

Look for High Quick Ratios

Max/Min

Max/min is just the stock's projected maximum gain and its projected minimum gain, both expressed as percentages. Though you already listed the projected high and low, sometimes the percentages make the situation more clear.

Ideal: Bigger is better for both maximum and minimum projections.

Where to Find It: *Value Line* prints projected price highs and lows, which you already used in the "Proj Hi/Lo" column of your worksheet. Right next to the high and low, *Value Line* translates the numbers into percentage changes for the next three to five years. Of course, you could always compute the percentage changes yourself using the current price and projected hi/lo from your worksheet.

The projections you use can come from a number of sources. You might find them in a magazine article, one of the financial papers, or on the Internet.

Track Your List

Now you know how to use the Stocks to Watch worksheet. It's your built-in filter that keeps your money away from hot tips and cold losses. Quite simply, whenever you encounter an investment idea, compare it to the companies on your list. If the new idea is better, strike one of the existing companies and add the new one. This process keeps your list of ideas streamlined and ready for action when opportunity presents itself.

Now let's look at three techniques you should use to track your list. Always compare competitors, ask why, and keep the information current.

Compare Competitors

There's no better way to judge a company than by looking at its closest competitors. When I first decided to buy Gateway 2000, I did so because I thought it was competing well against IBM, Compaq, and Dell. I didn't compare it to Ford or MCI, and I didn't choose it in a vacuum. It's critical to know where your investments stack up in their industries.

When you invest in a company, you want it to be the best of breed. You don't want just any computer company, you want IBM in the 1970s and Microsoft in the 1980s. You don't want just any milkshake stand, you want McDonald's in the

1960s. The way you find the best of breed is by looking among competitors.

If you're interested in McDonald's, conduct research on Wendy's. If you want Wal-Mart, don't forget to look at Kmart. Your favorite breakfast cereal might be from Kellogg, but don't invest in the company until you've read up on General Mills. If everybody's raving about Barnes & Noble, take a peek at Borders Group. Compare profit margins. Who keeps more of every dollar they sell? If the winner has been consistent, that's a good sign. If one company keeps its head above the rest year after year, that's the one you want to buy.

How do the ratios compare? You might pay a lot more for each dollar of sales at one company than at another. You might find that one company's management owns half of all the stock while another company's management doesn't invest a dime in their own company. Maybe one company's return on equity is twice that of its nearest competitor. Perhaps every company in an industry carries a lot of debt, except for one little gem. Does that little gem shine in other areas as well? If so, you might have found a new entry for your worksheet.

Find the Best of Breed

Sometimes you'll find a better option than the company first grabbing your attention.

Occasionally, you'll reach a stalemate and decide to split your money between two companies. Owning more than one company from the same industry is an especially good technique if it means you own the entire industry. For instance, investors buying shares of both Microsoft and Netscape will benefit no matter which Web browser people buy. Those companies make the only two browsers worth using. If somebody is going to browse the Web, they're going to use either Microsoft Internet Explorer or Netscape Navigator. Of course, much more would need to go into this investment decision, but as Web browser companies go they're the only two worth considering.

If you don't already know a company's prime competitors, you'll find them quickly as you conduct research. Articles will mention them. Sometimes you'll find competitors mentioned in annual reports or quarterly statements. If worse comes to worst, you can always call a company's investor-relations department and ask who the competitors are. If they hesitate, tell them you're organizing a boycott against all industry players except them and that you need a list of targets. That should get you some info.

Ask Why

As an investor, always question why a company's numbers are the way they are. Why is cash flow so low right now when it's been high in prior years? Perhaps you'll find in reading further into the annual report that the company is expanding overseas and has decided to create very flexible payment terms to attract new customers. If there's enough cash on hand to stay afloat while the new customers discover the company, the low cash flow is fine for a while.

Asking why is central to every investment decision. Growth investors want to know why a company is growing so quickly. They use that information to decide if the reason will maintain that growth in the future. Value investors always want to know why a company's price is depressed. If it's for a reason that won't go away anytime soon, nobody should invest. If it's for a reason that is disappearing, now might be the time to get in before the price rebounds to its former glory.

Beyond a general understanding of your companies—which you should always possess—you need to exercise a lot of per-

sonal judgment when investing. If a company appears good in every regard on your worksheet except for one, say five-year earnings gain, you need to know why that earnings gain has lagged and whether it's an acceptable explanation. Only you can answer such questions for your portfolio. These measurements aren't foolproof. There are millions of children with poor grades who achieve spectacular success in life. There is probably a better chance of finding successful people among the high-grade earners, but that doesn't mean we should brush off the low-grade earners. It works the same with stocks. For the most part, you should stick with those that shine on your worksheet. However, in some cases your better judgment will lead you to overrule the worksheet's verdict. Every investment rule gets broken from time to time.

Having written that, I must underscore the need to be prudent. Remember O'Shaughnessy's conclusions after studying the history of the stock market. Certain stories play out again and again and again. Your worksheet uses proven stock measurements. If you are going to overrule what they say about a company, you'd better have a darned good reason for doing so and be able to explain it in a heartbeat. That's why this section instructs you to ask why. In asking why, you'll find the answers you need to make wise decisions. There's a story behind all those numbers. Make sure you've read it.

Store Company Information in Folders

Once you've decided to add a company to your worksheet, start a folder for it. Place in the folder all the research material you used to convince yourself that the company is worthwhile. Your folders will contain annual reports, financial statements, photocopied pages from *Value Line* and *Standard & Poor's*, printouts from the Internet, notes to yourself, clipped magazine articles and newspaper stories, and maybe even a photo of you in front of corporate headquarters or using the  company product. My friends and I did that with Gateway 2000 computer boxes. In my picture I stood surrounded by cow-spotted boxes holding a handful of money. That was my company, after all. I was proud to be part of it.

Whenever you run across additional information about your companies, add it to their folders. Over time you'll build your own investment-research center. By opening your file cabinet and flipping through the alphabetized folders, you can remind yourself of why you like the companies on your list.

Keep the Information Current

Always keep your worksheet current. Update the information on it at least every quarter. It doesn't take long to do so, and the small effort will reveal valuable trends. There's a tendency to research a company one time and then rely on the results of that research for months, even years. Bad idea. Some of the best investments come about by finding good companies and then watching them for the right opportunity. If a company is perfect in all regard but stock price and that price drops by 50 percent just when sales are beginning to increase, you better start buying.

Similarly, good companies can go bad. Just because a company was good enough to make your list a year ago doesn't automatically mean it gets to stay there. This isn't a tenured membership. Your companies need to undergo constant scrutiny and comparison to eager wannabes. You can't make fair comparisons unless you have current information.

You found the information once and should have a file folder for every company on your worksheet. To refresh the info, make a quarterly trip back to your library or log on to the Internet and gather the information again. Refreshing your worksheet goes faster than finding the information the first time.

Use Your Reasons and Limits Worksheet

Once you've got a list of solid companies to work with, it's time to begin homing in on the select few you'll actually invest in. Here's where you need to make value and growth distinctions. Chances are good that you'll have some companies on your list that are beaten down in price, others that are pushing new highs and record earnings. My list always breaks down that way. My experience has never produced a list of growth companies only or a list of value companies only. I suppose if I insisted on a pure list, I could set out to find companies of one type or the other, but the natural tendency produces a mix.

By now you know that it's important to treat value investments differently than you treat growth investments. One of the most common differences is the way you should view the P/E ratio. In a high-flying growth stock, you'll pay less attention to P/E and more attention to earnings and relative strength. In a recovering value stock, you'll pay a lot of attention to P/E and price-to-book while accepting poor earnings and—by definition—a weak relative strength.

At first it bothered me to have both value and growth companies on my list. I continually read that the best investors are consistent in all markets. Pure momentum investors like Gary Pilgrim continue watching earnings and sales regardless of the market's preferences. He told me that switching strategies would unglue his entire operation. Strict value investors would say the same thing about switching from their strategy. So why is it that I, a mere part-timer working from my kitchen table, could stand a chance playing both sides of the coin?

Because the stocks to watch worksheet doesn't cater to one side over the other. It isn't a pure growth play or a pure value play, and no strict investor from either discipline would find the sheet useful. It's a 30,000-foot view of the land, allowing you to see different colored fields but few of the plants growing there. Gary Pilgrim, William O'Neil, Benjamin Graham, and Warren Buffett are flying crop dusters compared to our airliner. They see in much more detail and much faster the components of companies they're looking for. If they suddenly switched to look for something completely different, they'd be lost in the detailed information.

We Have a 30,000-foot View of the Investment Landscape

We, on the other hand, aren't surrounded by as much detail. It's relatively simple to look at a company's major characteristics and decide whether it's a growth or value bet. Once we've determined that, it's another simple task to focus on key measures appropriate to that type of company. That's what you're about to do with the reasons and limits worksheet, which I affectionately dub the R&L. It forces you to define reasons you're interested in a company and what would cause you to lose interest. The R&L worksheet is invaluable when emotions start kicking in and—surprise, surprise—the market really does begin fluctuating just like everybody said it would. It doesn't just happen to other people, it happens to you too.

So the stocks to watch worksheet is your consistency. It records the same measurements for every company. You'll always look at those measurements to identify a company as either a growth or value investment. Once that's complete, you'll focus on certain measurements to select the best growth companies and the best value companies from your list.

In this section I'll give a quick recap of discerning growth from value, then explain how to use your R&L worksheet.

Discerning Growth from Value

You should be familiar with these characterizations by now. Growth companies are those that are growing sales and earnings every year. Their stock prices are rising, their profit margins are big, and their expectations are high. Value companies are trading at low prices. The low prices are usually the result of tough times at the company but occasionally just because the market's a weird place. Preferably, you buy a value stock just when it has fixed its troubles and begins to profit again, or just before the market discovers its discount price.

Grow, Grow, Grow!

Often, the best growth investments are smaller companies. Of particular importance in evaluating growth companies are a high earnings record, high relative strength, and low price-to-sales ratios. Remember that O'Shaughnessy found price-to-sales a great measure to mix with traditional growth yardsticks because it keeps growth investors from getting too carried away with emotion and paying too much for a stock. Other growth investors, such as O'Neil, insist on ignoring measures of valuation completely.

The best value plays are usually large companies. Not always, but most of the time. Large companies don't change much, and that makes them prime candidates for bargain pricing. They're not going anywhere, after all, so they have no choice but to recover from whatever trouble they're in. These are the Chryslers and IBMs of the market. For such companies, traditional value measures will be your focus. Those are dividend yield, P/E, price-to-book, and price-to-sales.

It's simple to look at your stocks to watch worksheet and say, "Hmm, I see IBM, AT&T, Cisco Systems, and ATC Communications on here. I'd call IBM and AT&T value investments. Cisco and ATC are both growing like crazy, I guess they're growth investments." Yep, that's about as sophisticated as it gets.

Here's a cheat sheet of what measurements you should pay particular attention to for the different types of stocks:

All Stocks	Growth Stocks	Value Stocks
Net Profit Margin	Earnings	Price-to-Earnings
Debt	Relative Strength	Dividend Yield
Cash Flow	Sales	Price-to-Book
Price-to-Sales		Price-to-Cash Flow

How to Use the Reasons and Limits Worksheet

It's time to specify exactly why you like the company you're about to invest in and what would cause you to stop liking it. I got the idea for this worksheet from Peter Lynch, who uses what he calls the two-minute drill to identify company strengths and weaknesses. You can review the drill on page 66.

The worksheet is a snap to use. Photocopy it dozens of times because you'll need a copy for each stock in your portfolio. I recommend starting a separate folder for your portfolio information. In it you'll keep statements from your broker and R&L worksheets for each company. Your worksheet is in the back of the book. I explain each section of it below.

Growth or Value

Simply circle which type of investment this is, growth or value. You'd be surprised at the number of people you just surpassed. Differentiating between growth and value investments is a major step in keeping your expectations reasonable. It also helps make decisions later when things start getting hairy.

Company Strengths

Here you write in what attracts you to this company. Does it own a patent that nobody else can touch? Is it opening 500 new stores in Japan? Perhaps it just signed service contracts with every Dow company.

Company Challenges

Write in what you perceive as the major challenges facing this company. By the way, I'm not trying to be politically correct by calling them company challenges instead of company weak-

Ready to Meet Challenges?

nesses. Most of what faces a good company are outside pressures, things like fierce competitors, rising supply prices, and changing demographics. These are not weaknesses of the company; they're challenges for the company to meet. Hopefully, you won't be investing in companies that have excessive internal weaknesses. Your list is supposed to contain the industry-leading, best-of-breed profit machines. Thus, all mamby-pamby political correctness aside, you should be dealing with companies that have challenges instead of weaknesses.

Even the best companies face hurdles in their paths. As an investor, you want to be well apprised of such hurdles so you can see if they get bigger or if the company clears them with ease.

Why to Buy

Summarize why you're buying this stock. Presumably it's because you think the strengths are powerful enough to meet the challenges. To help jog your thoughts, I've included some common buy reasons for you to circle. Also write in any special developments in the world that you think will favor the company's industry, or move the company's product, or otherwise help matters.

Occasionally, I'll write in a measurement target in this section of the R&L worksheet. For instance, if I really like everything about a company but I think it's selling a bit too high at the moment, I'll pencil in all the things I like and conclude this section with a price target. If the stock hits that price, I buy. You can do this with ratios too, which can trigger a buy if either of the numbers involved moves in the right direction. If you want to invest in a company when it reaches a price-to-sales ratio of 1.5 instead of its current 2.0, a falling price or rising sale will bring you closer to your target.

Why to Sell

Certainly just as important as why you buy a stock is what will cause you to sell it. I've included some common sell reasons for you to circle. The most common reason to sell is that the stock reaches a price target. If you bought Mister Magazine at

$8.50, you might decide in advance that it has potential to double. So you write in a sell point at $17. When it reaches $17, you might reevaluate. Perhaps it's an even better company than when you bought it, or maybe it really has run its course. If in doubt, you could sell half your position and wait to see what happens.

Be careful of getting too price-centric in this section. Remember that all stock measurements change constantly, not just price. If the price doubles but the earnings triple, why in the world would you sell? I like to set sell points with ratios, just as I discussed in the why to buy section. Instead of saying you'll sell Mister Magazine at $17, say you'll sell it when the price-to-sales reaches twice its current measure or its P/E exceeds its growth rate. Combining factors provides you with a more complete picture. Remember, it's your company. You should know everything that's going on, not just the price of the stock.

Susan Byrne, manager of Westwood Equity mutual fund, shared her sell strategy in *Louis Rukeyser's Mutual Funds*: "We sell, basically, for two reasons: the stock reaches its price objective (which we target as [the P/E] being in excess of the company's growth rate) or something changes at the company that we don't really understand. We also will sell if we buy a stock and it goes down 15 percent on us in the first month; it's better to admit the error real fast." It's worth paying attention to Byrne. At the end of 1996, Westwood Equity returned an average 17 percent a year for the previous five years, 21 percent for the previous three years, and almost 27 percent in 1996. That's a market-beating performance in each time period. Notice that she doesn't go on price alone. She waits to sell when the P/E exceeds the growth rate.

There's More to a Stock Than Its Price

Sometimes you'll want to write in reasons to sell that aren't measured on your worksheet. I know a guy who bought Microsoft because he thought they were going to acquire Intuit, his favorite financial software company. The deal fell through. Looking back, he shouldn't have sold Microsoft because the company has done quite well without Intuit. But he bought the stock for a reason that never materialized, and he wanted to move his money to a company that did meet his reasons for buying. He might have written on his sheet, "Sell if the Intuit deal doesn't go through. Move all proceeds to Intuit stock."

Other common reasons to sell that don't involve measurements are the failure of medical upstarts to get approval for a new drug or piece of equipment, the departure of key management, and a sudden spate of lawsuits. You won't always know about these possibilities, but sometimes you'll read about them in your research. Pencil them in. It's good to be aware of such potholes in the path.

Buy Your Stocks

The big moment has arrived. First you learned to walk, then drink from a cup with no safety top, then speak in complete sentences, then drive a car, then ditch classes, and now you're about to buy your first shares of stock. Darwin would be so proud of you. In our Realm of Riches metaphor, you're about to hire your first henchman to send out of the fortress with money from your coffers to find fabulous wealth. You've researched his credentials and are convinced of his merits. All that remains is funding him and sending him on his way.

Choose a Market or Limit Order

You read about different types of stock orders on page 132. A market order buys at the current price, and a limit order buys at a price you specify. I almost always use limit orders because stocks bounce around so much that I can take advantage of that volatility to save a few bucks. In many cases you can figure out the exact price at which you want to buy, place a good-till-canceled limit order, and forget about it. If and when the stock hits your target, your broker will buy it and send you a statement. This technique has worked wonders for me. Indulge me a moment as I tell the story of buying Ericsson lower than almost everybody.

Ericsson Phones Were Everywhere

It was January 1996 and I'd been watching Ericsson a long time. The company is based in Sweden and competes against the likes of Nokia and Motorola. Ericsson is a leader in its field, having installed more telephone-switching systems worldwide than any other company and consistently producing the coolest little cell phones you've ever seen. Digital ones, too. I see Ericsson phones at the beach, in theaters, around malls, and in hundreds of briefcases. I see Ericsson phones in BMWs, Mercedes, Cadillacs, and Lexus coupes all around Hollywood. I figured that if I couldn't own one of those cars, I could at least own shares in the company that makes the phones in them. So that's what I did. I researched Ericsson, became convinced of its merits, and placed a GTC limit order to buy at $17.50 a share. It was trading at $23 at the time. Then I forgot about it. Two months later I received a statement saying that I'd picked up my specified number of shares at the target price plus the modest commission.

I didn't fully appreciate the value of that purchase until eight months later when I was in Manhattan talking to a hedge-fund manager who also liked Ericsson. He had a Bloomberg terminal handy and called up the price history of Ericsson. He asked what price I'd purchased the stock at. I told him $17.50. Then he laughed and pointed at the screen. There was a single thin line dropping down from the price history to a low of $17.25. The stock spiked down to my buy price in a single moment on that one day and I scooped up the shares. By the end of the week the stock had risen $2 already. A year after I purchased the stock, Ericsson traded around $34 a share. That's a 94 percent return in one year.

None of this is a tribute to any ingenious stock picking on my part. It's a tribute to the value of GTC limit orders. I love them. I could have placed a market order for Ericsson when I first decided to buy it. I would have invested at $23 per share. It would have still been a good investment, returning 48 percent in one year. But by simply deciding on a target price, typing it into the telephone, and forgetting about it, I saved $5.50 per share. Limit orders are a great way to circumvent your emotions.

Choose a Price,
Place the Order

Rather than get taken by the market's gyrations, you simply decide in a calm state of mind the price at which you want to invest. Then you instruct your discount broker to buy a certain number of shares at that price. If the stock never reaches the price, you don't buy. There are plenty of opportunities out there. If one gets away, move on to the next one. A rather terse woman I know has this to say about life: "Never chase a man, a bus, or a stock. There will be another one along in five minutes." The man I don't know about, and bus availability varies from city to city, but she's right about the stock. There are so many good ones day after day that there's never a reason to be upset about an opportunity lost. It's better to lose an opportunity than to lose money. So decide in advance what price is attractive to you and spell it out on a limit order.

Should you ever use market orders? Sure. There are times when you stumble on something that you think is so hot that it's not coming down for years. A limit order specifying a lower price than the current one might miss the chance to buy this rising star. I would caution you about jumping on something instanta-neously, though. I've discovered that what's a good buy today is usually still a good buy next week. The market moves around, but not as quickly as you might think. Emotions move a lot faster than the market. They also move faster than intelligent thoughts. So give the rational part of your brain time to catch up to your excited, frothy part. Never forget the power of clear thinking, pre-determined prices, and the limit order.

Make Gradual Purchases

From your reading of the master investors and the history of the stock market, you've come to see the importance of reacting intelligently to the market's moves. That means buying more of a good company on sale, and more of a good company that's on a roll. But you can never be absolutely sure you're investing in a company whose stock will perform well. That being the case, I recommend putting only a portion of your money into a stock you're considering. If it drops in price, you can reassess whether to move your remaining money in at the discount or steer clear until you're truly convinced that the stock has bottomed out and is on its way back up. O'Neil would shudder at that advice, but it has been a splendid technique for me. Good stocks drop in price frequently, and speculation bids the price of crummy stocks high on a regular basis. Because it's an unreasonable force causing such gyrations, you can't think your way through it. You can improve your odds by investing in the best companies out there, but you can't know what the unreasonable market will do.

So if Mister Magazine has you salivating over its awesome future and you've got $5,000 to invest, put only $2,500 in at first. If you happened to time it just wrong and the stock drops 50 percent with no significant changes in the company's fundamentals, move the remaining $2,500 in. Instead of just recouping your losses when the stock recovers, you'll double the value of your second $2,500.

Buy That Baby!

You've decided on your killer stock—certainly a hundred-bagger by anyone's reckoning—and you've chosen either a market or limit order. All that remains is contacting your broker. Because you've read this book and examined all the fine brokerage choices in Chapter 5, you probably have an account with a discount broker. Good for you!

Contact your broker by phone, computer, or in person. Specify your order and sit back a second. Soak it up. You've just become a business owner if you placed a market order, and you'll soon be a business owner if you placed a limit order and the stock hits your price. The next time you're in Omaha, stop by Berkshire Hathaway to swap a few stories with Warren Buffett. The two of you are in the same business now.

When the Market's Up, Down, and All Around

Flip forward a few pages in your calendar from that halcyon day of your first stock purchase. "Egads," you're thinking, "how did I ever let that Kelly guy talk me into this mess? My hundred-bagger is a minus twobagger and the headlines are getting worse." Yes, friend, I know what it's like to see that happen. The

Realm of Riches is a tough place. A lot of your henchmen will never come back. Those that do come back to the fortress are sometimes pretty beaten up. Others, like Sir Microsoft and Sir Cisco, never seem to have a scratch on their armor. Sir IBM has had a few long melees in recent years, but he's one determined fellow and swings a heavy sword. I funded him at his darkest hour and now he's standing strong again, bringing hordes of money back to the coffers in my fortress. Sir Apple, on the other hand, is drunk or something. Sir Netscape is facing the fight of his life against the ever glorious Sir Microsoft. What a saga.

But what do you care about all those henchmen? You're much more concerned about the fellows you hired to seek riches, some of whom are doing well but some of whom are not. That's what we'll explore in this section: volatility. The market rises and falls, your stocks rise and fall, your emotions rise and fall. It's time to get a handle on all of this.

Ignore the Gurus

Whatever your inclination, don't spend any time listening to so-called market gurus. They're also called experts, analysts, forecasters, pundits, and soothsayers. By and large they don't know anything more than what you and I know. Always keep in mind the market forecast of J. P. Morgan, "It will fluctuate." That's about all there is to say, and it's never wrong.

Just in case you are tempted to listen to the experts about the overall direction of the market, know that Warren Buffett never pays attention to the market. He looks at individual companies only. Ben Graham said that Mister Market is like a manic depressive. Sometimes he's happy and sometimes he's sad, and it's anyone's guess as to what he'll be next month or next year. Did you catch that last part? It's *anyone's* guess. The only difference between your guess and the guess of a guru is that you don't get paid for yours.

The Gurus Aren't as Important as They'd Have You Believe

You've probably heard about the major pundits. There's Elaine Garzarelli, who correctly predicted the crash of 1987. Her days in the sun ended in 1996, when she told people to get out of the market after a 400-point Dow slide—just as it started to rise again. There's Michael Metz, the chief investment strategist for Oppenheimer and Company, who warned investors of a stock market backslide in early 1995. The market gained 37.5 percent that year. So he repeated his warning in 1996. The market gained 23 percent. There's Ken and Daria Dolan, America's favorite financial couple, who said, "By the end of 1995, mutual funds will be the most despised investments." The average stock mutual fund gained 31 percent in 1995. There's Barton Biggs, Morgan Stanley's global strategist, who told everyone at the end of 1995 that a cyclical bear market would wipe us out and that aggressive mutual funds would be the worst investments. The average stock mutual fund gained 19.5 percent in 1996.

Are you convinced that your guess is as good as theirs? The worst thing that could happen is that you'd be wrong. Heck, that seems to be a requirement among gurus these days.

Forecasting or Marketing?

The truth, of course, is that none of the forecasts coming from newsletter writers and other guru types are intended to make you money. They're intended to sell a product. Nothing gets attention better than a panic-inducing outlook. If you're in the business of calling the market, it's always safer to call for it to crash than to soar. Here's why: if you call for it to crash and it doesn't, nobody is very upset because they made money when you said they wouldn't. But if you call for the market to soar and instead it crashes, watch out. Everybody who listened to you lost money because of your call, and they'll be slow to forget it.

Bear Markets Are the Safest Call

Following Elaine Garzarelli's July 23, 1996, sell alert, the *New York Times* wrote, "The most shrill voices often belong to people not backed by a major institution. Some attract attention by staking out extreme positions and by then being the quickest and the loudest to say they were right. And the prospect of a bear market is particularly enticing to them because it offers a once-in-a-market-cycle opportunity to seal their fortune as market gurus.

A well-timed market call could mean huge rewards as a highly paid investment strategist, a sought-after portfolio manager, or a popular newsletter writer."

Treat almost all market forecasts as infomercials. There's a lot of material there and some of it might be useful to you, but it's there to move a product. Your bottom line is never as important to the forecaster as her bottom line. The major institutions like Morgan Stanley, Oppenheimer, and Merrill Lynch are selling products as well. They don't sell newsletters, but they sell managed accounts. If one of their analysts scares the daylights out of everybody, people might want to open accounts there, where they incorrectly assume they'll be taken care of through the impending disaster.

We Could All Be Gurus

Beware the Shrill Voices

If you think about it, somebody's always going to be right. On any given day of the year, somebody is calling for the market to rise like a star and some other clown is calling for it to fall like a rock. One of them is going to be right eventually and when he is, it'll be printed on the outside of envelopes and at the top of marketing fliers. All that really happened is that the guru won a coin toss. It could have just as easily been the other guy.

Why listen to gurus? Your guess is as good as theirs. You knew going into the market that it has its good days and bad, good years and bad; indeed, it has good decades and bad. If you know your time frame and have a clear target in mind for each of your investments, you'll be fine. Long-term money can ride out fluctuations, and short-term money should be protected. That's all anybody can ever know.

You Knew This Was Coming, So Why Worry?

From all your reading to this point, you should be well aware that the market fluctuates. Always, friend. It won't stop because your money has finally arrived there. In fact, from your vantage point it will start fluctuating more than ever. It won't, of course, but somehow the numbers mean more when it's your money on the line.

Don't worry about it. Money you invest in stocks shouldn't be

money you need for groceries next month or
college tuition next year. If you define your
goals clearly and invest by those goals, you're
geared for whatever comes. The money you do
need for groceries is safely deposited in a bank
account. The money you do need for college
tuition next year might also be in a bank
account or perhaps a conservative mutual fund.
The money you have earmarked for long-term
goals such as retirement or a new home can

**Don't Invest Money
You Need for
Groceries**

withstand any short-term market fluctuations. It's a science. The
more time you have, the more risk you can take. The less time you
have, the less risk you can take.

If you still freak out when the market dips—or the market does
fine but your holdings dip—revisit page 123, where I discuss goal
planning and deciding on an appropriate risk level for you.

Review Your Reasons and Limits

At some point you're going to want to reevaluate your holdings. The hardest time to do so is when something serious has happened. That's not always a huge drop, by the way. Sometimes it's
a huge gain where your stock has pushed beyond your wildest
dreams. It's hard to make rational decisions when you've tripled
your money and want so badly to believe it'll happen several more
times. It might, but as with every "might" statement, it might not.

That's where your R&L worksheet comes into play. You
filled it out before you even owned the stock, so your emotions
were at a fairly even level. You were interested in the stock, but
you just completed thorough research and were making an objective decision. Now you own the thing, and it's
up, down, and all around. What should you
do?

Look at that R&L sheet. Pull out your
portfolio folder and scrutinize your every
scribble about this company. Did it reach your
price target, or one of your ratio targets? If so,
has anything changed to give you reason to
believe the stock still has legs?

If the stock is falling, has anything funda-

**Review Your R&L
Worksheet**

mental changed at the company? It might be the same company you first invested in, but at a cheaper price. Sometimes that's all it means when a stock drops in price. After checking over your R&L, it's time to follow the advice in the next section.

Reverse Your Emotions

Remember that Benjamin Graham said nobody ever knows what the market will do, but we can react intelligently to what it does do. Aha. If you're at a point where your investment has fallen into the mud, the words of Ben Graham are much more than ink on paper. They're good guidance indeed.

In "Where the Masters Agree" (page 87), I summarize the major agreements of our six master investors. They say to buy more of what's working and to take advantage of price dips. That seems to mean that no matter what's happening, you should buy more. That's only true regarding price. Are you starting to get the picture? Price is not really the most important thing. It seems to be and it's eventually the bottom line, but in the course of stock ownership there are a lot of things more important. For instance, Warren Buffett keeps an eye on profit margins and return on equity. If the company remains strong and keeps doing everything right, the market will eventually catch on and the price will rise.

You're beginning to see why it's so important to research your companies thoroughly and to have a clear understanding on your R&L sheet for why you invested. Such grounding enables you to see if the company is still as good, perhaps better, or worse than when you first invested.

If the price is rising and everything you liked about the company still persists, such as strong earnings, high margins, low debt, and steady cash flow, then you might decide to invest more. The market is finally recognizing what a great company you're invested in and people are beginning to buy. As William O'Neil recommends, you should move more money into that winner. Business owners buy more of what's working.

If the price is falling and everything you liked about the company still persists, you just stumbled onto a great company at a bargain price. It's incidental that you happen to already own shares purchased at a higher price; you still have the chance to buy a great company on sale. Think of owning property. Say you bought a 10-acre parcel at $5,000 an acre because of its beautiful meadows and stream. You build your dream home there. Two years later, another 10-acre parcel adjacent to yours goes on sale for only $2,000 an acre. It contains different parts of the same beautiful meadows and a different section of the same stream. Would you react by selling the land and home you already own? Of course not! It's still beautiful. Instead, you'd snap up the adjacent lot because of its identical beauty and

You Don't Sell Your Home When the Price Drops—Why Sell Your Stocks?

the fact that it's selling at 60 percent less than what you paid for the first parcel. That, in a sense, is exactly how you should react when a perfectly solid company drops in price without any fundamental reason for doing so.

React intelligently to the market. It freaks out from time to time, but you don't need to. If the market goes haywire and drops the price of your company for no reason, smile coolly and buy more shares. If the market goes haywire and drives the price of your stock through the clouds, buy more on the way up.

If you bought quality companies after conducting thorough research, you have little to fear in the markets. You will prosper over time. The market will rise and fall, gurus will claim to know where it's going and when, you will hold winners and losers, and by reacting intelligently to all this cacophony your profits will mount. Your henchmen will return to the fortress with more money than you spent to fund their excursions into the Realm of Riches.

Sell Your Stocks

Alas, the day will come when it's time to part with your stocks. You'll receive reports from the Realm about the successes and hardships of your henchmen. One day you'll decide to give one or two or all of them a rest. You'll sell your shares and place your profits in a tidy money-market account until the next happy henchmen come along.

Let's go over a few rules of selling, shall we?

Ignore Rumors and Popular Opinion

I've probably convinced you of the need to rely on yourself for decisions. Just in case, however, I must reiterate this point. Only you fully understand your goals and tolerance for risk. Nobody cares more about your money than you do. You worked hard for it, you searched the world for companies that meet your requirements, you became an owner of those companies, and you should count on yourself alone for the right time to sell.

Mailroom McGillicuddy

It's not always easy to stand alone. Imagine this common scenario. You go to work on an average day in November 1994, and there's big news in the hallway. Mark McGillicuddy in the mailroom read that the Pentium chip from Intel is defective. Imagine that! An Intel microprocessor that can't do math. He says, and is met by darkly nodding heads all around, that the company's days are over. Motorola is licking its chops over the opportunity. Cyrix and AMD are jumping for joy too. "Well," McGillicuddy sighs, "it's a worn story in American business. You just can't stay at the top of your game forever. Intel had it coming. I sold all my shares this morning. You guys better do the same." The hallway clears and you hear speaker phones come to life in every direction. There you stand, a previously proud owner of 300 shares of Intel stock. What do you do?

The first thing to do is confirm that McGillicuddy read the darned paper accurately. You'd be surprised at the number of times this simple step takes care of the problem. In so many cases the information is nothing more than a rumor. On the Intel Pentium fiasco, it turns out that McGillicuddy is correct. The first Pentiums did produce math errors in a few cases, and the problem was reported in November 1994.

Rather than join your colleagues at the speaker phones, you'd be a much happier investor if you paused to think back in your mind to that trusty R&L sheet. Can you remember what you wrote on it? Probably not. In that case, forget about it. That's right, just forget about the current situation all day long. When you go home that night, pull out your R&L and move on to the next section.

Rely on Your Reasons and Limits

With a copy of the newspaper in one hand and your Intel R&L sheet in the other, you can arrive at a prudent decision. The McGillicuddys of the world won't be offering their opinions, there won't be any speaker-phone beeps cluttering your thoughts, and you'll be oblivious to the impression that everybody but you has flown the coop just before the fox breaks in. And it is just an impression, by the way. Rarely is the entire world following the path of your acquaintances, but because your acquaintances form your little view of the world, it often appears that way. React intelligently, friend. Read that R&L sheet.

In your "Why to Sell" section, do you see anything about a Pentium math error? Of course not. Nobody saw that coming. Do you think for a moment that Intel, the biggest name in micro-processors, will crumble from the blow? Again, of course not. This is business, after all. Mistakes are inevitable. Restaurants deal with food poi-soning, amusement parks with guest injuries, automobile manufacturers with faulty engines, and semiconductor companies with math errors. All companies expect trouble along the way, and all are equipped to deal with it. Looking over your R&L, have any of Intel's strengths disappeared? None, with the pos-sible exception of the public's strong faith in its products. That chink in the armor—if it's a chink at all—will repair easily.

All Companies Face Trouble at Some Point

We now have the benefit of hindsight since that fateful bad Pentium day in November 1994. After its 4-point drop to around $29 in December, Intel stock rebounded nicely. By early Feb-ruary it was up to $36. By March it was still climbing at $42, and in July it hit $78. Thanks for the hot tip, McGillicuddy. At the end of 1996, Intel traded for $131. Had you followed your R&L, which would have revealed the fact that a Pentium math error did not change the core of Intel, you could have withstood the short-term volatility and done just fine. Once your R&L revealed that Intel was the same solid company that it was before the Pentium error, you might have chosen to invest more money at the tem-porarily low price. Let's see, 200 additional shares at $29 would have cost you $5,800 plus $20 commission. Seven months later, it would have been worth $15,600. At the end of 1996, it would have been worth $26,200. McGillicuddy would probably be convinced of the company's merits by then and resume investing.

Now, there will be times when you pull out your handy R&L and notice that one of your sell conditions has been met, or one of the company's key strengths has genuinely disappeared. If nothing has come along to balance out the change, sell. The R&L sheet is there to help you navigate difficult decisions in times of emotion. If it says to hold your stock, hold. If it says to sell your stock, sell. Unless new information is available that changes the conclusions you drew on the R&L sheet, pay attention to what you wrote there.

Review Your Stocks to Watch

Your R&L sheet is a good way to keep an eye on individual stocks. But it's all relative. Don't forget your stocks to watch worksheet. It's called that for a reason, namely, because you should watch those stocks.

Before you decide to sell, glance over your stocks to watch. Is there a better company available than the one you're currently holding? Often, that quick question combined with clear signals from your R&L sheet make the decision a breeze. For instance, if two of your R&L sheet's reasons to sell have been met in a company you own *and* a company you've been wanting to own just dropped 20 percent in price, sell the current holding and buy the stock to watch at a 20 percent discount. Sometimes, one of your stocks to watch will present such an outstanding opportunity that you'll sell the least attractive of your current holdings just to take advantage of the opportunity. That's a legitimate strategy. Just as the companies on your stocks to watch worksheet must withstand constant comparison to new stocks you encounter, so must your portfolio withstand constant comparison to your stocks to watch. It's survival of the fittest, and you want to own the best companies around.

Compare Your Current Holdings to Your Stocks to Watch

Even if there are no outstanding candidates on your stocks to watch worksheet, you might still elect to sell one of your current holdings. Often, a money-market account is a better place than certain stocks. But don't forget to take a look at your stocks to watch. Your decision might just be made for you.

Remember that you're managing a portfolio. In the Realm of Riches, you oversee a fortress of Dow companies. You also manage a team of henchmen who venture into the realm funded by money from your coffers. Those henchmen come from a select roster, your stocks to watch list. Don't make decisions in a vacuum. Know how every move will affect your little piece of the Realm. Sell one of your current holdings if a better one surfaces from your stocks to watch worksheet. Sell one of them if it reaches a predetermined reason to sell. If a stock drops dramatically but it is still a quality company, buy more shares or at least hold on to what you already own. That is, unless one of your stocks to watch is more deserving. In that case, move the money to the more deserving stock. See how it works? Everything is interwoven.

Choose a Market or Limit Order

You can place either a market order to sell at the current price or a limit order to sell at a price you specify. The same reasons I like limit orders for buying stock apply to selling stock as well. Even if the market has driven your stock to tremendous highs, a limit order placed just $1 higher usually comes through. If I think the stock is out of steam, I still like to tack on a little extra to cover commissions. Sometimes the stock backs off for a few days, but it usually creeps up to my target.

If you don't care about a few extra bucks and you just want to sell right away, place a market order. The beauty of an immediate sell is that you're not in limbo for an unspecified time period, unsure whether you've got cash in your account or will be waiting three months.

Make Gradual Sells

As with buying stock, I prefer to make gradual sells. The market is just as unpredictable when it comes to choosing the right time to sell as it is when choosing the right time to buy. If you move everything out because you're afraid of losing it all, how will you feel if the stock recovers to your buy price and then pushes beyond? If the stock doubles after you buy it and you sell everything, how will you feel when it becomes one of the legendary tenbaggers? In both cases you'll feel terrible. I know because I've been there. Gradual moves into and out of positions take some of the pressure off because everything doesn't need to happen just right for you to make money. Things can be a little fuzzy on the buy and sell. As long as you're making gradual moves, you'll be fine.

Combining gradual moves with limit orders is a good way to reduce investment stress. Let's say you own 200 shares of Mister Magazine. A couple of the R&L sheet's reasons to sell have been met, but the company has just opened a new distribution center that you didn't know about when you first bought. You're not sure if that's enough reason to hold on. The stock is trading for $30—three times what you paid for it. You feel comfortable taking that kind of profit now, but something about that new distribution center has you thinking the stock will go higher still.

If you sell nothing, you're going to blow a vessel if Mister Magazine drops to $12 a share. If you sell everything, you're going to blow a vessel if it rises to $40 a share, or even $32. So you compromise on both the sell price and the amount you're going to sell. You place a good till canceled limit order to sell 100 shares at $32. Then you go hiking, or golfing, or swimming, or take a run. Three weeks later while you're not paying any attention, Mister Magazine hits $32 and your broker sells 100 shares. Now, no matter where the stock goes, you can take comfort in your interim profits. If the price begins to drop, you will consider selling the remaining shares or buying additional shares with the money you just made at $32. If the price rises, you'll make even more profit on your remaining shares.

Place the Order, Then Blow Off Some Steam

Sell That Baby!

You've decided to sell some of your stock. Simply pick up

the phone, log onto the computer, or walk into your local brokerage branch and place the order. A market order will go
through that day with a confirmation statement mailed to you
immediately. A limit order will go through whenever your target
price is reached. You'll know about it when the confirmation
statement shows up in your mailbox.

Track Your Performance

The lord or lady of every fortress expects reports from the
field now and then. Most of your reports will be in the form of
periodic market updates, stock quotes, and statements from your
discount broker. In addition to those, however, you must track
your performance to find areas to improve.

I like to keep tabs on every stock to watch. If you followed
the advice from earlier in this chapter, that means you'll follow
around twenty stocks. You can do that in your spare time. I
track their prices from the time they make it on my stocks to
watch worksheet until they exit. If they exit at the same time I
sell them from my portfolio, I still track their prices for another
month or two just to see what happened to their prices after
I sold.

From there you're going to look at two
components of your performance. The first is
your overall portfolio profits, losses, and commissions. This is what most people mean
when they talk about performance, how they
did last year, who's a great investor, and so
on. But you're also going to drill a little further into your own performance by looking at
"the fearsome foursome," a term describing
four prices you'll use to gauge your individual
stock record.

**Track Your
Portfolio**

Portfolio Profits, Losses, and Commissions

Either in a software package or on a ledger page, record
what you paid for your stocks, what you sold them for, and the
commissions you paid. Periodically, say once a year, note how

the market performed as judged by the S&P 500 and compare your own performance. Are you ahead or behind?

Statements from your broker will help a lot in your calculations—especially if you consolidate all your investments at the same place, such as Fidelity or Schwab. You can see on your statement how much you started the year with and how much you ended with. Such numbers take everything into account including commissions. If you didn't invest any additional money, simply compare your ending balance with your beginning balance to see how your investments performed. If you did invest additional money, refer to your notebook or financial software for specific buy and sell prices.

I like using financial software. With predefined charts and reports I can press a button to see how my portfolio has done. It's also helpful to see your investments in context with your total financial picture. You might own $30,000 worth of stocks, but you also own a home, a car, and a piece of land in the sticks. Financial software will show it all in a few mouse clicks.

The Fearsome Foursome

Once you've got a handle on your overall performance, it's time to investigate how you've done on individual investments. For that I use an easy but strict system called the fearsome foursome. It's fearsome because it shows in no uncertain terms how you did.

It's a foursome because you write down four prices for every stock you've bought and sold: the price three months before you bought, your buy price, your sell price, and the price three months after you sold. The only one of these numbers that might not be handy is the price three months before you bought. If the stock was on your watch list and you tracked the price before you bought, then you'll have the number. Otherwise, you can call a broker to find out what it traded at, find its price history on the Internet, or consult a stock database on your computer. Here's what you might write down for Mister Magazine:

Mister Magazine Fearsome Foursome	
Three months before buy	$ 4
Buy price	$ 6
Sell price	$18
Three months after sell	$36

Well, you did the right thing on the buy. The stock had been rising and you picked it up before it rose too much. The sell, on the other hand, could use a little work. The stock doubled in the three months after you sold. Of course, gradual moves would have eased some of your pain since you might have left a little money in the stock to grab some of that journey to $36. But it's spilt milk now, and the best thing is to learn from it and move on. With this system you're looking to improve your buy points and your sell points.

Good Buy Points

Did you buy at a good time? For most growth investors, the price three months before the buy should be lower than the buy price. Growth investors expect to buy stocks on an upward move. For value investors, the price three months before the buy should be higher than the buy price. Value investors expect to buy when stocks go on sale.

Try to get your buy prices right around the price of three months before. That means you'll be buying growth at the beginning of its rise or value right near its bottom. It's rare to catch a stock at the absolute beginning of an upward launch or the bottom of a fall, but that's the ideal you're striving toward.

Good Sell Points

Did you sell at a good time? Everybody wants the same thing here: to sell at the top just before the stock dives to lower prices. Growth and value investors can agree on this point.

As with buying at the exact perfect moment, it's nearly impossible to sell at a stock's peak. They almost always bounce a little bit higher. By pushing your tracking period out to three months, you avoid killing yourself over a small uptick the day after you sell. Such occurrences are up to the whims of the universe, and no amount of studying prices will improve your odds of timing it right. That's why we look at three-month time frames. You're interested in trends, not flukes.

How to Improve Your Buy and Sell Points

I suppose the ultimate coup would be a sky-high price three months before the buy, a dirt-cheap buy price, a sky-high sell price, and a dirt-cheap price three months after the sell. You could brag about that one for years. To luxuriate in this dream a moment, pretend this is your very own fearsome foursome:

In Your Dreams Fearsome Foursome	
Three months before buy	$150
Buy price	$ 5
Sell price	$200
Three months after sell	$ 10

The Realm of Riches would whisper your name for eons. $10,000 became $400,000. You would have tricked them all by getting in just after a tremendous tumble and getting out just before another tremendous tumble. You could move that $400,000 back in at $10 for another recovery if your R&L sheet indicated that the company was still sound.

Now, back to reality. If there are drastic differences between the four numbers, go back to the file you keep on the company and see if you can recreate your thoughts at the buy and sell. Your folder should have clipped news stories, company mailings, updated research reports, and so on. Did you buy at the right time based on something you read? Perhaps you sold too soon because of a short-term scare that turned out fine in the end.

Find Your Bad Tendencies and Fix Them

Look over several fearsome foursomes for different stocks you've owned. Watch for trends. If you're consistently buying or selling too soon or too late, make note of that tendency. In many cases your fearsome foursome numbers will tell entirely different stories for different stocks. If so, there's little you can do because all the evidence is contradictory and that's par for this course. Every adage learned on the last stock will be reversed on the next.

That's why you're searching for trends. I discovered after looking over several fearsome foursome results from my own portfolio that I tend to sell too soon. My buy tendencies are too mixed to draw conclusions, but my sells almost invariably come early. That means I should trust my judgment in finding good companies and start letting them do their thing. I need to constantly read what Warren Buffett says: time helps wonderful businesses but destroys mediocre ones. Since discovering this tendency of mine to sell too soon, I've improved my returns by a few percentage points on the stocks I've sold. Others I haven't sold at all and am still holding onto as they continue mounting profits. Before the fearsome foursome analysis, I probably would have sold after they doubled.

You can do the same. Whenever you sell a stock, wait three months and write up the fearsome foursome results. Put the results in the company's folder when you're finished. Take a hard look at the numbers, compare them to your other results, and look for trends.

8 Bon Voyage!

That's about it. This book should help you get going safely with a stock-investment program. I like the fact that you won't run out and throw all your extra dollars into a $2 start-up because of something you read here. On the other hand, you won't languish for the next 20 years in Treasury bills for safety's sake. It's not safe to underperform inflation.

This Book's Strategy Is Your Friend for Life

For you this book's strategy is going to be a lifelong friend. It's not the only way to make money in stocks, but it's a way that anybody can follow from their kitchen table. You start gradually, perhaps in a bank savings account, then work your way into a discount broker's core money-market account, then into Dow stocks, and finally into the open market itself, where you'll search for stocks that measure up to high standards. It's a safe, profitable progression that allows you to learn more as you go without paying big money to do so.

I haven't made a complete killing in the market. My name isn't listed beside William O'Neil's, Peter Lynch's, Warren Buffett's, or Gary Pilgrim's. But what I have managed to do is beat the market over time, and have lots of fun in the process. I wish you the same.

E-mail Me Anytime, Baby: jkelly@ neatmoney.com

Drop me a line sometime. You can e-mail me directly, jkelly@neatmoney.com, or stop by *www.neatmoney.com* to send me a message from there.

Ever upward!

Reasons and Limits Worksheet

This investment is: GROWTH   VALUE

Company Name: **Ticker:**

Company Strengths

Why to Buy

Industry Leader   Growing Industry   Strong Sales Growth   Decreasing Debt   Increasing Margins   Superior Technology   New Management

Company Challenges

Why to Sell

Reached Price Target   Increased Competition   Declining Industry   Weakening Sales   Increasing Debt   Decreasing Margins   Legal Trouble

Stocks to Watch Worksheet

Company Name, Symbol, and Phone	Current Price	52 wk Hi/Lo	Market Cap	Day Dol Volume	Sales	Net Prof Margin	Cash	Total Debt	Sales /Share	Cash Fl /Share	Earning /Share	Div Yield	ROE	Insider buy/own	Stock buyback
[Example] Excellent Co. EXCO, 800-YOU-GAIN	10	12/5	$100 Mil	$1 Mil	$50 Mil	25% ◀▶	$10 Mil	$2.5 Mil	$15 ◀▶	$.45 ◀▶	$4 ◀▶	NA ◀▶	20%	10/30%	Yes
[Example] Terrible Co. EXCO, 800-YOU-LOSE	150	150/142	$100 Bil	$85 Mil	$20 Bil	2% ◀▶	$100 Mil	$5 Bil	$10 ◀▶	-$1.25 ◀▶	$3 ◀▶	.5% ◀▶	5%	0/3%	No
1)		/				◀▶			◀▶	◀▶	◀▶	◀▶		/	
2)		/				◀▶			◀▶	◀▶	◀▶	◀▶		/	
3)		/				◀▶			◀▶	◀▶	◀▶	◀▶		/	
4)		/				◀▶			◀▶	◀▶	◀▶	◀▶		/	
5)		/				◀▶			◀▶	◀▶	◀▶	◀▶		/	
6)		/				◀▶			◀▶	◀▶	◀▶	◀▶		/	
7)		/				◀▶			◀▶	◀▶	◀▶	◀▶		/	
8)		/				◀▶			◀▶	◀▶	◀▶	◀▶		/	
9)		/				◀▶			◀▶	◀▶	◀▶	◀▶		/	
10)		/				◀▶			◀▶	◀▶	◀▶	◀▶		/	

Company Name (cont. from above)	EPS Rank	RPS Rank	5 yr Sales	5 yr Price	Proj Sales	Proj Hi/Lo	Time Sale	STARS Fair Val	Current P/E	Average P/E	P/S	P/B	Current Ratio	Quick Ratio	Max Min
[Example] Excellent Co.	95	95	20%	900%	25%	100/60	1/2	5/5	2.5	5	0.67	0.5	10	2	900%/500%
[Example] Terrible Co.	25	25	2%	50%	3%	165/135	5/5	1/1	50	30	15	5	0.5	0.1	10%/-10%
1)						–	–	–							–
2)						–	–	–							–
3)						–	–	–							–
4)						–	–	–							–
5)						–	–	–							–
6)						–	–	–							–
7)						–	–	–							–
8)						–	–	–							–
9)						–	–	–							–
10)						–	–	–							–

About the Author

The publication of Jason Kelly's first book, *The Neatest Little Guide to Mutual Fund Investing,* launched him into a new career. He started NeatMoney, a company that offers a growing list of newsletters and booklets to help people manage their money. Jason presents seminars on mutual funds, stocks and money management, and teaches regularly in the Los Angeles area. He can also be seen as a frequent guest on CNN's financial network. For the latest information about Jason Kelly and NeatMoney, visit www.neatmoney.com on the World Wide Web or call 800-339-5671.

DUTTON **PLUME**

THE LATEST WORDS ON BUSINESS

☐ **WINNIE-THE-POOH ON PROBLEM SOLVING** *In which Pooh, Piglet and friends explore How to Solve Problems so you can too* **by Roger E. Allen and Stephen D. Allen.** Using the well-known adventures of Pooh and friends, this book teaches and explains the unique SOLVE Problem-Solving Method, a step-by-step system of identifying, analyzing, and resolving problems. Pooh, and you, learn all the principles of practical problem solving, which can be applied as easily to the many challenges that are part of today's rapidly changing and complex world. (940631—$17.95)

☐ **WINNIE-THE-POOH ON MANAGEMENT** *In which a Very Important Bear and his friends are introduced to a Very Important Subject* **by Roger E. Allen.** Using the characters and the stories of A.A. Milne to illustrate such principles as setting clear objectives, strong leadership, the need for accurate information, good communication, and other neglected basics of prudent management, the author offers sensible, time-honored advice in a captivating style. (938982—$17.95)

☐ **JUNGLE RULES** *How to Be a Tiger in Business* **by John P. Imlay, Jr., with Dennis Hamilton.** This compelling guide is not only about how to be a great manager yourself but how to build a great management team—picking the brightest and best and empowering them to conquer new territories on their own. All of the authors techniques are designed to enable people to be movers and shakers. "A must read for anyone who puts customers first and has the drive to succeed in a dynamic marketplace."—Harvey Mackay (271754—$13.95)

Prices slightly higher in Canada.

PLB2